THE
BALD TRUTH

KEITH SENIOR

My life in the world's hardest sport

WRITTEN WITH PETER SMITH

GREAT NORTHERN

Great Northern Books
PO Box 213, Ilkley, LS29 9WS
www.greatnorthernbooks.co.uk

ISBN: 978-1905080-92-2

Design and layout: David Burrill

Printed and bound by CPI Group (UK) Ltd, Croydon, CR0 4YY

CIP Data
A catalogue for this book is available from the British Library

CONTENTS

Acknowledgements

I would like to thank everyone who has contributed in any way to my playing career, particularly all the coaches I have worked under and players I have lined up with and against, from my first game as a nine-year-old, through to the pro' ranks with Sheffield and Leeds and into the international arena as well. Obviously they are far too numerous to mention by name, but the memories and friendships will last a lifetime. One person I would like to single out is Glenn Knight, who provided a route into the professional game and was my first rugby taxi driver.

Away from rugby, thanks go to my parents and family for their support throughout my life and career; Barnsby for supplying me with saddles and riding equipment and Caldene for riding clothing.

For their assistance in producing this book, I tip my hat to Richard Coomber, Ray Fletcher, Janet Harrison, Gary Hetherington, Stuart Martel and John Wray; Steve Riding and the photographers of the Yorkshire Evening Post, who kindly provided pictures, as did Dave Williams of RLphotos.com; plus Matt Johnson Photography for the cover shots; Patey Hats for the headgear used in the riding photo shoot; Barry Cox, David Burrill and everyone at Great Northern Books; Chubby Chandler and Liz at International Sports Management; Lee Westwood for his foreword and Kevin Sinfield for the afterword; my co-author Peter Smith, for hard work and coffees; and especially my partner Victoria Greetham for making me do it in the first place and for putting up with me for all these years, through the rough and the smooth.

FOREWORD

BY LEE WESTWOOD

As a rugby league fan I can only admire what Keith Senior has achieved in one of the world's toughest team sports.

His physical appearance alone – he is quite a frightening sight due to his size and trademark shaved head – command attention, but you have to be able to walk the walk as well as talk the talk and he has certainly done that, for Sheffield, Leeds, England and Great Britain.

For any supporter, the sight of Senior, with ball in hand, his long stride tormenting the opposition defence, is one of rugby league's most exciting images.

His record in Super League speaks for itself. Keith has made more appearances and scored more tries than anyone else and that is a remarkable achievement for someone who has bridged the gap between the old semi-pro era and the modern full-time game.

From my own experience, I am well aware of how much time and dedication it takes to get to the top in any sport. What the fans see during a tournament or a match is only a small part of the massive effort a leading player has to put in to compete on a consistent basis.

As a fellow professional sportsman, I have nothing but respect for the way Keith Senior has managed to perform so consistently at such a high level for so long.

To miss as few games as he has over 15 years or more in a physical collision sport like rugby league is a credit to Keith, to the way he looks after himself and his mental toughness.

As you will find out, he has made his fair share of mistakes on and off the pitch, but he has been able to put those behind him and come back stronger.

He is the sort of character a game like rugby league, which sometimes struggles to capture the media's attention, really needs.

Keith has always been something of a mystery and this book lifts the lid, with startling honesty, on some of the more colourful episodes in his career, including his eBay obsession, his inadvertent failed drugs test - something which will act as a warning to other athletes in any sport - and his unlikely transformation into a country gent.

Not all the headlines Keith has attracted have been positive ones, but in my view he has been a credit to the sport and to his various clubs and I am sure rugby league as a whole will miss him when he eventually hangs up his boots.

Lee Westwood is one of the world's top golfers, rising to No 1 in the rankings in 2010. He is also a keen rugby league fan.

INTRODUCTION

This is my first book and I have enjoyed it so much I plan reading one some day soon! When I left school if anyone had told me I'd end up penning my autobiography, I would have laughed at them. I didn't even read books, never mind write them.

So what makes me think you will be interested? It seems a bit egotistical to imagine anyone wants to read my life story, but I do think I have a tale to tell and it is a pretty unusual one at that.

I have been around in rugby league for a long time and there aren't many people playing today who made the cross-over from the old winter-based semi-professional game to the modern full-time summer Super League era.

I made my professional debut in 1994 and I was still playing at the top level 17 years later, which is an achievement I am proud of. That amounts to more than 500 games for two clubs – Sheffield Eagles and Leeds Rhinos - as well as Great Britain, England and Yorkshire. I don't think that's bad for a union convert whose first 13-a-side experience was in the depths of Pennine League parks rugby.

Do any job for that length of time and you are bound to meet interesting people; things will happen to you – good and bad – and you'll have stories to tell. That is definitely true in my case. I have had more than my fair share of triumphs and disasters, of victories and fiascos on and off the field.

I have won a Challenge Cup final at Wembley, but also lost one there – and three on other grounds. I have appeared in four Grand Finals and won the lot and I've played in Test match victories over Australia, but never beaten them in a series.

I would like to think I have earned the respect of players and fans on both sides of the world, but I have also made my fair share of enemies. There aren't too many referees who have my name on their Christmas card list – in fact, none - and I am practically banned from the town of Castleford, all because of a couple of punches thrown 13 years ago.

I have had my moments in my personal – and by that I mean non-rugby – life as well. When I see celebrities complaining about reporters and photographers hiding in the bushes outside their house I can sympathise, because it has happened to me. I think whenever the national press turn up in Halifax or Huddersfield, the two towns closest to where I live, the residents there automatically guess I have been up to something.

There have been three serious relationships in my life and I've messed things up in each of them. One resulted in a battle over child maintenance, another in a nasty divorce and the third, thankfully, is still going strong, but only after I almost blew it by getting caught up in a kiss-and-tell exposé. I have never revealed the full story of that before, but it is included in these pages.

Of course fame or notoriety has its plus points. Over the last few years I have been able to make a good living from flogging off my old rugby gear – even my used socks. Typically, not everybody approves and that earned me some negative headlines in the press as well, but I have learned that in life you can't please all the people all the time.

That's all right by me. I have never been one to lose much sleep over what other people think, but it is good to have an opportunity to set the record straight on a few issues. Maybe now people will stop asking what caused me to wallop Barrie-Jon Mather in a televised Challenge Cup tie back in 1998, or if I am really a drugs cheat, or what the true story is behind my marriage break-up? Did I really kick my wife out of the family home – and why were the media there to record the debacle as it unfolded? What was the truth behind me playing in the 2005 Challenge Cup final, when I clearly wasn't fit – and did I really retire from international rugby league, or was I pushed? Read on and you will find out.

Rugby league is a small world and everyone tends to know everyone else, so I have got some stories about people I have met along the way. It is not my intention to mock anyone or to upset friends or foes, but I have always been one for straight talking and I'm not going to change my ways now.

I realise most of the people who read this book will do so because they are interested in the rugby league side of my life, but there is a lot more to me than that and I have tried to get that across in these pages.

Not everyone who grows up on a council estate in Huddersfield ends up living on a country one a decade or so later. I may not be your typical country gent, but the outdoor lifestyle has become a big part of who I am and I think it will surprise a few people who only see me as a rough-arsed rugby player. Visit a north of England country show in the summer months and the chances are you'll see me there, grooming my horse Tommy or even doing a bit of eventing. I am told I look quite good in jodhpurs.

Over the years I have been asked several times to write my autobiography and in the past I have always declined. So why now? I am coming towards the end of my playing career and I think the time is right. It hasn't always been an easy process and some of the events included in here have been tough to write about, but I have not held anything back.

There are events in this book – one in particular - which don't show me in a good light, but once I decided to go ahead I set out to be totally honest. In a couple of cases I have recalled incidents without naming other people involved. I don't want to embarrass anyone over things that happened a long time ago, but those events are an important part of my story, which is why I have recounted them here.

This isn't a straight-forward rugby book and I haven't gone into a great deal of detail about individual games I have played in. I haven't rehashed match reports from past triumphs or disasters; those have been well covered elsewhere and I did not want to go over old ground, but I hope I have provided an insight into what makes me tick, my motivation and inspiration over a decade and a half at the top level of the toughest team sport of all and into some of the characters I have played with and against.

CHAPTER 1

FROM JAILBIRD TO EAGLE

I don't know the policeman's name and he certainly wouldn't remember me, but if he hadn't arrested me and chucked me in a cell, I probably wouldn't ever have played professional rugby league.

It's embarrassing to look back on it now, but I was a bit of a teenage tearaway and for a while, I was destined for a life on the wrong side of the tracks. As criminal masterminds go, I wasn't a huge success, but I did have a bit of an illegal operation running while I was at secondary school and there's no telling where that would have led.

It started in a low-key way, nicking sweets from local shops, in Huddersfield where I lived, with a few of my mates. I was pretty good at it and in time I graduated to bigger things, mainly stationery from stores like WH Smith's and Woolworth's. We used to pinch ballpoints, fountain pens, protractors and that sort of thing. It was easy, all I had to do was hide them up my sleeve and walk out of the shop.

I actually ended up getting a little business going at school, selling things on and even nicking to order. If anybody wanted a ruler or a pencil case, I'd go out and pinch one and then sell it to them for a tidy profit. That was about the only reason I ever turned up for lessons.

My 'business' was going pretty well and I was making good money, but of course one day I got spotted, pulled to one side and the police were called. This was in O'Neill's in Huddersfield and it happened on a weekend when my mum and dad had gone away on holiday, to the east coast. The police turned up, which was pretty embarrassing and I got handcuffed, which was even worse. I was thrown in the back of a car and taken to the local nick and then left in a cell.

My mum and dad were called and as you can imagine, they weren't best pleased. My dad basically told the copper, "just leave him there for the day". They were staying with my grandma and they'd only got there that morning, so they didn't fancy coming straight home, even to spring me from police custody.

Another reason was my dad had endured a similar experience when he was young. He did some stealing, told his sister about it and my grandma heard him. She marched him straight down to the police station and that sorted him out. When he heard what I'd done, he obviously thought 'right you little so and so, I'll teach you'.

I was left in a police cell all day and that's a memory that has stuck with me ever since. It's not a nice experience. The cell stank of piss, there was graffiti all over the walls, a mat for a bed and absolutely nothing to do. I was bored and terrified at the same time. Sitting there all day you can hear all sorts of things happening: cell doors banging, other inmates screaming and shouting. It is an intimidating environment. You can talk tough, but when you're on your own in that sort of situation, it's scary. I didn't know what was going to happen to me and to be honest, I thought I would end up in jail.

As a 15-year-old sitting in a police cell for eight hours, through the afternoon and into the evening, it gave me plenty of time to think. There's an old saying 'if you can't do the time, don't do the crime'. And I couldn't do the time. One day was bad enough and I decided there and then that a life of law-breaking wasn't for me. I was lucky, the police gave me an official warning and that was on my record for a time, but I didn't end up in court. The officers made it clear that if I went back, I would be in big trouble. The slap on the wrists worked, because I haven't stolen anything since.

Once my mum and dad turned up I had to go and see one of the PCs. I lied a bit and told them it was my first time shoplifting things. The copper didn't believe me, but he must have seen dozens of cases like that. It was a nightmare at the time, but in hindsight what happened was a blessing in disguise. If I had got away with it, I would have carried on and I suppose at some stage I'd have ended up in prison. As it was, that arrest was a turning point in my life. I was lucky that I got caught early on, before the consequences got too serious.

It's not something I'm proud of; in fact, I am ashamed of the whole business. It's strange how things turn out, but because of the reputation I've now got as a rugby player, I sometimes get asked to go and speak to young kids who have been in trouble with the law or are having a hard time at home. I can relate to them because I've been in their shoes. I can tell them it's not too late to turn things around. I don't know if it helps, but I hope it does.

The fiasco in the sports shop was actually the second time I got found out. The first, a few months earlier, led to another embarrassing episode and probably the least successful attempt to run away from home in human history. I got about 10 feet.

I got caught in Tesco's in Huddersfield, stealing items I didn't want or need. I was basically pinching things for something to do. I got pulled into the office there and the manager decided not to tell the police, but he did phone my mum, which was probably worse.

When I got home my mum was waiting. She sent me upstairs, told me I was grounded and said she was going to tell my dad when he got home from work. Every now and then, when I did something to upset my dad, the slipper or belt would come out and I'd get walloped. I was expecting a bit of a beating and I didn't fancy that, so I decided to do a runner.

Before my dad came home, I sneaked downstairs and took some money my mum and dad kept to pay their insurance. It was about £200, which was - and still is - a lot of cash. I went back upstairs, climbed out of the window and rode off on my bike.

Near where we lived there was a bit of an inland cliff face, overlooking the valley below. It was a nice warm, sunny day so I rode up there, sat on the hillside and spent quite a few hours just watching the world go by.

I could see our house from there and I spotted my dad arrive home; then, sure enough, a little while later, a police car turned up. They had reported me missing and they'd also told the police that some money had been stolen.

I can still remember sitting there thinking about what I'd done and wondering how I was going to get out of it. It had seemed like a good idea at the time, but I hadn't thought things through. That's a scenario that's come back to haunt me more than once during my rugby career. It began to get dark and cold and I had nowhere to go, so I did what came naturally and went home.

Bearing in mind the fact I had run away and I wasn't planning on going back to my mum and dad, I sneaked into an old coal cellar we had under the house. The plan was to stay there until I figured out what else I could do. On reflection, it wasn't the best scheme ever.

One of the problems was, in those days I used to talk in my sleep. I bedded down in the cellar, fell asleep and must have started chatting away. We had a dog, a doberman called Sly and he heard me and started barking. My mum and dad went to see what was going on, looked in the cellar and found me fast asleep, so that was the end of that. The police came back out, because I had stolen the money. They asked my parents if they wanted to press charges, but they decided not to.

Another time, I tried pinching a car, along with a couple of mates. Near where I lived in Longwood, in Huddersfield, was a street called Lam Hall Road. I had a paper round down there. One day I was wandering along, delivering papers, when I noticed a car with the keys left in the door. Without really thinking about it, I pocketed them.

I was about 15 at the time and I didn't know how to drive, but chatting to my mate Lee a bit later that day, we had the bright idea of going back and trying to nick the car. We roped in another mate who was a couple of years older, because he'd had a few driving lessons and we fancied going for a joyride.

We waited for it to get dark, then returned to the scene of my earlier crime. The car was still there, I had the keys in my pocket and everything was going to plan. We opened the car door, took the handbrake off and, being bright sparks, started pushing the car along the street, because we didn't want to start the engine and alert anybody.

Which wasn't a good plan, because we didn't realise the steering lock would come on. My older mate – I'll call him Jimmy - was behind the wheel and Lee and I were pushing. Jimmy was trying to steer, but nothing was happening and none of us had a clue what was going on. Panic ensued. We pushed the car up on to the kerb and into somebody's garden and then we heard a shout of "oi" from further down the street. We all scarpered, me and Lee were yelling at Jimmy and he was saying it wasn't his fault. That was my one and only – failed - attempt to steal a car.

I have had a few brushes with the law since my early, ill-fated days as a career criminal, mostly when I've been nicked for fighting on nights out. One time was in Wakefield, when I was with a few of the Sheffield Eagles boys. There were four or five of us in a group and one nightclub we turned up at wouldn't let us in. Ricky Wright took exception to that and got into a bit of a tussle with one of the bouncers. I got involved, the police came and I got chucked into the back of a van and carted off to spend a night in the cells. They didn't charge me, too much paperwork I think; I just got woken up and kicked out at 6 in the morning.

Another time, when I was working as an apprentice HGV mechanic, my brother John needed an MoT certificate. Like an idiot, I offered to get him one. Someone I knew had a stockpile. I didn't know how to fill it out properly, so I messed it up. When my brother went to produce it, to tax his car, the Post Office staff called the police. John told them where he had got it from and I got a caution for that. I was only 17 at the time. A while later, the police made a dramatic visit to my house when I got divorced, but that's another story and I'll talk about that later.

I was born in Deighton, just off Leeds Road in Huddersfield, close to where Galpharm Stadium is now. We were nomads, though. We used to move house all the time, though always in the Huddersfield area. After Deighton we lived in Moldgreen, then Waterloo, Outlane and finally Longwood, which was where I spent my teenage years.

I made mates in those days who I am still in touch with now, including Lee Mallinson, of car-pinching fame. A small group of us used to hang around on the streets and in the local park, which backed on to my house. There was myself, Lee, Shaun and Chris Joyce and two sisters from the big houses at the top of Longwood, Carolyn and Kimberley Wood. They were the subject of my first real crushes, though nothing ever came of it.

My first meeting with the local lads was a strange business. They used to play football in the park behind where I lived. One day I sneaked into the park and hid up a tree, watching the game. When they had finished playing they all sat down on the grass for a breather and a chat. Suddenly there was a loud crack and the next thing I knew, I was lying flat on my back on the ground, surrounded by leaves and branches. They were all pretty shocked, but I didn't hang around, I leaped to my feet and ran off. At least that gave them something to laugh about, it broke the ice and the next time I saw them they invited me to join in the footy.

I wasn't a bad kid, just easily bored and that's what led me to do a lot of stupid things, like the car-stealing incident. Another activity we liked to indulge in was hedge-hopping, which involved dashing through people's back gardens, climbing through and over the hedges any way we could. We had our regular runs, until the time one of the local residents got his revenge by putting barbed wire all the way through his eight-foot high hedge. You can imagine the cuts and scrapes we got when we tried to plunge through that. We didn't do it again.

Another game, which I suppose most kids have tried, was knocking on doors and running away. That also ended in disaster. There was one particular guy who would chase after anyone who tried the 'knock a door run' game at his house. We adopted a new tactic of chucking stones at his windows, but he turned out to be a nutcase – and a speedy one at that. He came tearing out of his front door, chased us down the street and caught us. We were all locked in his garden shed until the police came to give us a ticking off. Our new friend left us to stew for a while before he called them, so we were imprisoned for a fair few hours.

Not all the scrapes I got into involved what would these days be called anti-social behaviour. For some reason, on one occasion I decided to trim my eyebrows. I made a complete mess of it and ended up shaving the whole lot off. I looked ridiculous, so I tried to draw some back on with a permanent marker. As you can imagine, that didn't really help the situation and I got plenty of stick from my pals. I was reminded of that during the 2011 rugby season when one of my team-mates, Kylie Leuluai, tried to trim his sideburns, but went a bit too high. He used a marker pen to cover up his mistake, just like I did. The difference is, I was 13 when I tried it – and he was 32.

At one stage in my youth we lived close to my grandma's home and she was the only person who could control my dad. He was a bit of a lad, he used to go for nights out and he would say he hadn't had a good time if he didn't get into a fight at some stage. It was that type of environment.

I remember once, when I was about four or five, I was with him when he had a bit of a disagreement with one of the neighbours, after he'd had a few pints. It all escalated and they ended up having a punch-up. My dad was like the meat in a sandwich. He was lying on top of the neighbour in their garden, pummelling away, while the other bloke's wife was lying on my dad's back, hitting him. That was the type of thing my dad used to get up to.

There was a pub at the end of the road called the Wise Owl and my dad - who is called Michael - used to spend quite a bit of time in there. My mum would go and try and get him to come home, but he'd be busy playing dominoes or whatever and he wouldn't take any notice. So then it would be time to call in the cavalry and grandma would go and fetch him. My dad was scared stiff of gran: he'd be sitting in the pub having a good time, she would walk in and he'd be off home before his feet could touch the ground.

I know all this is going to sound like he was a bad dad, but he wasn't really. It wasn't a very disciplined environment to grow up in, but the reason my dad was away so often was because he wanted to earn enough money to give us a decent standard of living. He was a proud man and if we wanted something, he would provide it. I wish he had been around more often, but I understand now that he was, in his own way, trying to do the best for us. It was his method of providing for his family. He hasn't changed, he still works every hour God sends and he's not far off retirement age. He is a no-nonsense sort of a bloke and most people will say that's how I've turned out as well.

He did try to spend some time with us at weekends. He used to take me to football and rugby, which is something I'm thankful for. He played amateur rugby and a bit of local football and he was keen for me and my older brother John to play sports. He was a goalkeeper and I was the same, though when I was growing up I never even thought about making a living out of sport.

With my dad away most of the time, it was up to my mum, Janet, to look after us, which wasn't easy. John and I used to fight all the time and because he was older and bigger, I was the one who always got beaten up.

John, who lives in America now, only came off second best once. He was beating the living daylights out of me, as usual, and my dad jumped in the middle. He grabbed John and I saw my chance, so I punched him in the face. John had one arm free at that stage and he tried to fight back, but Dad pinned his other arm and I managed to land another one, so he ended up with two black eyes. We get on all right now, but that's a memory that always makes me smile.

I wasn't a saint at school either, when I bothered to turn up. I started at Moldgreen Junior School, then went to Outlane Junior School, then Salendine Nook High School. I hated it, I wasn't very bright and I used to skive a lot. I was a bit of a disruptive influence. A couple of times I even went into class drunk. I'd go home at lunchtime, break into the booze cabinet, have a few drinks and then go back.

I did drink a bit, but I only tried drugs once. That came about as a dare between a group of us. Lee and I shared half of an ecstasy tablet and it was a strange experience and not something either of us wanted to try again.

I got away with a lot of things, because my mum was a bit of a soft touch. If she tried to stop me doing something, I'd just laugh at her. John and I would basically do whatever we wanted and then when my dad came home we'd get a bit of a telling off. My mum and dad didn't really get on, because he was working all the time. They are divorced now, but they were married for 20 years and they fought like cat and dog for most of it.

The only thing that got me interested at school was PE. I played football and a bit of rugby, but academic lessons didn't make much of an impression on me. I am not sure how, but I did manage to get a couple of GCSEs, in maths and English, so it wasn't a complete waste of time.

One thing about sport is it does teach you discipline. Funnily enough, it wasn't rugby that started to straighten me out: Thai boxing did that. Lee was into martial arts and he got me interested. I was pretty keen at one stage and the things I learned - not just the physical contact part of it - have stood me in good stead. It's maybe something I would have liked to take further, but I had to stop when I began taking rugby more seriously.

The Thai boxing definitely helped calm me down and learn to control, or maybe channel is a better word, the aggressive side of my nature. It also gave me some of the discipline I was missing at home. In martial arts you basically have to do what you're told: don't chat when the instructor's talking, don't stand with your arms folded, always wear the right equipment and that sort of thing. It was really the first time I'd taken any notice of those sort of rules. It is all about respect and at that stage in my life I didn't have much of that for anybody.

Thai boxing began to sort out that particular character defect and playing rugby helped with the process, though in the early days sport was never more than a hobby and a way of letting off steam.

My dad will tell anyone who brings up the subject – and plenty of people who don't – that our John was a much better rugby player than me. Playing at Wembley for Sheffield Eagles in 1998 was probably the highlight of my career, but John beat me to it by 13 years and that's what really got me interested in the sport.

Every year two under-11 schoolboy teams get to play in a curtain-raiser to rugby league's Challenge Cup final, at the national stadium. In 1985 it was Huddersfield Schools' turn and John – who was at Moldgreen Junior School at the time - got selected. They played Leigh Schools and the Huddersfield team also included Nathan Sykes and Darren Turner, who both went on to play in Super League. John played centre or second-row and I think he could have made it in the professional game, but he didn't really have the ambition or the desire. We are like chalk and cheese and he was the quiet one with all the brains. He did well at school and got all his GCSEs and I don't think rugby was that important to him, even though he did have some talent.

As I moved up the age groups I enjoyed the social side of things as much as the game itself, but John liked to turn up, play the match and go home. Eventually, when he got to 17 and the social part of it became more important, he packed in playing, so he didn't really fulfil his potential. I think with hindsight, having seen what I've gone on to achieve, he might do things differently if he had his time again, but on the other hand he is happy enough, so good on him.

I was nine at the time of John's big day and I didn't go to Wembley, but

I watched it on TV. The final that year, Wigan against Hull, was one of the greatest-ever and watching that and John's game – plus the whole atmosphere of the occasion - gave me the rugby bug. John was playing for a local junior rugby league team at the time, but I went to the nearest club, which was Huddersfield YMCA rugby union.

At that age rugby is rugby. It's all about running around and having fun with your mates and I wasn't even aware that there were two different codes of the game. I enjoyed the contact side of it and I was quite fast as a young kid, so it suited me.

I stayed with Huddersfield YMCA right through the age groups, until after I left school at 16 and I would probably still be there now if the club hadn't run into problems. The coach got fed up and there was no team for my age group, so the side I had come through with disbanded and I drifted away.

At the time I was working as an HGV mechanic for Continental Wines and Foods, on Leeds Road in Huddersfield. If you've been to a game at Galpharm Stadium you'll have been past it. It was an Italian company and my dad also worked there, as a driver.

In those days you had to do two weeks' work placement during your final year at school. Initially I got sent to Poundstretcher, which wasn't regarded as a cool assignment. All my mates laughed at me and there was no way I could stick at that, with all the embarrassment it caused, so I had a word with my dad and he got me in at Continental. He had been there for something like 15 years, so they probably thought they owed him a favour.

I did a couple of weeks as a tea boy and tidy-upper and then they offered me a job on the Youth Training Scheme, which was basically very cheap labour. I didn't have any idea what I wanted to do when I left school – and there was no way I was ever going to go to university - so that seemed as good as anything.

I had taken the Army entrance exam and that was an option, but when Continental offered me the YTS, I decided to take it. Being on the YTS I did four days a week, plus one at college and I used to work weekends as well, when I had the chance. I can still do a bit of tinkering with engines, but I would class myself more as a fitter than a mechanic. If someone tells me what a problem is, I can usually sort it out, but engines have changed completely since my day and I'd probably be lost if I went back to my old job now.

Not that I would. We did work on plant machinery as well as trucks and you'd find yourself in 10-inch deep mud, working under JCBs, with oil and muck and water dripping on to you all the time. I enjoyed it for a while, but I wouldn't want to go back; because it was hard work for not much pay. I used to stink of diesel oil – some of it got under my skin and is still there - and I was filthy all the time, which isn't great for any 16 or 17-year-old.

Fortunately, one of the truck drivers played for Milnsbridge in Pennine League Division Four. He knew I had played a bit of rugby and was without a team, so he invited me to go training with them. I was keen to get back into the game and I was missing the social aspect of it, so I went along. That was the first time I'd had anything to do with rugby league and I took to it straight away.

To be honest, it wasn't a great standard. One of the props there was nicknamed Nine Bellies. When you are in a team with a front-rower called Nine Bellies, you know you aren't going to be winning many trophies. Funnily enough, he also went on to a career in Super League – he is now the mascot at Huddersfield Giants, Big G. I still see him every now and then and we have a chat about the good old days.

I had never really achieved anything in union. I played centre and a few games at flanker, but it was just a hobby, a bit of fun. I went for Yorkshire trials, but never got selected. It was clear my face didn't fit. I enjoyed the game and the craic afterwards, but there wasn't much chance of me going any further than the level I was playing at and I didn't have aspirations to do anything other than play as an amateur for Huddersfield YMCA.

If you had told me then that I could go on and make a living out of the game, I would have laughed at you. For a lot of players nowadays it is all they have ever wanted to do, since they started in an under-six team or whatever. Someone like Kevin Sinfield was always destined to be a professional player, but I sort of drifted into it, as much by luck as judgement.

I had a few training sessions with Milnsbridge and then played a few games once the season started and I ripped it up. A few of the players in the team told me I was much too good to be playing in that division and they said I should be trying to get in at a professional club.

One of the Milnsbridge guys knew Glenn Knight, a former Huddersfield half-back who was then a scout for Sheffield Eagles. Glenn lived in Huddersfield and he took me to training at Sheffield. I owe him a lot, because he used to taxi me all over the place, to training and matches.

It wasn't a case of the Eagles scouting me or me being head-hunted.

They didn't have the biggest squad and they were probably short of players, so Glenn said "come down and we'll have a look at you". I didn't have anything to lose and neither did they, so I went along. To me, that was the best thing since sliced bread. I actually felt that I was finally getting somewhere, though I still didn't think I was good enough to play professional.

In my first year at Sheffield I played nearly a full season in the academy and the reserve grade alliance team. Paul Daley, who is a bit of a legend in rugby league as an old-style coach, was in charge of the academy team at the time. Paul, who is still involved in the game at Leeds and Hunslet, taught me the basics of the sport, along with the other Eagles lower grade coaches.

I was very green, but I had speed and size on my side and I think the other thing in my favour was I was prepared to work hard and learn. I trained with the team, but I also put a lot of time in working on my own individual skills, which really paid off in the long run.

Richard Chapman and Dean Lawford, who both went on to have decent careers, were in Eagles' academy ranks at the same time as me and we had a decent team, which helped me because I hadn't been playing league long. The club obviously thought I had got something to offer as, after I'd been there a year, the coach and club owner Gary Hetherington came to my house with a big-money contract. Gary, who is now chief executive at Leeds, founded the Sheffield club in 1984 after he got turned down as coach of York. He thought 'if they won't give me a job, I'll form my own club'.

They started on a shoestring budget and had some really tough times for their first few years, but by the time I came along they were an established top-flight club who were beginning to achieve some success, though they still hadn't really captured the local public's imagination.

Gary offered me and Dave Larder a contract at the same time. Dave turned his down and went on to play for Keighley Cougars, but I signed on the dotted line. My first professional deal was for the princely sum of £3,000 – for three years. So I was on a grand a year! That was the first of many contract negotiations I have been involved in with Gary and not a lot has changed. The sums have gone up a bit over the years, but not by much.

Still, I was a professional rugby player and for me at the time, being paid to play the game was like a dream come true. I snapped Gary's hand off. He was offering me £1,000 a year to do something I would have been happy to do for nothing, though obviously I didn't tell him that. Even at that stage I didn't think I was good enough to play professional rugby league, so any sum of money was a bonus. And as I was on a Youth Training Scheme wage of £29.50 a week for the HGV work, anything else was a bonus.

I wasn't a semi-professional player for very long before I went full-time, but I can tell you, in comparison Super League is a picnic. My basic wage at Continental was for a 40-hour week, but I was working 60 or 70 hours to get a fairly decent pay packet. I was working all hours, getting up at the crack of dawn and grafting sometimes until 3am the following day.

It was hellish and when I started training at Sheffield that just added to the workload. I was still doing more or less the same hours, but with breaks for training two nights a week, on Tuesdays and Thursdays.

I was exhausted pretty much all the time and on one occasion it caught up with me, with an almost fatal result. Living and working in Huddersfield, I used to drive over to Sheffield for training in my brother's car. I didn't have my own motor at the time and, to be honest, I never bothered getting insured to drive John's.

One evening I was on my way to South Yorkshire and I fell asleep at the wheel. Nearly 20 years later it still brings me out in a cold sweat thinking about it. I went straight across a junction, through a red light and into the side of another car.

Luckily, nobody was hurt and there was only minor damage to John's car and the other vehicle. We exchanged details and the other driver's husband phoned a couple of days later. He said "I've heard you're only a young kid, do you want to pay cash for the damage to our car, or shall I put it through the insurance?"

Maybe he guessed I wasn't insured and he didn't want all the aggro that would have caused, but I agreed straight away, even though it was a struggle getting the money together. I was really lucky. If he hadn't said that it could have ended up costing me thousands. If the police had got involved I might have landed myself in court and that could have cost me my licence, which I needed for getting to training and for driving trucks at work, as I sometimes went out delivering. Before the crash I didn't think it was worth paying for insurance, but I definitely learned my lesson. It was a bit too close for comfort, but I carried on and went to training after the crash, which shows how keen I was.

I signed for Sheffield on September 1, 1994 and I played 23 games for the first team that season; 20 of them in the starting line-up, which was a pretty good return for a young kid. My debut was at home to Widnes, on October 2 and it wasn't the most auspicious of starts – we lost 22-0. It was the first time Sheffield had ever been nilled. I played on the wing and I'm not saying the coaching staff didn't have much faith in me, but they had another winger, Bright Sodje, on the bench in case I messed up. I really enjoyed it and from what I remember, I played quite well. I didn't score, but I did some good things, caught a few high bombs under pressure and held my own in defence, even though, from a team point of view, it was a bit of a nightmare.

Sheffield weren't a massive club and Don Valley Stadium was one of the worst places in the country to play rugby. The training facilities were excellent, but it wasn't the best of pitches, crowds were pretty small and it is basically an athletics venue so the fans were a long way away from the action, which meant there was never much of an atmosphere. The biggest home crowd Sheffield played in front of that season was 7,450 for a tour match against Australia – which we lost 80-2. I didn't play in that one, because Gary thought going up against the Aussies might shatter my confidence. The average gate that year was 2,661, so it wasn't exactly the big time, but it was still professional rugby league in the top tier and it was a long way from Pennine League Division Four.

There were times early in my career when I played two games in a day, for the academy team and the alliance. The first time I was involved with the senior side was a friendly against Castleford, when I was on the bench – and I played the full 80 minutes in the academy side immediately before that. I think Gary wanted to make sure he was getting his money's worth. When you're paying a player £1,000 per year, you want to keep him busy.

I scored three tries in that debut season. My first came in a game against Halifax at their old Thrum Hall ground. To be honest, I can't recall anything about that touchdown, but the first one I remember was in a game away to Salford, at the Willows, after I had come off the substitutes' bench. It wasn't a spectacular score, but the game was on TV and it sticks in my memory for that reason. Strangely enough, we lost both those games by the same score, 24-20 and Ryan Sheridan and Anthony Farrell, who later played with me at Leeds, scored in each of them as well.

My third try was in another away game, at Featherstone Rovers, at the start of November. We managed to win that one, 24-14. Sheffield finished eighth out of 16 in the Stones Bitter Championship that year so, all in all, it wasn't a bad start. For me, the highlight was probably a game against

Leeds at Don Valley Stadium in March. We must have been hard up in the forwards, because I played in the second-row. I had a good game and we won, 31-22, which was a good effort as Leeds finished as runners-up to Wigan that season.

My second year as a professional, 1995, was a bit of a disappointment. I only played 11 games, scoring three more tries, because I injured my back. The medics couldn't fathom out what was wrong with me and the problem kept coming and going. To be honest, I probably wouldn't have played that much anyway, because I was still very much one of the fringe squad men. It was 1996 and the start of Super League when things began to take off for me.

CHAPTER 2
TALKING ABOUT A REVOLUTION

It's not often you can say you were in at the start of a revolution, but Sheffield Eagles were. Maybe because the authorities thought the new boys had a chance of beating us, we were chosen as Paris St Germain's opponents in the first-ever Super League match, on March 29, 1996.

That was the year rugby league changed from a winter sport to a summer one and it was probably the best thing the game has ever done. It was all part of the new Super League era, paid for by Sky TV, and the big difference from the players' point of view was that we all went full-time. Until then, only Wigan and Leeds had been fully professional and players at other clubs worked during the day - if they were lucky enough to have a job - and trained on an evening a couple of times a week.

I was a pioneer, or guinea pig, because I actually went full-time, for about seven days, before most of the Eagles squad. In other words, I gave up the day job. I lodged with a couple called Pete and Glynys and it was one of the best weeks of my life. I got seriously pampered. They were a family who sponsored the club; they were big Sheffield fans and they wanted to help out, so they offered to put me up at their home in the city, which saved me having to drive over from Huddersfield every day.

I was pretty keen to get out of my mechanic's job and Gary Hetherington saw an opportunity to make me full-time, which meant I could concentrate 100 per cent on my rugby. As a newcomer to the game I needed that more than most of the other guys, who had been round the block a time or two. That first full-time contract was for £7,000.

Unfortunately, it didn't work out. Sheffield only had about five full-time players and they were doing development work in schools. I didn't get that opportunity, so there wasn't anything for me to do during the day, apart from go to the gym. It was pretty boring, to be honest. It sounds good, but after a few days it was driving me up the wall, so I went back to work. I had a mate who worked at Allied Colloids in Bradford and he got me a job there, which paid very well compared to what I was earning from mechanicing and my rugby income. I was a labourer, laying electric pipes and doing some welding.

I was there from 1995 until I went full-time again with the rest of the Sheffield squad when Super League started. That contract was for £14,000 per year, which was a big step up from what I had been on, but I took a pay cut because I lost what I'd been earning at Allied Colloids. I was actually worse off when I became a full-time professional player.

The first Super League game in Paris is pretty famous, because they beat us and it got a massive crowd, more than 17,000. It was exciting to be part of it, but looking back, my main memory of the start of Super League is just how tiring it was.

What happened was this: We had a short winter league season from August to January; then the Challenge Cup and straight into Super League after that, which meant there was no break or pre-season. We just went from one campaign to another. By the start of the season we had already been playing for eight months and everybody was knackered.

Paris was a good occasion, though, and I am pleased I was part of it. There was a long build-up and Sheffield – who didn't get much coverage in the media - worked hard to take advantage of all the free publicity. We had a French player, Jean-Marc Garcia, and he bore the brunt of it. I remember getting roped into a photo call which involved him cooking an omelette, French-style, for some fans. He was a fully-qualified chef, so he knew what he was doing. On another occasion a couple of the other players, Mark Aston and Paul Carr, got kitted out in authentic French gear - berets and strings of onions, to have their picture taken with someone from the local French community. The berets were Army surplus and the onions came from the Crucible Theatre's props department. That's what it was like at Sheffield, make do and mend.

The game itself was live on Sky TV and it was the biggest crowd I had ever played in front of. There was a lot of razzmatazz, which was unusual at the time: we came out on to the pitch as our names were called out, with fireworks going off in the background and that wasn't something we were used to, though it's pretty common now. The Paris club and the RFL hyped it up and to be fair, they did a very good job of it. The majority of the tickets were given away, but the French crowd created a terrific atmosphere and it was a great environment to play in.

I had only been abroad once before, to Lanzarote on a family holiday - out of season - when I was a kid, so that was a big thing for me. I was on the bench but fortunately I got on quite early when big Joe Dakuitoga got injured. He was the right-winger and I ended up coming on in his place. I played quite well and scored the last try. The game had gone by then, but it was good for me to get over the line and it wasn't a bad try. It was a disappointing night for the Eagles, but a decent one for me personally and scoring in the first game was my little piece of history.

It was also the start of a breakthrough year which ended with me making my Test debut for Great Britain, something I wouldn't even have dreamed about that night in Paris. Going full-time definitely helped me, but Big Joe's injury didn't do me any harm either. It got my foot in the door and I managed to take the chance when it came. I played in all 22 games that season and started in 21 of them. I began the year as a fringe man and ended up as one of the first team regulars.

I started on the wing and moved into the centre as the campaign went on. I scored 17 tries, which I was happy with, and I felt like I had really got somewhere at last. People were starting to talk about me as one of the main men in the team and that was a good boost to the ego and a real lift for my confidence.

At the time I was described as being the 'next Daryl Powell', which still makes me laugh. Daryl was a big Sheffield hero: He was Eagles' first signing and maybe their best-ever player, but - apart from playing in a similar position - we are nothing like each other. We have a totally different playing style, though Daryl achieved a lot in the game, not least winning 33 Great Britain caps, and he was a good person to be compared to.

We had a decent side in those days and we did okay in the first Super League season, finishing seventh out of 11. There were some good characters in the team, like Dale Laughton, a big raw-boned prop from Barnsley. We used to call him Cushty - after the expression Del Boy uses in the TV comedy Only Fools and Horses. Dale was a good bloke and a bit of a wheeler dealer; he was the one in the team you went to if you wanted something. Dale and his brother Ronnie are both into rugby league, but they are like chalk and cheese. Dale was a hot-head on the pitch and a wide-boy off it, while Ronnie is a rugby league referee - and his full-time job is in the Police force.

I am not sure how Dale managed in Paris, but his team-mates needed a translator to understand what he was on about. He has got the broadest South Yorkshire accent you have ever heard. I remember one time – after we had won the Challenge Cup - he did an interview on Calendar, the local Yorkshire ITV news programme. I don't think the interviewer or anyone watching had the faintest idea what he was talking about, it was hilarious. Johnny Lawless does a superb impression of it. Dale won't mind me saying he's not the brightest bulb in the box; he used his physical attributes to get what he wanted, but he was a great bloke to have around.

Another of the main players was Mark Aston, the scrum-half. He was Sheffield Eagles through and through. When the club merged with Huddersfield in 2000 - which was more of a take-over - he hung around and formed a new club; one that is still going and doing pretty well, considering they haven't got any resources and not much support.

Mark is known by everybody in the game as Tubby. He was a good player and I think he deserved more of a shot at Test rugby than he actually got. He earned only one cap for Great Britain, in 1991. He came off the bench and played for about 10 minutes so he wasn't given much of a chance, but he proved how good he was when he won the Lance Todd Trophy, as man of the match, at Wembley in 1998.

Anthony Farrell – a Huddersfield lad who I later played with at Leeds - summed up what we had at Sheffield at the start of Super League. He wasn't the best of trainers and as soon as a game had finished he'd be round the back of the changing rooms having a shifty cigarette. But get him out on the field and he was a rock, just the sort of player you would want in your team. In the off-season we used to train at Ponte Park, on the middle of Pontefract Racecourse. One time the conditioner sent us off on a run round the track. I was in a group with Faz and Mark Gamson. Half way round they decided to go on a detour - straight across Ponte Park to join at the back of the rest of the group. We got our wrists slapped for that, but that's the type of trainers they were. That's why there's a difference between training fitness and match fitness. A lot of it is down to attitude; if you have the right attitude you can perform to the highest level whether you are fit or not.

Another of the characters at Sheffield, who I also played alongside at Leeds, was Dean Lawford. He wouldn't be in anybody's list of the top 100 Super League players, but he was as talented as virtually anyone I've ever played with. He could have been a world-beater if he had applied himself a bit more. We played in the same academy side and went through together into the first team. Dean had his problems. He was a short, fat, ginger kid, so he wasn't blessed with good looks or athletic ability - like I am - but he could play. He was second-choice half-back behind Ryan Sheridan and he also filled in a bit at hooker. He could pass either side and find his man with inch-perfect precision, but unfortunately, he didn't have the dedication to really make it. That happens with a lot of the most skilful players. I think because they've got the talent they reckon they don't need the work ethic as much.

There are loads of Dean stories – like the time he ordered his pizza cut into four pieces because he couldn't eat eight – but my favourite happened at training one day when our conditioner Simon Worsnop was in charge. Dean was in the bad books for some reason or other and he had to do 100 metre sprints at the end of the session. He did the first one, then the second, but on the third he ran straight past the goal line, carried on, got straight into his car and drove off. He is the only player I have ever seen walk, or more accurately run, out of a training session.

When he was at Leeds, Dean once told Franny Cummins and me he could make himself sneeze. How he found this out I have no idea, but if he scratched a certain point on his forehead, it made him sneeze. He did it until he literally had no skin left and he made himself bleed. Dean got on really well with Anthony Farrell and they ended up playing together at Halifax.

Gary Hetherington was the Eagles' team boss for the first Super League season and he would probably admit he is not the most technical of coaches. Here's an example of what he was like. For one game, he came up with a plan to catch the opposition napping from the kick-off. The idea was that Tubby would kick off and Ryan Sheridan would chase the kick. Gary told Tubby: "I want you to kick off, aim for the crossbar and the ball will bounce back. Shez will chase, he'll catch the ball and he'll score - because the defence won't be expecting that!"

So we tried this bright idea at training. Tubby kicked off, Shez chased and the ball dropped short. So try again. Tubby kicks off, Shez chases like mad and the ball misses the crossbar again. Have another go - same thing and by this time Shez is blowing out of his backside. "It's not working this," says Gary. "Try it one more time." Again, Shez runs like mad for 40 metres and the kick misses the woodwork. "Right," says Gary, "That's it - we'll try something else". And that was the last we heard of that idea.

Gary did have another, angrier side. I remember once when we played Halifax at their old Thrum Hall ground, which is long gone now, thank goodness. We had a bad first half and Gary wasn't in a happy mood when we got into the changing room at half-time. We were all sitting around and for some reason I was looking down at the floor. Gary didn't like that; he thought I wasn't listening to what he had to say, so he punched me on the top of my head. Looking back, that's quite funny, but at the time it was a bit of a shock. I didn't know what to do, so I just sat there and took it. If it happened now, I'd more than likely jump up and smack him one back. That shows how passionate Gary was about his team, though he's not that aggressive most of the time.

Gary was never going to win any coaching awards, but he created a good spirit in the camp and he managed to get everyone playing to the best of their ability, which is what it's all about. As well as coaching, Gary was basically running the club and he kept tight hold of the purse strings. He's a good businessman but he wasn't the sort to splash out cash he didn't have for big-name stars. What we did have was a hard-working side, full of experienced pro's coming to the end of their career, or young lads like me who were trying to make a name in the game.

The way Gary ran things was good for me, because maybe if the club had been better off financially and they had been able to bring in some big-money signings, I wouldn't have got a chance. They needed to produce home-grown talent and they took a punt on me because they could see I had potential - and I wasn't going to cost a fortune.

Sheffield didn't have many resources, but they did have fantastic training facilities at Don Valley Stadium. We had a state-of-the-art gym and an indoor track to train on and that was something that really helped us.

In 1996 I won quite a lot of club awards - player of the year, players' player of the year, most improved and that sort of thing. Getting picked for Great Britain was totally out of the blue and it wasn't something I expected, especially playing for Sheffield. We weren't a glamour team and we tended to get ignored when it came to international selection, though Paul Broadbent, one of our props and another leading player, got picked on the same tour.

All in all, it was an encouraging year for us and we thought we could kick on in 1997, but Gary left at the end of the '96 season to go to Leeds as their new chief executive and we got a fresh coach in Phil Larder, which wasn't the best thing that could have happened.

The 1997 season itself was mixed. We finished eighth, but we had a handful of good wins, including doing the double over Leeds. I remember a young kid with a big forehead and a sloping brow making his debut for them. He made a couple of breaks and from one of them all he had to do was draw the full-back and pass, but he dummied, went himself and got tackled. I spoke to him afterwards and he said he'd got a bollocking from their coach, Dean Bell, for messing up. I thought he looked like he could become a decent player, if he learned how to read a game. I checked his name on their team sheet and it was Kevin Sinfield.

Those wins over Leeds were probably the highlights of what proved to be Phil Larder's only year in charge at Sheffield. You get many different types of coaches in this game and Phil Larder likes to put the fear of God into you. As a player he had been nicknamed Soft Centre, but as a coach there was nothing soft about him. If you dropped a ball, in practice or a game, you knew about it and so did everybody else because you'd have Phil raving at you. It got to the point where you didn't want to try anything in training because you knew what would happen if it went wrong. It was a bit like being in boot camp.

He liked to train with the players, to prove he could still do it better than we could. He was massively competitive, which is obviously a good thing in professional sport, but I don't think his methods worked, not with the players we had at Sheffield anyway. He'd like to beat you in fitness training and demoralise you that way.

As a fairly young kid still, I found that type of coaching method quite intimidating. If I had a coach like that now it would be water off a duck's back, but when you are scared to make a mistake it doesn't encourage you to try new things, to take risks or to develop your game.

I haven't got any complaints about Phil's technical ability and he had a good background. He has a sport science degree, he played union and league to a good standard and he coached Widnes and Keighley - as well as England and Great Britain – before arriving at Sheffield. He knows his stuff, but I wasn't a fan of his style of man-management. It takes a lot to be a good coach; you need a mixed bag of attributes, not just technical nouse.

I think player power played a part in him getting sacked. A lot of us felt the same; it was like being in an army barracks and that wasn't great for team spirit or morale. There were a lot of unhappy people there at the time. Phil had done well at Widnes - who were a big club - and with Keighley when they were on the up and trying to get themselves into Super League, but at Sheffield we didn't have any star players or resources to support the team. I think he had unrealistic expectations about what we could achieve. The team didn't fit the coach and the coach didn't fit the team. We were happy to be a mid-table outfit, but Phil wasn't. Maybe if we had been a top side things would have worked out better for him. As players, we didn't respond to his methods and the first half of 1997 was a bit of a disaster. We only won four games and eventually the axe fell.

A few players, Paul Carr was one, had had enough and they made their views known. I didn't have anything to do with it, because I was still young and relatively new to the game, but the board decided enough was enough and Phil found himself out of a job.

As it happened, that was probably the best thing that could have happened to him. He went back into rugby union with Sale and then Leicester and Clive Woodward pulled him into the England coaching set-up. He was defence coach when they won the World Cup in 2003 - he got the MBE for that - and he also went on a couple of British Lions tours, so he did well for himself.

That didn't surprise me, I always thought he was a good coach, but for me he didn't have the right way of getting his ideas across. Phil's departure also had a positive effect at the Eagles because John Kear took over and that appointment paved the way for the best day of my career.

A few years ago the Rugby Football League held a vote among fans to pick the greatest Challenge Cup surprise of all time and Sheffield's Wembley victory over Wigan Warriors in 1998 walked away with it.

That's something I am hugely proud to have been part of and I am not at all upset that people look back on us as a team of no-hopers who happened to come good on the day. Of course that's not the full story, but I'll happily admit Wigan were a better team than us, with better individuals. They went on to lift the Super League trophy that season, finishing top of the table and winning the inaugural Grand Final against Leeds. We ended up eighth and that was a fair reflection of the two sides' relative strengths.

We had some good players and a couple of great ones, but we were a mid-table team and we tended to lose more games than we won. What we did have was a fantastic team spirit and a quality coach who knew how to get his players up for the big occasion.

Probably our best player in 1998 was Dave Watson, who had wonderful skill, but was also as mad as a box of frogs and was always in trouble. He didn't have any money at all when he came over to this country from his native New Zealand and he liked to enjoy himself off the field a bit too much. To prove it, he had served a ban earlier in his career for taking cannabis.

He was the nicest bloke you could meet when he was sober, but once he'd had a drink you had to be quite wary of him, because he could just flip. He was always after money. One time he asked the Eagles chairman, Tim Adams, if he could borrow some cash to fill his car up with petrol. Tim asked him how much he needed - and he said 500 quid!

As a player he was absolutely exceptional and I don't know if we would have won that Cup final without him; he kept us in the game a few times. He didn't train much, but once he got out on the field he could do whatever he wanted.

Dave was our go-to player, but John Kear's arrival, in place of Phil Larder, was the most important piece in the jigsaw. Of all the team bosses I have worked with, John was my favourite personality, though he wasn't the most technically gifted of coaches. One time Mark Aston and I were talking to Darren Turner about running lines - how to run on inside shoulders and that sort of thing. John came over and said "there's no need to bother about all that - just run over the top of them"!

John really does his homework. He prepares for games in depth and he definitely can get you motivated, though it's hard to describe how that works. It is probably different for different people, but in John's case it is his passion which really shines through. He cares and he makes you care.

He is from Castleford, which is rock-solid rugby league country, and he is massively passionate about the game. He really cares about his players, his teams and the sport itself. He has a lot of love for the game and that rubs off on other people. As Eagles' coach, John knew how to get his message across, without being too technical and confusing everybody. He is a fully qualified teacher and I think that probably helped with his coaching career.

On one later occasion, when he was the international coach and we were playing New Zealand, he had the idea of coming into a team meeting and ripping up a Kiwi shirt. He didn't do it - which is a good thing, because we'd probably have wet ourselves laughing - but that shows how passionate he is.

He is also someone a player can approach and talk to. At times it is like he is your mate rather than the boss. That doesn't always work but it did for Sheffield in 1998. We were men on a mission that year. Right from the first meeting in pre-season, John said "we are going to win the Challenge Cup". If anyone else had told us that, we wouldn't have believed them, but John was confident we could do it and that seeped through to everybody in the camp. I think John was being realistic. He knew, and we knew, that we were never going to win the league. You have to be consistent over a whole season to do that and we weren't good enough, but we could pull out good performances every now and then - and that's what the Challenge Cup is all about.

You also need a bit of luck with the draw. In the first round we got Leigh, who finished bottom of Division One that season. We beat them 66-11 and I got over for a try. In the next round we drew an amateur team, Egremont, at home and hammered them 84-6, with me crossing for a couple of touchdowns. Then it began to get tough. We had to go to Castleford Tigers, who really fancied their chances of winning the Cup. They had already won at Leeds and beaten Bradford Bulls, so they were in red hot form and full of confidence after knocking two of the big guns out.

Like us, they probably weren't strong enough to win the league so they had also targeted the Challenge Cup. The tie was televised on the BBC and the Grandstand coverage certainly got me noticed, though not for all the right reasons. Even all these years later people still come up to me and ask about my run-in with Castleford's Barrie-Jon Mather. It was my 15 minutes of fame and what happened was this: We were trying to clear our lines and someone threw a pass out, which BJ intercepted to score. My team-mate Darren 'Rocky' Turner, being a dirty little so and so, went in with his knees as BJ touched down; they had a bit of a set to and Dean Sampson, the big Castleford prop, came in to have a go at Rocky. I pushed Dean, we got into an argument and out of the corner of my eye I saw BJ - who is about 12 feet tall - coming towards me. I thought I was going to get thumped, so I decided to get my retaliation in first.

I actually had hold of the referee, Robert Connolly, with my right hand and I punched BJ with my left. I caught him sweetly on the chin and he went down like a sack of spuds. I should have been sent off, but I didn't even get a caution. I don't know what the referee was doing! All this was captured by the TV cameras and there was uproar about it, on the terraces and in several million living rooms all over the country. To rub salt into Cas' wounds, I went on to score two tries and we won the game, 32-22, which was a fantastic victory for us because nobody had expected us to get through. It was supposed to be Tigers' year, but we went there and spoiled the party. I still get abuse about it every time I go to Castleford now and there was a huge fuss after the game, when my clash with BJ dominated the headlines.

The incident with BJ was a career-defining moment, but isn't something I am proud of. I had been on tour with him in 1996 and though we weren't exactly mates, we got on okay. I was disappointed with myself afterwards because he is a nice bloke, a real gentle giant. He hasn't got a bad word to say about anybody, though I don't think I was his favourite person that evening.

I went up to him after the game and apologised and I really meant it. He was nice enough about it, though he must have been fuming about missing out on a possible trip to Wembley. A few days later the club got a letter from a young fan who had seen us talking. The same fan also wrote to the Rugby Football League, saying the fact we could have a chat about it afterwards showed what a great game it was and also appealing for them to be lenient with me. They didn't take any notice, of course. After the RFL's disciplinary experts had a look at the video I got called to a hearing and handed a four-match ban. It was probably deserved, but Cas did everything they could to make sure I copped it. Their medical report said that BJ had twisted his knee when he'd been knocked down and that I had fractured his jaw. Before the disciplinary meeting, John Kear was pretty confident I'd get a two-match suspension and it would be reduced to one on appeal, because we were going to plead self-defence. If it hadn't been a televised game I might have had a bit of success, but I think the panel felt they had to do something, after all the furore the incident had caused.

My punch on BJ caused a lot of ill feeling at the time and that hasn't gone away, though I don't think he bears a grudge. At one time I lived in Normanton, which is mid-way between Castleford and Wakefield. The first time I popped into Cas to do some shopping it was like walking behind enemy lines. I had only been there five minutes when someone came up to me and said "What do you think you're doing here? You're not welcome after what you did to us." That was the first of many such remarks and after an afternoon of comments like that, I got the message and hightailed it out of Dodge.

The ban could have been a lot worse, but it meant I couldn't play in the semi-final against Salford at Leeds' Headingley Stadium. That was an awful afternoon for me. Salford were the favourites and they were in front 18-10 with just 15 minutes left. It looked like we were going to miss out on an appearance at Wembley and if that had happened, I would have blamed myself. As it turned out, Tubby got a try to get us back in the game and then Dale Laughton crashed over with seven minutes left and we hung on to win 22-18.

It was terrible having to watch from the sidelines. When the final hooter went, Salford made a break and a lot of our players stopped and began celebrating, rather than playing to the whistle. Matty Crowther chased back and made a cover tackle to save the day. I'll be forever grateful to him for that.

Salford fans invaded the pitch at the end and one of them attacked the referee, Stuart Cummings. I ran on to the field to celebrate and found myself in the middle of an angry mob, all of whom were drunk and some of them in tears. I thought my time had come. I ended up managing to worm my way out and scarper off the pitch. The whole day was a strange experience. I was massively pleased that we'd won, but because I hadn't played I didn't feel part of it. You don't experience the same elation as you do when you have been involved. I was relieved more than anything else.

We had four games between the semi-final and Wembley and we lost three of them, but off the field our preparations couldn't have been much better. The film The Full Monty, about a group of male strippers in Sheffield, was a big hit at the time and that was our theme. Coincidentally, one of the characters in the film wears an Eagles shirt, which was great publicity for the club, and it felt like a bit of an omen.

The club made the most of the exposure the Wembley appearance and the film created. And exposure is the right word. A week or so before the game we went to the club where the movie was shot and we all got naked for a photo call, John Kear and everybody in the team. We were given rugby balls to protect our modesty and if you look at the picture, you can see the one they gave me was extra-large.

It was a good build up and the main emphasis for us was enjoyment. We were determined to go to Wembley and have fun. The team meeting before the game was really emotional: John made a motivational speech and when I looked over at Matty Crowther, his bottom lip was quivering. We were both nearly in tears.

You can sense when you're going to win a game and we just knew we would come out on top, even though we were playing Wigan, who were the Cup kings. They had a much stronger squad, full of internationals and players who had been in finals before, but from the Cas game onwards everything just seemed to fall into place for us. It was an emotionally-charged squad, we had a great team spirit and we really believed in ourselves. It was our destiny.

I have never been to Wembley as a spectator, so the walkabout on the pitch the day before the game was something special. I couldn't quite believe I was there. Nobody expected us to win and that was a good thing as far as we were concerned. The bookies had us as 14-1 underdogs, which was also a good thing. Like several of the boys, I had a few quid on us to win the Cup and the chairman Tim Adams also had a big bet. We were on

£3,000 each from the club to win, so the gamble made a big difference to our match fees. Tim paid our bonuses out of the winnings from the wager he had placed.

The day itself was special. Before we walked out, John said "if you see your family in the crowd, wave at them". Normally teams walk out of the tunnel stern faced, with heads down, trying to shut out the atmosphere. We were the opposite. We wanted to soak it all up. We all knew we might never play in a final again, so we were determined to make the most of it. We loved the occasion. It was a warm, sunny day, the atmosphere was electric and the walk-on was one of my favourite moments of the entire event.

The game went exactly to plan. We scored after just four minutes when Nick Pinkney got above Jason Robinson to go over the line from Mark Aston's bomb and then Matty Crowther scored: Rod Doyle passed to me and I got poleaxed by their winger, Mark Bell, who came flying out of the line. That created a gap and Matty picked up to go in and touch down.

Mark Aston kicked a goal and a drop goal and we were 11-2 up at half-time. We were all focused and confident in the changing room during the break. Wigan were going to hit back at us, we realised that, but we knew if we kept doing what we'd done in the opening 40, we'd be all right. In the second half they did come really hard at us, but Darren Turner went in for our third try and Tubby kicked another conversion, so that made it 17-2. They got a try and a goal back, but we held on quite comfortably to win 17-8.

I was happy with how I played. I didn't get a try myself, but I put Matty away a couple of times and I made a few strong runs. From a team point of view, the way our game plan worked was really pleasing. We targeted Jason Robinson because he wasn't the biggest of blokes and that was how Nick scored the first try. When that worked, we knew we had the tools to beat them.

Near the end Andy Farrell had a try disallowed and got penalised for spitting his dummy out at the referee and that was the moment when I knew we were going to win the game. Wigan threw everything at us in the second half and at one stage I looked up and I could see pigeons pecking at the grass in the Warriors' part of the field. We managed to clear our line with a kick and all the birds flew off.

When Rocky got his try we knew it was going to take something special from them to turn it around. They were a very good side, but we had the edge on the day. At the hooter, the feeling was one of immense joy. Paul

Broadbent was bawling his eyes out because it meant so much to him. He was a workmanlike player who took the game very seriously. If we lost a match, he'd sit in a corner of the changing room and sulk. He was coming towards the end of his playing career so to have achieved something like that was fantastic. In those days players' kids were allowed on the pitch to join in the celebrations and that was another nice moment.

We had a party back at a hotel in London afterwards, which was a big night and the free beer went down very well. We all ended up getting naked again, standing on the tables doing our Full Monty bit. Even Tim Adams joined in that time. There's a time and a place for drinking and our team hotel that night was the time and place.

I've gone on to achieve a lot more in my career, but that is still the stand-out highlight, the one I'd like to live through again if I had the chance. It was particularly special because we had been written off so much. At Leeds, there's a different type of pressure as you're expected to win things. At Sheffield the only pressure was what we put on ourselves. I spoke to Ray French, the BBC TV commentator, afterwards and he admitted he hadn't given us a chance and everybody else in the media felt the same.

The rest of that season was a huge anti-climax. We played Wigan at home in the league the week after Wembley and got battered, 36-6. I scored our only try. Nobody, in our camp at least, cared. We had achieved our goal and anything after that was going to be a bonus. We still went out and tried to perform at our best, but if we lost, our attitude was 'oh well, it's not the end of the world'.

The sad thing is that Eagles never kicked on after Wembley. The club was in debt and the owner, Paul Thompson, was financing it himself. We thought winning at Wembley would capture the public imagination in Sheffield and transform us into a big club, but it didn't really happen and we were soon back down to crowds of 3,000 again. That was really disappointing. We finished eighth in the table again in Super League II, which wasn't too bad, but a terminal decline set in after the Cup final and the club only lasted one more year before the ill-fated merger with Huddersfield. The idea then was that the club, Huddersfield-Sheffield Giants, would split itself between playing at the Galpharm Stadium and Bramall Lane. People called it Shuddersfield, but the Shud bit got neglected and the Steel City element was eventually dropped altogether, though Mark Aston's re-formed club are still alive and kicking.

I had moved on by the time of the merger. At the start of 1999 I was being linked with Wigan and Leeds. Andy Goodway, who had coached me at Test level, was in charge of the Warriors team and Gary Hetherington was chief executive at Rhinos, so they both knew me and what I could do and I was aware of what they were all about. Being chased by the two biggest clubs in the game is a nice situation to be in.

Wigan didn't get around to actually making me an offer. Negotiations didn't get that far because they opted to sign Steve Renouf, one of the great Australian Test centres, instead and the club didn't need both of us. I wasn't too bothered, because I had been speaking to Gary for a while and I was coming round to the idea of going to Leeds.

Sheffield didn't want me to go, but I asked for a transfer and they were in such a dire situation financially, they couldn't afford to hang on to me. I started talking to Leeds at the beginning of the year, but didn't sign until the very end. Believe it or not, I didn't move for the money. I was one of the top earners at the Eagles and I took a cut to switch to Headingley, but I saw Leeds as a big club with much more potential; they were very keen to get me and having worked with Gary before, I knew what sort of environment I'd be going in to.

Rhinos won the Challenge Cup in 1999, while I was talking to them about a move, but at the time they were the game's sleeping giants. Gary had big plans and he sold me on what he thought the club could achieve over the next few years. He was talking about winning Super League titles and becoming the dominant force in the game and, though it took a while, to be fair to him he was spot on.

To an extent, I talked my way out of Sheffield. I played 25 games in 1999 and scored 19 tries, so it was a good season for me personally. But I wasn't happy with the direction the team was heading in. In sport when times get hard you often have a circle of truth, which means you all sit round and tell each other what you think is going wrong, why it's going wrong and what can be done about it. It is a chance to get things off your chest and I am a bit notorious for speaking my mind in meetings like that.

I'd been at the club a while, I had achieved international status and got a Cup winner's medal and I wanted more. Towards the end of the year we circled the wagons and I told a few home truths. I had a dig at the coaching staff, which was still led by John Kear, with Simon Worsnop as conditioner.

Simon was very knowledgeable, but he struggled to put things across. What amazed me was, he was taking us for defensive drills in training, something he knew absolutely nothing about. I criticised him and had plenty to say about John and his assistant Steve Deakin. One of the things I said about John was that his heart wasn't in it.

It was basically a breakdown in our relationship and not long after that, I found myself at Leeds. John had said they needed me at the club and he wasn't going to let me go, but after that meeting he changed his mind and I was basically told to pack my bags.

Late in the season, we played Leeds away. I was getting linked with the Rhinos in the papers and I did a press interview in which I said I thought we were playing "boring" rugby. The paper made a headline out of that and as you can imagine, it didn't go down too well with John and some of the other players.

We had a team meeting as usual before the match, at The Village hotel in Headingley, and John was steaming. He told the rest of the team: "Just give Keith the ball and we'll see what he can do with it." We won 36-22, I scored and had an absolute stormer, one of my best games of the year, so at least the Rhinos fans could see they weren't getting a total numpty.

I don't want it to sound like I left Sheffield on bad terms, though, because that wasn't the case. The Eagles club and the people there, including - and probably especially - John Kear, were good to and for me and without them I wouldn't have gone as far in the game as I have.

I have got some great memories from my spell at the Eagles and I learned a lot from John Kear. I have worked with him since and I've still got a lot of time for him, as a bloke and a coach. He told me when I left that he had no hard feelings and I was the same way. It was just time for a change.

CHAPTER 3

TOUR-TURE AND TAKING ON THE WORLD

If you were following rugby league in 1996 you probably knew about my first international call-up before I did! In those days the system for notifying players about Test duty was a farce. The team management usually announced the squad at a press conference and the players would get an official letter a few days later, giving full details of what was going on. The players, in other words, were the last to know.

Tony Smith tidied things up when he was in charge, but before that it was a case of getting the news off Teletext, reading it in the newspapers or hearing from a journalist who called you for a comment.

At the end of the first Super League season Gary Hetherington, who was the Great Britain assistant-coach, gave me a heads-up that I was in the frame for a place on that autumn's tour to Papua New Guinea, Fiji and New Zealand. Apparently it was down to a choice between me and Warrington's Jon Roper, who was playing out of his skin at the time. I don't know if it was because of Gary's influence, but I got the nod first. Jon got a call-up anyway when a few of the original picks dropped out, though I think later on he wished he hadn't.

I only knew for sure that I was in the squad when I read it on Teletext. The stories in the press said I was a surprise choice - and that was true. I was more shocked than anybody. It was the first time I'd had a sniff of representative selection at any level and until Gary tipped me off I hadn't the faintest idea I was even a candidate. I was still trying to find my feet in the game and I hadn't given international honours a second thought.

I had only been playing the game seriously for a couple of years and was still basically as green as grass. I had enjoyed a good season, but luck had played a big part in that because if Joe Dakuitoga hadn't got injured on that opening night in Paris, I might not have got much of a look in. I couldn't help feeling it had come a bit too soon and that assessment turned out to be right.

Still, you can't look a gift horse in the mouth so off I went on my first big rugby adventure. We had a couple of training sessions, including one at Huddersfield YMCA, then we were straight into it and right from the start it was a tough tour.

Not being much of a world traveller - up to that point my globetrotting experience added up to one holiday in Lanzarote and the opening Super League game in Paris - I didn't even know where Papua New Guinea and Fiji were. I can tell you now they are a long, long way away! It took us 47 hours to get to PNG and flying in economy it wasn't a lot of fun.

The first leg, to Singapore, was pretty straightforward. We had a 12-hour stopover and the first thing we saw when we got out of the airport was somebody dead in the middle of the street. There had been a road accident and the body was still lying there, in a pool of blood, so that didn't really do much for anybody's mood.

Phil Larder was the Great Britain coach and he decided we would use the stopover for a training session. Phil trained with us and we got absolutely flogged. We were all pretty stiff after the flight, it was red hot and so humid you could hardly breathe. That decision wasn't very popular with the players and I think what happened during the stopover set the tone for the rest of the tour. At one stage Phil had a pep talk with Jon Roper and he told him "You're a good player, you just need to learn how to catch a ball." That was Phil's idea of how to motivate someone. It totally blew Jon's legs off and shot his confidence to pieces. Things like that don't make for a happy camp.

After Singapore we flew to Port Moresby, in Papua New Guinea, and we had to wait there in the baking heat for five hours before we got a connection on to Lae. Having never been outside Europe before, Papua New Guinea was a massive culture shock for me. It is a pretty wild, untamed place, the heat is incredible and the living conditions are basic. We had been due to go to the PNG Cup final as soon as we arrived, but because we were delayed getting there we had to give that a miss, which turned out to be a good thing. Rugby league is the national sport in PNG and the locals are obsessed by the game. It is a violent country, crowd trouble is common and that Cup final was marred by a huge riot among the spectators. We heard later that several fans had been shot and that tear gas had been fired into the crowd. Nobody in PNG thought that was unusual.

Papua New Guinea itself was a real eye opener. When we first landed at the airport there were thousands of people just sitting around, waiting for something to happen. The national obsession, apart from rugby, is a drug called betel nut, which you chew and then spit out. There are red stains everywhere - and at first I thought it was blood!

Most British rugby league players could walk down the street anywhere in the country outside Yorkshire, Lancashire and Cumbria and not get recognised, but thousands of miles away in PNG everybody knew who we were. Obviously there aren't too many 6ft 4ins white blokes wandering around, so all the locals knew what we were there for and that could be quite intimidating.

A group of us went for a walk outside the hotel one evening and by the time we got back there must have been 200 people following us. We were told it wasn't safe to walk around on your own, but we didn't have any trouble at all. The locals just wanted to look at us and touch us. It was all very surreal.

The hotel was surrounded by a 6ft high barbed wire fence, patrolled by armed security men, with very big, fierce dogs. We had to spend most of our time cooped up there so we didn't get to see much of the countryside. Not that you felt much like doing anything, it was so hot and humid. The buildings we were in were air conditioned, but going outside was like walking into a blast furnace. We spent a lot of time in and around the pool. The media were staying with us, including Ray French, the BBC TV commentator. He had a comb-over hairstyle at the time and we enjoyed a good laugh at him swimming, with about three feet of hair trailing behind him.

The first game on the tour was against the PNG President's team, up at Mount Hagen. I played in the centre, scored a try and set up a couple more in a 34-8 win. Playing in that game was a good experience for me, but it was definitely outside my comfort zone. Being at altitude it was a bit cooler than in Lae, but harder to breathe because the air was so thin.

We changed in a hotel and then rode to the ground in a minibus. The local fans were amazing. Some of them had walked for days through the jungle just to watch the game. There were people clinging to trees all round the pitch, because most of them couldn't afford to pay to get in. That's not the sort of thing that happens at Don Valley Stadium, though it's not unheard of in the Pennine League.

The referee was a local and he did his best to give the home side as much help as possible. They got every 50-50 decision and quite a few 10-90 ones. The crowd invaded the pitch after the final whistle and the referee got his nose broken, because the locals thought he was too biased to us. I don't know what the score would have finished up as if that had been the case.

It was a pretty intimidating environment and not just for the players.

Dave Hadfield, of the Independent, was one of the few journalists on the trip. We got straight on to the minibus after the game, but Dave isn't the quickest of blokes and he almost got left behind. As we set off we saw him running after us, with a big gang of Papua New Guineans chasing after him. Dave was convinced they were lining him up to be that day's lunch. I still have a laugh with Dave about that now.

I didn't play in the Test match, which GB won 32-30, mainly thanks to Bobbie Goulding's goal kicking. Marcus Bai, a top fella who I teamed up with a few years later at Leeds, played for PNG that day. The Papua New Guinea national team are always tough and awkward to play against; they aren't the biggest, but they are totally fearless and they really do put their body on the line. They've got some skill as well, so even though it was close, it wasn't a bad result for us.

After PNG we jetted off to Fiji, which was a lot more relaxed. That's a beautiful place and I've been back since on holiday. We were based in the touristy area around Nadi and Fiji holds happy memories for me because it was where I made my Test debut. I played in a warm-up game against the Fiji President's XIII, scoring another try, and after that Phil Larder told me I'd be on the bench for the one-off Test, which was the first time Great Britain had played Fiji. We won 72-4 and I scored our 13th and final try, which made it three games and three touchdowns on the tour so far.

I was really nervous beforehand. I was one of the new boys in the squad, I was only 20 and I didn't really know what to expect. I was a bit in awe of some of the other players out there and I only really knew the Sheffield guys: Beans, as Paul Broadbent is known - as in broad beans - and Daryl Powell. I wasn't the most outgoing of people and I tended to be one of the quiet ones, sitting on my own in a corner. Making my Test debut was a proud moment, but it didn't seem real. I kept thinking 'this can't really be happening'.

The most memorable thing about that game against Fiji was a huge punch-up which erupted midway through the first half. Denis Betts got into a dust-up with one of the Fijians and everybody else joined in. Denis and the Fijian, Livai Nalagilagi, got sin-binned, but then it all kicked off again.

One of the Fijians, Mal Yasa, who played with me at Sheffield at the time, got upset at something that was said to him and ran out of the line to try and attack Bobbie Goulding. He got sent-off as a result and that made the afternoon's work a lot easier for us.

Mal was a big, naturally tough prop. He had done some time in prison and came out as a born-again Christian. He was a massive guy, but didn't have any technique; his game was based on pure strength. The Mal I knew at Sheffield was one of the nicest, most placid guys you could meet, a real gentle giant. But when he went, he went. It took half their team to hold him back and stop him killing Bobbie and that was a side of him I hadn't seen before. Bobbie is the sort of person who can easily wind people up and he certainly did it that day, to good effect.

The Fiji team included three Sheffield players, with Waisale Sovatabua at full-back and big Joe Dakuitoga playing in the second-row, which made it even more special for me. Luckily I was on the bench at the time of the fight, but I got introduced about 10 minutes later. Joe saw me enter the action so he ran straight at me and I missed him. My tackle stats for the game were no tackles, one miss. The try made up for that a bit. I was playing on the wing and Daryl Powell, who was my centre, put me over.

I was happy with the way it went and it was a thrilling moment when I pulled on a GB jersey in a Test match for the first time, though it didn't need washing afterwards! I've got a picture of myself, Daryl, Beans and the three Fijians, which was taken after the game. The others are all covered in mud and my shirt looks like new, which says something about my total involvement, or lack of it.

After a couple of weeks in Papua New Guinea and Fiji we headed off to New Zealand for the final leg of the tour. Things had gone pretty well up to then, the team spirit was good and we were unbeaten, but we knew the Kiwis would be a different class. That's when things started to go downhill and the trip turned into a bit of an embarrassment.

The New Zealand leg of the tour was awful. We began with a warm-up game against a Red Lions XIII, which we drew 22-22. I was rested for that one, but came into the starting line-up for the next match, in Wellington against a New Zealand select team. Phil named what he saw as his Test side and we lost 30-22. It was a disaster for the team in general, but I did okay, well enough to be named on the bench for the first Test.

In those days to get a cap you had to play two games against teams like PNG or Fiji or one against the Aussies or Kiwis, so it was a bit like making a second Test debut. In all honesty, it was a step too far for me. I'd gone okay against lesser opposition on the tour and I was learning all the time, but I wasn't ready for that level of rugby and it showed.

When I went on to replace Stuart Spruce, after 56 minutes, we were leading 12-2. Adrian Morley was sent on a few minutes later and we were still eight points in front, but he got sin-binned with eight minutes to go and the Kiwis scored 13 late points to win 17-12.

I was sent on in the centre, inside Anthony Sullivan. He played a different style of defence to the one I was used to and we hadn't really developed an understanding because we hadn't been tested in the warm-up games. The Kiwis had a good team and they were smart; they saw a young kid in the centre and they attacked him. I didn't deal with the pressure because I was too inexperienced. They targeted me and I failed to cope. John Timu scored two tries in three minutes and I got plenty of the blame from the fans and the media, though not from the coaching staff.

Moz also copped a lot of stick for his yellow card, but that was unfair. He was following orders from Phil Larder to slow them down at the ruck and he got sin-binned for it. It wasn't his fault. I roomed with Moz for the whole tour, so we had to console each other afterwards. He is a good bloke and he was a lot more at ease with the whole situation than I was. He knew a few more of the players and he was a bit more outgoing than me. He likes a drink and he enjoyed getting stuck into the social side of things a bit more than I did. We got on pretty well and it was good to have someone like that to talk to when things weren't going well.

I felt really bad about what had happened, but in hindsight it was probably a good thing. It showed me where I was and how far I had to go to get myself up to international level. I wasn't good enough, at that stage, to be playing in Test matches against teams like New Zealand. What happened was a kick up the backside for me. It also taught me how to cope with criticism, so looking back it was a blessing in disguise and it definitely made me stronger.

I had a chance to get back on the horse a few days later when we took on New Zealand Maori in a midweek game before the second Test. We should have won that one easily, but we had a nightmare and we ended up losing 40-28. That was the last non-Test game on the tour and we were told afterwards that half the squad were being sent home early to save money. That was a real bombshell. The media reported it as though we were all devastated and angry about the decision, but that was an exaggeration. Actually a lot of us were happy and relieved. I know I was.

Phil Lowe, who was the team manager, drew up a list of 12 players deemed surplus to requirements and my name was on it. I was delighted. I had been away from home a long time, I was homesick and things weren't going well on the field. I couldn't wait to get on the plane. Morale in the camp wasn't at its highest by that stage and to celebrate our release those of us who were heading home went out for a night on the town in Auckland, which developed into a morning on the town. When I finally staggered back to my hotel room in the not-so-small hours there was a message waiting for me from Phil Lowe, saying I was needed as cover and telling me to fly down to Palmeston North where the Test squad were based.

I had mixed feelings about that. I had enjoyed the experience of the tour and it had been a real eye-opener for a young kid, but it hadn't gone as smoothly as I had hoped and I wanted to go home. It was devastating watching the rest of them fly back to England, but on the other hand, I fancied another crack at the Kiwis and chance to makes amends for the first Test.

I flew down to join up with the players who were staying on, but as it turned out I might as well not have bothered because I didn't get into the team. I had to act as water-carrier instead. We lost the second Test 18-15 after leading for most of it and we were hammered 32-12 in the third and final game, which brought the tour to an end.

If we had come home after the PNG and Fiji legs it would have been seen as a big success, but what happened in New Zealand showed how far behind we were at the elite level, which has been a bit of a recurring theme throughout my international career.

The tour was definitely a learning curve for me, but on balance it was a good experience, despite the disappointments. The spirit in the camp was good, though morale suffered as the tour went on and things began going against us. The press, particularly in Australia and New Zealand, had a field day and that was hard to take, even if things like that can pull you closer together. Once half the squad had been sent home, that turned the tour into a mockery and we became a bit of a laughing stock.

It is the camaraderie I remember the most, though, which is inevitable when you are spending so much time with characters like Rowland Phillips and Neil Harmon. Neil had acquired a Scream mask, like the bad guy wears in the horror film of the same name. One night he managed to get hold of Anthony Sullivan's room key. Sully was fast asleep when Neil, with a big group of us peering through the crack in the door, sneaked into his room wearing the mask and a long black cape. Sully woke up with a start, saw this figure leaning over him and swung a punch which nearly knocked Neil's head off. That went well, so we tried the same trick with Moz, but Sully's screaming had woken him up and he was ready for us. Which was probably a good job. You don't want to be on the end of one of Moz's hay makers, as plenty of opponents have found out.

So that was my first experience of international rugby and after being so badly out of my depth, I had to wait a couple of years for my next chance. I wasn't selected for the 1997 Super League Ashes series, but when New Zealand toured this country the following year I was back in.

Having travelled all the way to Papua New Guinea to make my Great Britain debut, my first Test appearance in this county came within walking distance of my house, at Huddersfield's Galpharm Stadium. Typically, the series was a failure from a GB point of view, as the Kiwis beat us in two of the matches and the third was a draw. But it was another good learning experience for me and the first lesson I picked up was that this Test lark isn't all it's cracked up to be.

The Great Britain team were staying in a hotel at Brighouse, close to Huddersfield, and I roomed with Paul Newlove, one of the stars of the team and a hugely experienced player. I was due to play on the wing, with him as my centre. That was a great opportunity to pick things up off one of the best-regarded three-quarters in world rugby league. I was really looking forward to gaining some tips from him. He arrived before me and when I turned up in the room, full of enthusiasm and dying to meet one of my heroes, he was sitting on his bed, head in hands, moaning "I've got too much to do, I shouldn't be here". He had got a lot of work on at home and playing for Great Britain was putting extra pressure on him at the time. I was a bit shocked, but a decade later I could understand where he had been coming from.

There was a single bed in the room and a double bed and I thought I'd get the small one, but he gave me the double, which was another surprise. He was a senior pro and I was shocked he wasn't playing the big I-am with a young kid just getting on to the international scene.

The time I spent with Paul did make a lasting impression on me. Don't get me wrong, he was totally committed to the cause, but he had a laid-back approach which took some getting used to. He wasn't the best of trainers, but he had bags of natural talent. I'd be on his wing, asking him what plays were on, what's happening, what's going off? All I'd get back was a shrug of the shoulders and the response "I don't know". I think some of that rubbed off on me. Since the time I spent with him in that series, I definitely got more relaxed about the game. I like a laugh and a joke and I let everything unfold, play off the cuff and see what happens, which was how he approached things.

It wasn't a case of him not being bothered, it's just the way he was and it worked for him. Paul wasn't the best in the gym and he didn't train much, but he had inbuilt ability. You see some gifted athletes come and go, but others stay around for a long time and he was one of the latter.

Gary Connolly, who was the other first-choice centre in that series, was the same, so I was training with the two best in the game. Gaz is one of the most relaxed people you could ever meet and if there had been a Great Britain drinking team, he would have been in that as well. But a fantastic player and a great person to watch and learn from.

So that was, for me, the biggest thing to come out of the series, a personal insight into two of my role-models, people I was striving to emulate and – eventually – take over from: Paul Newlove, who was so laid back he was practically in a coma and hadn't got a clue what was going on most of the time, and Gary Connolly, a complete piss-head. They might not have been typical sporting superstars, but what those two achieved in the game was remarkable and I am still a big fan of both of them.

Making my UK Test debut on my hometown pitch was a bit of a dream come true because a lot of my friends and family were there to cheer me on. When Galpharm – which was originally called McAlpine – Stadium was built it was one of the best things that happened in my career because it meant big games were being played in Huddersfield again. The old Fartown ground used to stage Test matches and semi-finals, but it was quite primitive and Huddersfield moved out in the early 1990s. They shared the old Leeds Road ground with Huddersfield Town for a while and then moved next door when the new stadium was built. The Galpharm is a cracking ground with good facilities, so it is a popular venue with the RFL and I have been lucky enough to play some of the most important matches of my career on home turf.

That first Test was a disappointment result-wise. We lost 22-16, but we might have got a draw if I had been awarded a penalty try near the end. I jumped for a high kick from Andy Farrell, caught it and was taken out in mid-air by Robbie Paul, who pushed me into touch. The referee Bill Harrigan spoke to his touch judge and awarded us a penalty, though a lot of people reckoned we should have got a four-pointer from it. I'm not sure whether I would have scored or not if I hadn't been tackled in the air, but I would have taken the try if I'd been given it. It would have been my second of the game, after I got over earlier in the half, which was a good moment.

The defeat was controversial, but it was our fault. We were 6-2 behind when the half-time hooter sounded. We stopped, but the Kiwi full-back Richie Barnett, who was playing the ball, played on. Joe Vagana picked up and rumbled over for a converted try which proved the difference in the end. We were furious, but Harrigan hadn't blown for time and, as players are frequently told, you should always play to the whistle.

I was in the centre for the second Test, at Bolton, which we lost 36-16. Paul Newlove pulled out with a leg injury and Leeds' Franny Cummins made his debut on the left wing alongside me. We were 16-8 up at the break and looking good, but the second half was a disaster.

That meant the series was dead going into the third game, played – for some reason - at Watford. That was one of the more enjoyable Tests I've been involved in. We were losing 10-2 at half-time and 22-10 with a quarter of the game left, but we showed some fight and Tony 'Casper' Smith booted a drop goal right at the end to salvage a 23-23 draw.

I had a try ruled out by the video ref, got sin-binned – harshly – for interference at a play-the-ball and helped create a vital try for Casper just before his equalising kick, but for me, the game was most memorable for my Leeds team-mate Darren Fleary squaring up to big Joe Vagana. Daz is a legend; he's a big, physically imposing bloke and a menacing sight. He went into the prison service after he packed in playing, which shows he doesn't take any nonsense, but he has a squeaky high-pitched voice, a bit of a lisp and he can't fight for toffee. Big Joe is a proper tough guy and he does know how to rumble. Something kicked off, I got into the thick of it, turned around and there was Daz, bouncing up and down, yelling "come on, come on" at Joe. I couldn't throw punches for laughing.

The following year, just after I joined Leeds, I was picked for the first Tri-Nations series in Australia and New Zealand. For some reason, we were Great Britain & Ireland on that trip, though the only real Irish connection any of us had was the odd stag do in Dublin.

The opening game was a warm-up against an Aussie team called Burleigh Bears, the Queensland Cup champions. It was a bit like Australia playing a practice game against Featherstone Rovers. Of all the hundreds of games I've played, that was one I remember more than most. It was a meaningless match, but an absolute nightmare and almost a huge embarrassment.

Stuart Fielden took one of the first hit-ups and got belted, popping his rib cartilage. That set the tone for the rest of the match. The Bears must have had 30 players and that didn't help our cause. I played the full game and I remember being in the defensive line, trying to talk and get things organised. I looked up and their full team was getting subbed – 13 off and 13 on. And they did that about every 15 minutes. I have never seen anything like it. The regular rests meant they weren't getting fatigued and by the end we were on our knees. Everybody came out of the woodwork to play for them, current players, past players, blokes down the pub. We were a major tourist attraction and it was a case of if you wanted a game, put a shirt on.

We were an international team and to only just scrape a win, 10-6, was quite humiliating, though if we had lost we would never have heard the end of it. They were winning 6-4 with 20 minutes left, but Andy Farrell scored a try for us and kicked the goal to get us home. I'm still grateful to him for that now, but it didn't bode too well for the rest of the tour. Funnily enough, despite the near-disaster, I enjoyed it and I felt I played well.

One of the biggest rollickings I've ever had came after we lost the first Test to Australia – and I am still not sure what I did, or didn't do, to deserve it. We were completely out-played, as simple as that. The Aussies beat us 42-6, after it had been 10-6 at half-time. I played left centre and I wasn't brilliant, but I certainly wasn't worse than anyone else. It was a scratchy performance from everybody and a painful experience, especially for Ryan Sheridan who got absolutely smashed by the Aussie half-back Matthew Johns. Iestyn Harris scored our only try, but it was a dispiriting day and – at the time - Great Britain's worst defeat in Australia. It isn't anymore, but that's another story.

When I arrived at the post-game meeting there was a chair put to one side at the front and Andy Goodway, the coach, told me to sit in that. I thought he was joking and I went to take a place with everyone else, but he said "no, I want you to sit there". I was like a naughty schoolboy pulled out to the front of the class. Once the meeting began, he pulled my performance apart and basically blamed me for the defeat, which I didn't think was just. I had heard some rumours that Goodway wasn't happy about the way I had played, but I wasn't expecting a public execution. He absolutely slated me; anything that happened, it was my fault. On one occasion, Iestyn had put in a poor kick, Darren Lockyer tidied it up and made some big metres up field - and I got the blame for that.

I was in the backs' group and I found out later that the forwards' meeting was about me as well and about how badly I had played. I was pretty annoyed about it, because I didn't deserve singling out after a lousy team effort. It was one of those meetings which could have absolutely destroyed somebody. I have always been able to take things like that on the chin, but players are human and not everybody can handle it in that way. Things like that have tended to make me stronger. It seemed I was the scapegoat and I never did find out why I got the blame, but the strange thing is, I kept my place for the game the week after. In fact, we played five matches on that tour and I was in the starting line-up for all of them.

After we got destroyed by the Aussies, we played New Zealand in Auckland. Because the Kiwis' lost to the Kangaroos in the opening game we could still qualify for the final if we won by at least 20 points. We were pretty confident we'd at least get close to that, but it all went pear-shaped – again – and we were beaten 26-4.

The rugby on that tour was terrible, but it had its moments socially. There was a big motorsport street race going on when we were based on Australia's Gold Coast and we got a pass-out to have a few beers and enjoy the fun. Casper was in the squad and he's a livewire, a bit of a joker who is always chatting. My old Sheffield team-mate Dale Laughton was there as well and he is the opposite, a raw-boned Yorkshireman who could teach me a thing or two about not spending money. He's as tight as a duck's backside and the only bloke in rugby history ever to go on tour and return with more cash than when he left. He didn't spend anything. He saved all his expenses and never parted with a penny. We had our food paid for and most of us went out and treated ourselves to some clothes, a laptop, that sort of thing, but Dale didn't put his hand in his pocket once.

On the motor racing night out, Casper had a beer or two and he got even more loud-mouthed than usual. Unfortunately, he decided to take the mickey out of Dale. Dale took it for a while, until eventually he'd had enough. Enraged, he went up to Casper and told him – in his broad Yorkshire accent - "If tha doesn't shut tha mouth, I'm going to kill thee!" I have never seen anyone shut up as quickly as Casper did. We didn't get another peep out of him for the rest of the night. Dale scared the living daylights out of him and that made him very popular with the rest of us. It was the highlight of the trip, which tells you what sort of tour it was.

After getting battered by Australia and New Zealand, we picked up the booby prize. The Aussies and Kiwis met in the final in Auckland and we had to take on New Zealand Maori in a curtain-raiser. I don't know who at the RFL agreed to that, but it was a complete humiliation – a bit like being in an under-11s match.

The two finalists got the main changing rooms and we had to get stripped somewhere else and then walk down a load of steps to the pitch. We fielded a strong team and won 22-12, but it felt like a punishment. It was a rotten way to finish a disappointing few weeks, though I felt I had played all right.

Touring is not the glamorous experience people imagine. I have got to visit some interesting places which I wouldn't have seen if I hadn't been a professional rugby player and I am grateful for that, but a lot of the time being away is pretty miserable. It's boring, it's hard work and you miss your friends and family.

Even on a short tour, like the 1999 Tri-Nations, you're away from home for at least a month. Living out of a suitcase isn't much fun and no matter how well you get on with your team-mates, everyone is sick of each other's company by the end of it. It is a tough life; you train most mornings and then you're left to kick your heels. There are only so many sights you can see, so many cafes to visit and shops to plunder. The old days of playing, having a few days on the beer and then playing again are gone. Social events are organised, like team dinners, 10-pin bowling nights and so on and occasionally you are unleashed to have a drink or two, but there's an awful lot of sitting around in hotel rooms, which becomes soul-destroying after a while.

You do try to do some sight-seeing, but you don't have your own transport and you have to be back at the hotel at set times for meals and meetings. It can get quite mind-numbing. Poker is a big hobby on tours and non-card players tend to get themselves into coffee clubs. People talk about cliques forming on tours and of course, certain groups get together, but that's only natural. On most tours I have been on there has been a 'take the next seat' policy, so when you turn up for dinner or to a team meeting, you sit next to the previous person to arrive.

But in time off it is only natural to stick with the people you know and you feel most comfortable with. In Test squads there tends to be a large group of players from one or two teams and those blokes hang around together. It's not a case of snubbing anyone else, it's just human nature. You have a lot of spare time to fill, so you spend it with your mates. It is a great life experience and you learn how to look after yourself, but touring is a hard slog, especially when results aren't going your way, which in Great Britain's case is most of the time.

The best international trip I have ever been on was in 2000, before that year's World Cup. The tournament and the England team were sponsored by Lincoln, an American company. As a warm-up they treated us to a trip to Disneyland Resort in Florida. It was superb. We stayed in massive condos, with three separate bedrooms and a huge living area. The main bedroom even had a Jacuzzi. It was luxury and the first time I had ever felt I was being treated like an international. We went to the theme parks and were allowed in an hour before they opened to the public, so we had the rides to ourselves. When it got to the official opening time we were ushered straight to the front of the queues. We played a game over there against the United States and we won something like 114-0, so all round it was a brilliant trip.

One player who didn't enjoy it all was Adrian Morley. On the journey out he was given some sleeping pills. It's an 11-hour flight and they were handing out free booze, so Moz had a couple of bevvies. He wasn't drunk by a long way, but the alcohol combined with the pills and knocked him out and it took him a while to recover. He was practically in a coma for the first few days we were there. If it had been Paul Newlove, nobody would have noticed.

The World Cup tournament itself, played in the UK and France, was a flop and cost the RFL a packet. It was a disaster waiting to happen; from the start it was badly thought out, there were too many below-par teams, too many one-sided matches and games were played at a poor choice of venues, so crowds were low throughout. The ticket arrangements were chaotic - from what I was told afterwards - and to add to all that, it chucked it down virtually the entire time.

That said, from an England team point of view I thought we did a bit better than we were given credit for. We were competitive in our opening game against Australia, losing 22-2 in the first rugby league game played at Twickenham. I played in the centre, with Chev Walker making his debut as my wingman, though I had a spell in the second-row as the game went on. Kev Sinfield played too. I did reasonably well that night. They scored four tries and we had to settle for a penalty goal, but we were far from disgraced.

After that we thumped Russia 76-4, in what was a bit of an embarrassing evening for me. Kev grabbed a hat-trick of tries and Chev and Andy Hay also scored, so the Leeds lads were in the thick of it, but I didn't get over the whitewash. I got the mickey taken out of me a bit after that. I didn't play in the next game against Fiji, but I was back for the quarter-final, against Ireland. That was played at Headingley and it was a good occasion because there were so many Leeds boys involved. I scored the opening try of our 26-16 win. Darren Rogers, the Castleford winger, caught the ball and slipped it to me and I scored in the corner. Chev also crossed. Moz was in the England team as well and Ryan Sheridan, Barrie McDermott, Jamie Mathiou and David Barnhill – who was a Rhinos player at the time - all turned out for Ireland. I think they qualified through having been to Ireland on holiday, or drinking Guinness, or something like that. Ireland were the surprise package of the tournament and they pushed us really close. Those are the best games to play in, so I enjoyed that one.

We let ourselves down big style in our semi-final, getting smashed 49-6 by New Zealand – who went on to lose to the Aussies in the final – at Bolton, which hasn't been a happy hunting ground. The highlight from our point of view was when their centre Nigel Vagana made a long distance break and Jamie Peacock chased back and pulled him down just short of the line. That was a superb effort, but unfortunately Vagana played the ball to Lesley Vainikolo, who fell over the line for yet another try. Tonie Carroll, who had just signed for Leeds, played in the centre and he showed what we could look forward to with some big hits and powerful running.

That was about the only encouraging aspect from my point of view. After that, we all went back to Leeds for the post-tournament booze-up. The after-match is often better when you've lost and you're drowning your sorrows. We had a cracking night in the Skyrack, a popular rugby pub in Headingley. David Howes was the team manager and he appreciated the effort we'd put in throughout the tournament, even though we came up short. He had an RFL credit card and he turned it over to us for the evening. He said "have some fun – you deserve it" so it was my kind of night. Mind you, Howesy hasn't been tour manager since!

England got slated for failing to reach the final and that was a big disappointment, especially on home soil, but a lot of pluses came out of the tournament. We played well in the opening game and were good against Russia and Fiji, though admittedly the opposition wasn't up to much. Some young players, like Stuart Fielden, Jamie Peacock, Kev Sinfield and Chev really made a mark and established themselves as international class and I thought we could come away with our heads held high. I reckon I played all right and I enjoyed working with John Kear, who was the coach, again. It perhaps came a bit early for John, but he did a reasonable job and I'm sure he would have liked another crack at the England job a few years down the line, when he had a bit more experience under his belt.

Our opening game at Twickenham was a famous occasion, but my preparation for that match was probably unique in the sport's history - I spent the morning of the game at a London police station, giving evidence to support one of my England squad mates, who had been accused of rape.

We were holed up in a hotel in Staines, west London, quite close to the ground. The night before the game the players who weren't due to face Australia were allowed out for the evening, to let their hair down. That's a policy which was abandoned quite a while ago. I was under a curfew, so I spent most of the evening in my hotel room, watching porn on TV and chatting to my roommate, Kevin Sinfield.

The following morning, when we got up for breakfast, there was police tape across the door of the adjoining room. We went downstairs and saw David Howes, who told us one of the England players had been accused of rape. He was the player in the next room to ours. We'd been in our room all evening and we knew nothing illegal or untoward had gone on, so we told Dave and he asked us to give some details to the Old Bill. So that's how Kevin and I spent the afternoon before one of the most important games of our lives. The police investigated the incident, decided there was nothing in it and the case was dropped, which was the right outcome and is why I'm not mentioning the name of the player involved, who hadn't done anything wrong.

Later during the World Cup we were in camp in Leeds. Like every other camp, we were bored rigid for a lot of the time, because there was so little to do. One evening a few of us – me, Kev and Darren Fleary - decided to nip into Headingley, which is the big student area in Leeds, to hire a DVD from Blockbusters. That's how bored we were.

We went in my car, a silver Renault. There are two lay-bys in Headingley and I parked in the one furthest away from the shop. When we'd chosen a film and we came out of the shop, Daz looked in the nearest lay-by and said "where's your car – it has been pinched". I fell for it completely. Kev and Daz obviously knew I was looking in the wrong lay-by and they were falling about laughing, but I was getting madder and madder because I really did think it had been stolen. I couldn't understand why they thought it was so funny and I was on the point or smacking one or both of them when they pointed the vehicle out, parked further down the road.

CHAPTER 4

RHINO WOE

At this point I would like to tell you about how I became an instant success at Leeds Rhinos and the way I had their fans chanting my name after a glorious first appearance. I'd like to, but it would be a load of rubbish. And if anyone was yelling my name, it was along the lines of: "Get back to Sheffield Senior we don't want you!"

The process of joining Leeds took virtually the whole of the 1999 season and by the time I arrived the entire situation had become so hyped up, the weight of expectation was massive. Leeds, along with Wigan, showed an interest right at the start of the year and I eventually put pen to paper at lunchtime on September 10 - the day of Rhinos' last league game.

Once Gary Hetherington left Sheffield to become chief executive at Leeds, it was probably inevitable I was going to wind up at Headingley at some stage. Gary rated me and I enjoyed working with him. His take-over, along with the chairman Paul Caddick, put some money back into the Rhinos' coffers and they were able to splash out a bit of cash to bring players in, not that Gary has ever been one to pay big wages. I could have got more money staying at Sheffield, where I was under contract, but I was attracted by the idea of playing for a bigger club in front of much larger crowds and the prospect of winning some silverware.

Sadly, Sheffield didn't kick on after the Wembley triumph in 1998, but by the following year Leeds were the Challenge Cup holders and it looked like they could go on to enjoy a period of sustained success, though if you scratched the surface it became obvious they had some real problems there too. The media linked me with Leeds throughout the year, but when journalists asked me what was going on I could honestly say I didn't know. The move was continually on and off because Sheffield wanted a fee and Leeds weren't keen to pay.

Eventually, a deal was done; I came over for lunch in Leeds on a Friday afternoon, signed a contract and made my debut that evening, eight hours later, thus putting a couple of noses out of joint.

One belonged to the Aussie centre Brad Godden, who had been at Leeds a couple of years and was a big favourite with the fans. He had already announced he was leaving at the end of the year and the final league game was going to be his big farewell, but he got dropped to make way for me and obviously that was a big setback for him.

Chev Walker wasn't best pleased either. He had broken into the side that year and made four appearances. He was on a bonus for playing in five first team games and he reckons that my coming along scuppered that. He had come off the bench and scored a try in the previous match and he was expecting to play that night, but when I signed he got a phone call saying he was dropped, on the afternoon of the game. Godden came back in for our two games in the play-offs, but Chev was left out of those as well, so he didn't get his cash. He still blames me for that whenever I see him now, even though it wasn't really my fault. Marcus St Hilaire was the substitute back for the final three games of the year, so Chev should be blaming him instead!

I've learned plenty of lessons during my career and one of them is that it is not a good idea to make your debut for a team eight hours after you've joined them. I went into the game, against London Broncos, blind, but I sort of muddled through and we scraped a win, 14-8, after being behind for most of the match.

I played okay considering the circumstances and I remember a decent tackle on Ady Spencer late on, when London were trying to pull the game from the fire. I got a pretty good reception from the fans so it wasn't too bad a day, but things went downhill after that.

Graham Murray was the Leeds coach and he was on his way out as I came in. Earlier in the year he had announced that he would leave at the end of the season to coach a club in Australia. From what I can tell, he didn't really want to go and the fans and players were certainly keen to keep him. Ironically, the job he had resigned at Leeds to take had fallen through, but by then Rhinos had already confirmed a replacement, Dean Lance, so Murray was leaving a club he wanted to stay at - and who had been willing to keep him - without having anywhere else to go. It was a strange situation for me to come into.

The team had been struggling since their Wembley win and it was an ageing side. The season fizzled out and after finishing third in the table we lost both games in the play-offs, at St Helens and home to Castleford Tigers. I started in both of those, but I didn't score and didn't play particularly well and even at that early stage some of the fans were starting to turn against me. I came into a team that was on a downward spiral, they'd lost their focus after winning the Challenge Cup and the coach was on his way out. They weren't performing very well and when I signed the expectations on me were massive. The feeling around the place was 'we've made a big-money signing, so everything's going to be okay'. People expected me to turn things around and unfortunately it just doesn't work like that. I was only 23 at the time and I was trying to find my feet in a big club and a very different environment to what I was used to.

I hadn't trained with the boys before my first appearance and I didn't know Leeds' attacking or defensive structures. They might as well have thrown me on to a soccer pitch and told me to get on with that. I didn't know what was going on and all I could do was try and muck in, get my head down and pick things up really quickly. That's hard enough when a team's going well, but nearly impossible in a struggling side.

The rest of the players were okay with me. There was no resentment from anyone else, even though Chev was a bit peed off, but it was a tough environment to settle into and the way the season ended on such a low didn't help. It was the only time during Graham Murray's spell in charge that they lost two successive games. To make things more difficult, I was selected for Great Britain's tour Down Under that autumn so I missed a big chunk of pre-season ahead of the 2000 campaign, which was the last thing I needed as I tried to adjust to my new surroundings.

Dean Lance came in as coach to take over from Graham Murray and one of the first things he did was sign a centre, Paul Bell, from his old club Perth. I got the No 4 jersey - and he was 15 - but he started the season in the centre, with me shoved out of position on the wing. I thought I had been brought in as a first-choice centre and I reckoned I would do a better job, but maybe Dean thought that as Paul was an Aussie he must be a superior player. That's an attitude most English players will have come across at some stage. As it happened, Bell only played four games before he got badly injured - he dislocated a shoulder and damaged his collar bone - and was released, so I switched back into the centre and that helped me settle in.

We started the season off really well in the Challenge Cup, getting through to the final which was against Bradford Bulls at Murrayfield, but we couldn't buy a win in the league, losing our first five. If we hadn't beaten the merged Shuddersfield at home the week before the final, we'd have travelled to Edinburgh bottom of the table.

I copped plenty of stick from the supporters, who thought I wasn't pulling my weight. I came with a reputation as a try scorer, but it took me seven games to get my first touchdown, in a defeat at Halifax. I was trying my socks off, but the Leeds public were expecting a lot more from me than they were getting. I was used to playing in front of crowds of 3,000, who applauded you off at the end win, lose or draw. In my 140 appearances for the Eagles I think we got booed from the field twice.

The crowd at Leeds were much more sceptical. There was a lot more of them and after cheering me on my debut, they turned against me quite quickly, which was pressure I wasn't used to. If the team had been going okay I might have got away with it, but one thing about playing for Leeds is you learn to become thick skinned. Leeds is a big club and you're always in the media spotlight. Players always say they don't read the papers, but they do. It's nice to get praise, but when things are going wrong you just have to put the press talk to one side. If you took everything that was written about you to heart you wouldn't last long - everyone would hang their boots up and we wouldn't have a game. I have had a lot of negative coverage over the years and that season in particular I got a lot of abuse from the national media, as well as the fans.

It took me until half way through the season to really settle in, but I scored four tries in a good win over Halifax in June and that changed things overnight. Instead of booing me, suddenly the crowd were singing my name and ever since, they've been really good to me. Obviously you can't please all of the people all of the time, but I like to think I've developed a good relationship with the Headingley faithful.

Mind you, the game before that Halifax one I copped some of the worst stick of my entire career, though – fortunately – it wasn't from the Rhinos fans. We were playing Wakefield in a match at their run-down and hostile ground, Belle Vue. One of the Wakefield players got injured and there was a long stoppage in play. I was chatting to my winger, Karl Pratt, about something and we both had a bit of a chuckle. Being on the flank, we were right in front of the Wakefield supporters and they must have thought we were laughing about the player who was hurt. The abuse started flying so we did the only thing you can in circumstances like that, we smiled and gave them a wave back. That made things worse and then a steward came on and told us he'd get the police to arrest us both if we didn't stop inciting the crowd!

I've always found it a bit galling that so-called fans seem to be able to throw whatever insults they like at players, but if you so much as look back at them you're in trouble. At least Pratty and I got out of the situation unscathed. I played for Sheffield in a game at Belle Vue once when the referee, Karl Kirkpatrick, upset the home fans so much he got chased off the field at the end. Disgraceful behaviour – but it still makes me smile whenever I think about it.

One of the advantages of joining Leeds was it meant I didn't have to play against Barrie McDermott any more. Barrie is a top bloke but a nightmare to play against and, as it turned out, with. At least when he's among the opposition you know he's going to come head hunting for you.

Barrie was basically big and fat; he wasn't the fittest of players and whenever he got tired, which was usually after about five minutes, his head started to wobble. That was the cue to keep out of his way. When Barrie got tired, his arm used to swing. Nine times out of 10 he'd come third man into a tackle, arm swinging and head wobbling and he'd end up clouting his own player. I had more black eyes playing with Barrie than when he was on the other team. After making a tackle Barrie wanted to see someone sitting on their backside and he wasn't too bothered whether it was friend or foe.

I remember playing against him in a Roses match at Headingley, when I was on the Yorkshire team and he was with Lancashire. He had been on the field for three or four sets, so he was just about exhausted and he moved over into the centre, opposite me, for a bit of a breather. I came into first receiver and I was screaming at the dummy-half to give me the ball so I could run at him. Unfortunately the play kept heading in the opposite direction, but he never lets me forget that. He reckons we'd had an agreement to keep out of each other's way; he wasn't going to smack me and I wasn't going to put some footwork on and make him look silly.

That 2000 season wasn't the happiest for me or the team, but it was certainly eventful. The Challenge Cup semi-final ended in a riot, after we had beaten Hull at Huddersfield. The Hull fans – some of whom had been drinking all day - weren't best pleased to see their team miss out on the final and they invaded the pitch at the end, pulling down the goal posts. Fortunately we were tucked up in the changing rooms by then, so we were well out of it. Hull fans have got a bit of a reputation for that sort of thing, but to be fair to most of them they are passionate and knowledgeable as well. I always enjoy playing against either Hull club, Rovers or FC, because you're guaranteed a decent turn out and a good atmosphere, but those scenes were embarrassing for everyone involved in the game.

The final itself almost didn't happen. On the Thursday morning as we were en-route to Murrayfield - it was while Wembley was being rebuilt and the Cup decider had to be played elsewhere - we got news that the river which runs past the stadium had burst its banks and the pitch was under four feet of water. The staff up there did an amazing job getting the field cleared and the game went ahead, though it was in doubt until 24 hours before kick-off on the Saturday afternoon.

Given the finalists' respective form, nobody expected us to win and we didn't. We lost 24-18, but high-flying Bradford were wobbling and we weren't too far away from snatching it towards the end. Losing that game was my first big disappointment, though strangely the booze-up afterwards was a highlight of the weekend. After a victory, everything is a bit of an anti-climax, but when you've lost you want to drown your sorrows and it usually turns into a good night, though it hurts when you wake up in the morning.

Kevin Sinfield got dropped for the final, after playing in every game up to then. At the time I thought it was the wrong decision and I still do. Kev was 19 at the time and it could have ruined his career, but the way he handled it proved to everyone at the club what a top professional he was going to become. It really hurt him, but he turned it around and used it as a positive, which is the type of player he is. He got a kick in the teeth but he climbed back off the floor. A few years later he spoke about that in a Great Britain team meeting and how adversity can make you stronger, so I know it made a lasting impression on him.

One player whose career it did finish was Leroy Rivett. A year earlier, almost to the day, he had been Leeds' Wembley hero, scoring four tries in their Cup final win over London. Sadly, it all went wrong for him in Edinburgh. Bulls peppered him with high kicks, he literally couldn't handle it and he became the scapegoat for our defeat. Dean dropped him for the next game - when in my opinion the better option would have been to pick him and let him get back on the horse - and he didn't play for the club again. That just shows how quickly fortunes can change in professional rugby league. Leroy drifted around the lower divisions for a while and then ended up back at his old amateur club, East Leeds. I've been playing for so long I have seen highly-rated kids come and go, but it was a shame for Leroy because he had great talent and after his man of the match performance at Wembley, the world should have been his oyster. He was a good kid but his career was a case of what might have been.

Maybe if we had won that day things might have turned out differently for Dean Lance as well, but he struggled big time. He found it hard to get his game plan across to the players and I think he lacked a bit of confidence, which is something every coach needs. You have to believe in yourself and what you are doing, or else how can the troops believe in you and be expected to follow your instructions?

Graham Murray was a tough act to follow and whoever came in after him was always going to have his work cut out. Leeds hadn't won anything for years and Murray had transformed them into a side who could regularly reach big finals. Dean was expected to build on that, but he couldn't do it. It wasn't entirely his fault because, as I have said, the team was getting on a bit and he also had to contend with a terrible injury list, but having said that, I don't think he was the right man for the job. I think he was a bit overawed by how big a club Leeds is. There is a lot of pressure at Headingley and a lot of expectation and when you're the coach you get the blame if things are going wrong. It was bad for me early on, but it must have been much worse for Dean, who away from the club was a good bloke. As a team boss you have to be able to take it all on the chin and to deflect criticism away from your players. Dean wasn't really able to do that.

Training dropped off while he was in charge; the coach was struggling and the team struggled as well. Training became a bit of a circus and we'd all turn up whistling the big top theme. It all turned into something of a joke at times. It is hard to maintain discipline when a coach loses the changing room. You all start to do your own thing and play as individuals. When you do that, every now and then you can pull certain things out of the bag. But when you start looking at each other and you aren't playing to a set pattern, team spirit goes down and morale suffers. You end up going through the motions and just ticking boxes - attended training, tick; played in the game, tick; went to the gym, tick. It's hard to enjoy what you're doing once that happens.

Dean had his faults as a coach but he wasn't a racist. One of the problems in the background that year was his relationship with our winger Paul Sterling. Sterlo is a pretty strong-minded character and on his day he was a superb finisher. Dean, though, didn't see him as part of his plans. He left Sterlo out of the side at the start of the season and Sterlo reckoned that was down to the colour of his skin. He took the club to an industrial tribunal and won a partial victory, which wasn't exactly good for team morale. I don't think racism had anything to do with it. Sometimes coaches rate players and sometimes they don't. If players went to court every time they were dropped they'd spend all of their time in tribunals and none out on the pitch.

Having that sort of thing going on in the background wasn't good for team harmony, but though we struggled for most of Dean's reign, it wasn't all doom and gloom. Things picked up, slowly, after the Cup final and in the middle of the season we won 13 games on the bounce. We had a great victory at Castleford, battling back to snatch it in the last minute after being a long way behind at half time and we also pipped Bradford 28-26 at Odsal, which was one of the most satisfying games I've played in. Ironically, that good spell coincided with Sterlo's return to the team. It clawed us up into the top five and people started to say we could be on course for the Grand Final, but then it all went pear-shaped again and we lost five of our last seven games. We finished fourth in the table and got knocked out of the play-offs at Bradford.

That play-off was Adrian Morley's last game for Leeds before he went off to Australia to join Sydney City Roosters, which was a big loss. It cost the RFL a packet as well, in all the fines they missed out on. The Aussie judiciary must have been rubbing their hands together when they heard he was going over there. He was always getting into fights and being sent-off, but away from the field he is one of the nicest blokes you could wish to meet. He likes a drink and enjoys socialising, but it has never affected him. On the pitch he never takes a backward step and he is always willing to do the hard yards and get stuck in. He's one of the few Brits who has gone over to the NRL and taken the Aussies on at their own game. It suited him to a T over there. He has a good engine, he's very fit and he likes the physical stuff as well. He was a huge favourite Down Under and he deserved all the success he had. I have a lot of respect for him as a player and a friend.

Despite all the problems we had in 2000, Dean was given another chance and to my surprise we started the 2001 season with him in charge. For a while it looked like things were going to work out. We went on a pre-season camp to America, playing Huddersfield and Halifax in a mini-tournament at the Jaguars' gridiron stadium in Jacksonville, Florida. That was a good experience and it paid off when we came home and beat Swinton 106-10 in the Challenge Cup, which is a club record score.

I signed a contract extension, until the end of 2004, soon after that and I was feeling good about things. We had strengthened the team with overseas recruits Robbie Mears, Bradley Clyde, Brett Mullins and Tonie Carroll all coming in and it looked like we were on the up. But Robbie got hurt in that game at Swinton and Brad and Mullo spent just about the whole year injured. After winning our first five matches, including really good Cup victories at Castleford and Hull, we lost the next four, among them a really heart-breaking defeat against Saints in the Cup semi-final. If we'd won that maybe Dean would have hung on, but we got pipped at the post and then lost to Hull in our next game and after that he finally got the boot.

My feeling was one of relief. He had lost the dressing room and we needed a change at the top. We weren't getting any direction and I think it was the right move by the club, though obviously it was tough on Dean and his family. It's never nice when anyone loses their job, but unfortunately it comes with the territory. To be honest, I think it was probably a massive weight off Dean's shoulders. He went back home and got a job as assistant-coach at Melbourne Storm which suited him a lot better. I wished him well but I was glad he had gone. That was a situation I found myself in again about 10 years later.

CHAPTER 5
NEARLY MEN

Probably the best game I ever played in was a Challenge Cup semi-final at Huddersfield's Galpharm Stadium in 2003. We beat St Helens 33-26 after extra-time and it was one of those matches that comes along once in a blue moon.

What made it all the more special was the fact Saints had beaten us at the same stage in each of the two previous years; narrowly in 2001 and with embarrassing ease 12 months later. We fancied our chances going into the 2002 semi, but losing 42-16 was a total humiliation. We scored a late try and as we returned to our marks for the restart the Saints fans at that end of the ground all stood up and cheered. They weren't being sporting, they were taking the mickey. You try to shrug things like that off, but it does hurt when people are laughing at you and that was at the back of our minds when we got drawn against them yet again a year later.

We went into the 2003 game unbeaten and played really well on the day, but again it didn't look like being our afternoon. With a couple of minutes left Darren Smith scored a try for them to make it 26-20. Standing behind the posts waiting for the conversion, we could see Leeds fans at the other end of the stadium flooding out of the exits. If Paul Sculthorpe had kicked the goal Saints would have been through to the final. But he missed and we were, just about, still in it. We took a short restart, they knocked on and we got the ball back from the scrum, then a penalty. That took us up to their line and Danny McGuire, who was just breaking through into the first team that season, dummied over at the corner. Danny's try made it 26-24 with time up and the kick still to come. It was from flush on the right hand touchline, but Kev Sinfield showed nerves of steel to send the ball between the posts, levelling the scores with the final kick of the 80 minutes. That had the Leeds fans who were in the car park by that stage rushing back.

Kev kicked a drop goal in extra-time and then with two minutes left Danny scored a great try, converted by Kev, to win it for us. Afterwards, the pundits were calling it the greatest Challenge Cup tie of all time. It was a privilege to play in a game like that and we thought we had finally cracked it and we were about to win a trophy at long last. We went into the Cup final, against Bradford at Cardiff's Millennium Stadium, on a run of 10 straight wins. All good things come to an end, but we picked the worst possible time for our record to be broken.

Bulls beat us 22-20 and Kev made the headlines again, for the wrong reasons this time. With a few minutes left we got a penalty close to their posts. If Kev had converted it the two points would have levelled the scores, the game would probably have been drawn and the final would have gone to a replay. But instead of kicking for goal he opted to take a tap and Bradford held out.

Kev got some terrible criticism from fans and the media for that, but nobody in the team has ever blamed him. We were on a bit of a roll at the time and they were out on their feet. We were confident that with another six tackles on their line we'd find a way through. We had gone there to win the game and we felt that if we got in front, we were strong enough to hang on to a four point lead. If Kev had taken the two points, we might have messed up from the restart and given away a penalty or a drop goal, so we'd have been back to square one.

We were at a point when we were in control of the game and we were turning the screw. Hindsight is a wonderful thing, but to this day Kev stands by his decision and I still back him 100 per cent. He's the captain, he makes the decisions and I have always trusted him to do the right thing. Nothing happened that day to change that. Anyway, not taking the kick wasn't the reason we lost the game. You have to look at the bigger picture and other incidents had an equal, if not greater, influence on the result. It was one of those things, we were on the front foot and we felt we could score and finish the game off. It didn't happen and credit to Bradford for holding out.

That was the closest we got to winning something during Daryl Powell's time as Leeds coach. He was in charge for two and a half years and, to be fair, he didn't have much luck. He took over with us at a low ebb after Dean Lance left and we definitely improved under Daryl. We seemed to be on the verge of a breakthrough on a few occasions, but it never quite happened. And then the year after he left we finished top of the table and won the Grand Final. He probably didn't know whether to laugh or cry.

Daryl did a lot of good things, one of which was bringing through some young kids who went on to become established first team players. The likes of Rob Burrow, Danny McGuire, Mark Calderwood, Ryan Bailey, Richie Mathers and Nick Scruton all became regulars under Daryl. That wasn't completely by choice. We had some bad injuries to key players, particularly in 2001, and some of our big-name signings failed to do the business. Daryl inherited imports Brett Mullins, Bradley Clyde, Robbie Mears and Tonie

Carroll and three of them went home after just one season.

I would have loved to have played more with Brett Mullins. You could see he had talent; whenever he touched the ball it was like it was glued to his hands, but he spent most of his only season with us on the treatment table or in the Skyrack, a pub just around the corner from Headingley. That was his second home. If he had been fit he would have been great for us, but he only managed 12 appearances and we never saw anything like the best of him. He went back to Australia and ripped it up, winning a Grand Final with Sydney City Roosters in the same team as Adrian Morley.

It was a similar scenario with Bradley Clyde, but he was just unlucky. He had a fantastic career in Australia, but by the time he arrived in Leeds his body was beginning to give up on him. Like Mullo, he was injured for most of the year, but when he did play, all of 15 times, he was sensational. He got a lot of abuse off the fans, who were expecting big things, but the criticism wasn't really deserved. He wanted to do his best. He was our best trainer that year, he trained the house down, but every time it looked like he was going to come in and do big things, he got hurt again. It was just a year too far for him, but I could see he was a class act and it would have been great to have played alongside him in his prime.

Robbie Mears was another injury-prone Aussie. He genuinely wanted to do well, but he was really unlucky on and off the field. After he got hurt in that huge Cup win at Swinton he was out of action for a long time, then he came back and suffered a broken jaw in the second to last league game of the season, away to St Helens. Sonny Nickle caught him with a high shot and seriously spoiled his good looks.

Robbie never really settled into the lifestyle over here and every time we had a game his house got robbed, so that didn't help. Obviously some local scumbag knew who he was and had a copy of the fixture list and he got targeted on a regular basis. He didn't have the best of times and he went back home after one season.

Tonie Carroll did a bit better. He lasted two years before he hightailed it back to Australia. At least he managed to get out on the field on a regular basis and he proved he could walk the walk, as well as talk the talk. He had played for New Zealand in the World Cup final in 2000 and I played against him in that tournament, but the first time I ever met Tonza - Tonie's nickname - was at a pre-season fans' function at a working men's club in Leeds.

He definitely made an impression on me. He was there when I arrived, so I went over to meet him, shook hands, said "how are you doing", like you do and all he replied to me was, "It's a good job you've already got that No 4 shirt, because I would have taken it off you." Then he walked away. I'm not often lost for words, but I was then.

Tonie is the most confident person you will ever meet; confident about his ability and - for some reason I never understood - his looks. He thought he was God's gift, even though he had the biggest chin in the world. When you got tired at training, you could sit on it. He exaggerated that by growing a goatee, but that was the type of person he was.

To come up to a new team-mate and stamp your authority straight away like that takes a bit of nerve. I didn't know him and I had no idea how to react. As a season goes on you gradually get to know new blokes' personalities and I realised that was just what he was like. He wasn't trying to cause offence, he was just saying here I am, I am going to make a big impression.

I used to room with him a lot. I'm not sure if he used to do it just to wind me up, but every morning he would wake up and then sing a song in the mirror to himself. It went something like "Here I am, I am the greatest in the land, my name is Tonza, I am the greatest in the land." I never did work out if he was doing it for my benefit, or if he'd carry on like that even when he didn't have a roommate.

The thing about Tonie was, he could play. He was our top scorer in 2001 with 23 tries in 28 appearances, which is good going. He also had a habit of getting knocked out a lot. Once when we were playing Wakefield away, he banged his head just before half-time and when he came to his senses after the break he emerged from the changing rooms as if he was going to go back on, which the medical staff soon put a stop to. Another time we played Wigan at the JJB Stadium and he slid into the advertising hoardings in spectacular fashion.

He was a big, horrible, strong thing and tackling was his main forte. He had a massive defensive game and if you ran straight at him, you'd know about it. I played against him a few times, but I wasn't daft enough to try and challenge him head-on. After his stint with us he returned to Brisbane Broncos and went on to play for Australia, which proves that he was just as good as he told everyone he was. There are not many players who have turned out for both the Kiwis and Kangaroos.

The mid-season change of coach from Dean Lance to Daryl probably didn't help any of our overseas contingent. It's part of the game, but they had come over expecting to be coached by an Aussie, Dean Lance, and ended up with an Englishman in charge. Daryl got the job much earlier than he expected and I think he would probably admit it came a bit too soon. He was someone we all had respect for, but it is the hardest thing in the world going from poacher to gamekeeper. One minute he was one of the lads, the next he had become the boss.

Daryl hung his boots up at the end of the 2000 season to take over as head of Rhinos' youth department - basically academy coach - but by April 2001 he was in charge of the first team. It must have been tough for him and it was hard for us to adjust as well. It is human nature to try and take liberties and you think you can push a bit harder when someone you know is making all the decisions.

It was a weird scenario and that was probably one of the reasons it didn't really work. Daryl used to come on some of our nights out and once the truth serum started taking effect, people began talking with a bit of honesty. One time Daryl came up to me and claimed I was against him; he thought because I had played with him for so long - at Sheffield as well as Leeds and internationally - I wasn't working with him. He had got it into his head that anything he wanted to do, I was trying to sabotage. He believed if he came up with a game plan, I was bad-mouthing it behind his back to the other players. There was a bit of conflict between us because of that, but the accusation wasn't true. It was a tough time when Daryl came in, he didn't inherit the best of cultures and he hadn't done a lot of coaching at that stage. His back was against the wall straight away, especially as he had taken over from someone who had lost the plot and the changing room. To be thrown straight into being Leeds Rhinos coach was a massive job and a huge ask. Daryl probably needed a couple of seasons somewhere else first. As I mentioned earlier, I had always been regarded as the "next Daryl Powell" when I was at Sheffield and I think that got to him a bit. But I always looked up to Daryl and when he accused me of stabbing him in the back that was quite hurtful. He questioned my professionalism and I was upset about that as well.

We did have some good wins in 2001 and the highlight was a 74-16 victory over St Helens, when I scored one of my favourites tries, going the length of the field from a scrum near our own line. That result was a bit of a flash in the pan though. We ended up finishing fifth and we went out of the play-offs in our first game, away to Saints. That was the famous Foot of God match. We were pressing on their line near the end of the game when Tommy Martyn spotted a spare ball on the pitch and kicked it in-field so the referee had to stop play to have it removed. That break gave them chance to reorganise and they held us out to win by eight points. Someone asked him about it afterwards and he said it was down to the "Foot of God". It was annoying at the time, but I suppose we would all have done the same thing in similar circumstances.

One player who left the club at the end of 2001 was Jamie Mathiou, our Aussie super sub who holds the record for most bench appearances for Leeds. When I scored a hat-trick away to London at the start of that season I passed to Jimmy (as we called him) so he could go over for a very rare touchdown and some of the boys refused to talk to me for days.

Jimmy was a strange character. He was a proper name-dropper and I think maybe he thought he was a bit better than he actually was. From what I could tell he was on a good contract, better than a lot of the other boys, and that didn't make him the most popular member of the squad. He was what I'd call a typical Australian, very loud and very in your face. It's no secret that Barrie McDermott and Jimmy didn't get on. They nearly had a fight at training before the Challenge Cup semi-final in 2001, but I also remember Chev Walker coming close to blows with Jimmy at our old Tetley's training ground in Leeds.

It was in pre-season, on a really muddy day. Chev was larking about, throwing mud bombs at Jimmy. He took offence and tried to wrestle Chev to the ground, but that was a big mistake. Chev's a freak of nature, a real athlete and it was Jimmy who ended up in the dirt, which embarrassed him deeply. To be honest, I thought Jimmy was a likeable character, but if you spent more than 10 minutes with him he was a bit of a pain in the bum.

We prepared for the 2002 season by going to South Africa for a pre-season camp, which was an experience in itself. The fun and games started at Heathrow Airport, when Karl Pratt - my winger - realised his passport was out of date. That caused a real kerfuffle, as you can imagine. We were all crowded round, watching and taking the mickey, especially Jamie Jones-Buchanan. He was taunting Pratty, calling him all the names under the sun for being such an idiot – and then when he got to the check-in desk he discovered his passport was out of date too. They both had to catch a train back to Leeds, go to the passport office in Liverpool, then back down to London for a later flight to Johannesburg. The headline in the paper said "Pratt by name…"

We played Widnes in an exhibition game in Johannesburg at the end of the camp, which we lost in the worst conditions I have ever seen. There was torrential rain, plus thunder and lightning, from start to finish. It was pretty scary, but we had a good drink afterwards to cheer ourselves up and to celebrate going home. Camps like that are good, but it is always nice when they are over. We hit a few of the local bars, which was quite unnerving. It was made clear that the black lads in our group weren't welcome, so we stuck together and moved on. The racism was quite shocking. At one of the bars we did hang around in, we ended up pouring huge jugs of Coke over each other, because it was so cheap.

When we got back to the hotel we saw the other side, quite literally, of Kevin Sinfield. Kev's probably the ultimate professional and he doesn't drink very often, but when he does, he's massively entertaining. For one thing, he likes to throw things. It's bizarre, once he gets a few beers down his neck, missiles start flying - peanuts, ice cubes, anything he can get his hands on. As the night wore on, things were starting to get a bit messy. In the early hours Gary Hetherington turned up, to give us a bit of a bollocking and tell us to go to bed. We were all sitting in the foyer, which had a staircase at one end. Gary had his back to the stairs and as he was lecturing us, Kev suddenly appeared, stark naked, behind him. We all started chuckling, so Gary turned around and Kev hit the deck. Gary couldn't see anything, so he turned back to us and carried on with the telling off, while Kev got back up and started dancing around again. It went on like that for about five minutes and by the end we were all rolling around on the floor. To this day, I don't think Gary knows what was going on.

Daz Fleary and I both bought diamonds when we were in South Africa. Through someone on the staff at the hotel we got in touch with one of the local precious stone dealers. He turned up with bags full of diamonds and a hand gun for protection. There was a casino attached to the hotel we stayed in and I remember a sign at the entrance warning that firearms were not allowed inside.

We had a decent year in 2002, reaching that disastrous Cup semi-final and finishing fourth in the league table, before getting walloped at Wigan in the play-offs. Dave Furner played for them that day, before joining us for the following season. He proved to be a big influence and was one of the reasons we eventually went on to achieve some success.

At the end of that year Daryl set about changing the culture of the club, starting by getting rid of Andy Hay, Ryan Sheridan and Karl Pratt. I think he regarded them as bad eggs and he probably saw me in the same light.

Shez was the grumpiest bloke you could ever meet, even more so than me, which takes some doing. If you had me, Matt Diskin and Shez in one room on our own, you'd have to take away our shoelaces and belts and put a suicide watch on the door. What Daryl did was get rid of the opinionated ones. Pratty had a lot of talent, but he wasn't too bothered about how he used it, while Shez and Andy were both getting towards the end of their career and they tended to speak their mind.

The culture at the club in those days was a lot looser than it is now. It wasn't exactly a drinking culture, but we did know how to party. It was the era of the Dews Fest - Dews as in Dewsbury, the town between Leeds and Huddersfield and scene of some dubious goings on involving the Leeds Rhinos squad, including me. A group of us - 20 or 30 strong - would go into the centre of Dewsbury or the neighbouring town of Batley, invade the scruffiest pub we could find and basically take over the place. We didn't go out looking to cause fights, but we did like to see what we could get away with. There was one time when we borrowed a dartboard. We were running off down the road with it when the landlord came out after us, saying "don't nick that board, it's brand new - here take this old one instead". So we did a swap in the street. On another infamous occasion Danny Ward attempted to kidnap a dog. He picked up a Labrador and tried to walk out of the pub with it, but it bit him. He had to go for a tetanus shot - and I'm not sure what happened to Wardy.

Another time we were out with one of Wardy's mates, known as Star. I was one of the oldest there and Star was having a bit of a pop at me, trying to take the mick. I had got into a big argument with Nick Scruton about dressing room respect. When you first join a club, you wait for everyone to get their peg, then you see what's left. Scroots was fresh in the first team and he was basically saying he didn't care; if he wanted Barrie McDermott's peg, he'd take it. I was telling him that, in my opinion, that was wrong. People like Barrie have been in the game so long even if you think you are doing better than them, you have to have respect for the senior players. It all got heated and in the end, I went for Scroots. Disko was sitting next to me and he grabbed me by the arms, a couple of the other boys jumped on top of me and Scroots scarpered, until I had calmed down.

Then Star came over and decided he'd join in. He got into my face, taunting me and saying over and over "you won't hit me". I told him to go away, but he kept saying it and eventually I lost my temper and proved him wrong. I knocked him through a door into the pub toilet, breaking his nose.

I felt terrible about it. He got himself cleaned up, came up to me and said "There was no need for that now, was there?"

We never did anything to hurt anybody outside the group, but we did behave like proper old-school rugger buggers and there was a bit of a competition to see how many complaints we could get. I remember one night when we took over a pub's dance floor for a wrestling competition. It was all good natured, but if you're in a pub and you see 20 rugby players in a big heap, wrestling, I can understand why it would be a little bit frightening.

We chose the sort of pubs where you wiped your feet on the way out, because we knew we'd be able to get away with doing whatever we wanted. We had a green jacket and whoever was the most entertaining individual on the night out got the jacket to wear next time. The club received quite a few complaints, but there was never any backlash.

Dews Fests, which always took place on a Sunday, got abolished when Tony Smith took over from Daryl as coach. The club, quite rightly, clamped down at the end of 2003, when Ryan Bailey and Chev Walker were both locked up following an incident on a night out in Leeds.

That wasn't a Dews Fest, but I think it did bring home the implications of what could happen if a night on the town got out of hand. We did get targeted when we went out and there was often a lot of abuse thrown at us. People are usually all right early on, but when the booze takes hold later, they can turn nasty. Instead of pointing and staring, which you get all the time, people start coming up to you and the occasional challenge gets issued. I don't know how many times I've been asked to arm wrestle or to tackle somebody, but I wish I had a pound for every one. After what happened with Chev and Bailey, we basically got banned by the club from going out in Leeds, barred from visiting nightclubs and there was a midnight curfew. We had to ask permission if we wanted to go out.

We all thought Chev and Bails were harshly treated by the courts and it's tough when something like that happens to a close mate. I went to visit Chev in Doncaster prison and it was a surreal experience. He was pointing out lads who were in there for murder, armed robbery, you name it. It was tough enough going to visit him, so I can't imagine what he went through. What they did was wrong, but I thought the punishment was too severe. Their case came up not long after an infamous trial involving some Leeds United footballers – who were acquitted - and I think it was a case of making an example of them because they were in the public eye.

The court hearing overshadowed the 2003 campaign, which was a case of what might have been. After the Cup final defeat to Bradford we finished second to them in the league table and then lost both our play-offs games, which meant we were the first team from inside the top-two not to go through to the Grand Final. We played Bradford five times that year and lost them all, including the Grand Final qualifier at Odsal. We should have beaten Wigan in the final eliminator, at home. We were well in front a couple of times, but couldn't finish them off. Brian Carney, their Irish winger, scored two great tries and Danny Tickle booted the winning drop goal with three minutes left. I felt bitter about that at the time and still do. We should have had a penalty for interference on Willie Poching, but the referee - Steve Ganson - awarded a scrum instead and Tickle kicked his one-pointer in the resulting set. After losing narrowly to Bradford so many times that year, I felt we had it in us to beat them once and I'd have been confident of doing it in the Grand Final at Old Trafford, if we'd had the chance.

CHAPTER 6

TESTING TIMES

A lot of people think our national coach should be an Englishman, but to be honest I couldn't care less if a Martian got the job, as long as he showed us how to beat Australia. In 2001 the RFL bit the bullet and named David Waite – a former Australia Test player – as the new Great Britain coach, taking over from Andy Goodway.

David's appointment caused a heap of controversy, because it was the first time an overseas coach had taken charge of the GB team and a lot of people thought an Aussie couldn't have enough passion for the role. But when he came in, David was a breath of fresh air; though he might well really have been from a different planet for all the sense he made during some of his team talks.

As I've said, I don't have any great objection to a foreigner coaching England or Great Britain. It is a massive role and you have to find the right person for the job. At the time David was appointed we had been through all the best English coaches and the RFL were probably looking for someone a bit different. David had been a big success at St George-Illawarra in the NRL, coaching them to a couple of Grand Finals against the odds, so he had the right credentials. There was probably also an element of 'if you can't beat them, join them'. A lot of people involved in the game in this country are star-struck when it comes to Aussies, and to a lesser extent Kiwis. They believe if you have an Aussie accent, you must automatically be better than a home-grown Brit, whether that's as a coach or a player. I am all for appointing the best-qualified individual and you can worry about where he comes from later.

David's problem wasn't that he was born in Australia. He was just too technical. It took a couple of years of playing under him to understand fully his way of doing things. A lot of the time it was hard to understand what he was talking about. In coaching, knowing your stuff is one thing, but being able to put that across to the players is just as important.

When you are in charge of a club you have plenty of time to do that – a full pre-season and then nine months of working with the players, day in and day out. But at international level everything has to be done in a limited number of sessions. So to a large extent you have to keep things simple. In a three-match series there isn't much opportunity for trial and error.

Despite those reservations, in my opinion David was a very good coach and I enjoyed my time working with him. I definitely learned a lot from him and became a better player. He was one of those who wasn't a particularly good player, but excelled on the management side of things. I think that's probably because bad players have to think about things a bit more!

His first challenge was the biggest one, playing Australia with the Ashes up for grabs. The 2001 Test series nearly didn't happen, because of the terrorist attacks on New York that September, a month before the Aussies were due to arrive in this country. Australia were initially due to come over for a mini-tour, playing three Tests and a handful of club games, including one against Leeds, but their players got together and some of them decided they didn't want to travel to England, due to the terrorist threat.

One of their props, Robbie Kearns, came out with a famous quote about being worried that English landmarks like the Eiffel Tower would become terrorist targets. It takes a front-rower to say something like that. I could understand why they were concerned, but cancelling the tour wouldn't have been the right thing to do. Fortunately a deal was agreed and the Test series went ahead without the club matches. That was a big relief to everybody in the game. I was pleased to get an opportunity to test myself against the best players in the world and apparently the RFL was so heavily in debt following the 2000 World Cup fiasco they desperately needed the revenue to keep the game in this country afloat.

It was a really memorable series. The first Test was played in Huddersfield and we won 20-12, which broke my duck against Australia. For some reason I wore the No 5 shirt and I was listed on the team sheet as one of the wingers, but I played in the centre as usual. The game went well for us from the start when Jamie Peacock scored inside the opening couple of minutes. We were 12-0 up at half-time and they came back at us after the break, but we sealed it when Paul Sculthorpe scored with four minutes to go. He got over the line, stood up and kicked the ball into the crowd as the rest of us jumped on him. That was one of the greatest moments of my career, knowing we were about to beat Australia, in my home town, with a lot of my friends and family in the stands.

Over the years Great Britain have managed to win one Test against Australia on a fairly regular basis, but doing it twice in a series has been the problem. I don't think we over-celebrated that day, but it did feel like we had achieved something, when we would probably have been better just waving to the crowd and then getting off and starting to think about the next match.

The Aussies had only been in the country a week before the first Test and I am honest enough to admit that helped us. It takes longer than that to acclimatise fully and get over the jetlag, as we found out to our cost just a few months later. By the time the second game came around, a week later, they were much better prepared.

Unfortunately that game was played at Bolton, which has never been a happy hunting ground for Great Britain/England. We got hammered there by the Kiwis in the 2000 World Cup and the 1999 Test series and it was the same story as Australia thrashed us 40-12. We went into the game with high hopes, but the Kangaroos were 40-0 up after 55 minutes before they eased off and we scored a couple of consolation tries. Scully crossed for the first of them in similar style to the one the previous week, but without all the celebrations.

I have always enjoyed playing at the DW Stadium in Wigan, or the JJB as it used to be known. I seem to play well there and I got Man of the Match for us in the third Test, but I would definitely have swapped it for a win. The final result was 28-8 to Australia, but we went ahead early on and were a lot more competitive that the 20-point margin suggests. It was a strange situation after the game. We were gutted because we had lost yet another series and the Aussies were sombre too, after their coach Chris Anderson was taken ill at half-time. We found out later that he had suffered a heart attack during the first half and had been rushed to hospital. Things like that put rugby matches into perspective. Fortunately he made a full recovery.

I felt like I had played well. I made a couple of good tackles and one or two decent breaks, so there was some personal satisfaction and at least we had restored a bit of pride after the previous week's drubbing. But losing the series after winning the opening game and playing so well in that one was really disappointing.

The media built us up after the Huddersfield game and they knocked us back down again the following week, which is what happens in this country. It's the nature of the British press, in any sport. Before the 2010 football World Cup, Wayne Rooney was hyped up into being the best player on the planet, but he under-performed, all the newspapers stuck the boot in and it was doom and gloom. In rugby league we don't get anything like that amount of attention, but it is a similar scenario. I don't think the rugby league media are deliberately negative and I'm sure they'd love us to be successful, but there's never any in-between – you are either fantastic or rubbish.

After losing the 2001 Ashes series we faced the Aussies again the following July, in completely different circumstances. I don't know if it was a trade-off for Australia agreeing to go ahead with the previous year's tour, but as stupid ideas go, flying to Sydney for a mid-season, one-off Test must be pretty near the top of the list. It was one of the low points of my Great Britain career and I get depressed thinking about it even now.

At first it seemed like an enjoyable experience - mainly because we got to fly business class for the first time, rather than at the back of the plane in cattle. That was great; I actually felt like an international player, which hadn't happened before. If we had stayed on the plane and come straight home again it would have been okay, but getting off and playing the game ruined it.

It wasn't a realistic concept and I'm not surprised it hasn't been tried since. We would have needed a couple of weeks' preparation to be competitive against a team as good as the Kangaroos. As it turned out, we were Lions to the slaughter, literally. For the first few days in Sydney it was just a case of trying to get over the flight and adjust to the time difference. Being wide awake at 3am and exhausted by mid-afternoon isn't an ideal way to prepare for a Test match against Australia.

Even in the luxury of business class, a 24 hour plane journey doesn't do your body much good. In the first training session, the day after we arrived, I got injured. We were doing some weights and I pulled my back. It went into spasm and I was out of action for a couple of days. For a while I didn't think I was going to be fit to play. In the end, I had to have a muscle-relaxing injection and that got me through. It would have been a long way to go just to sit on the sidelines, though as it turned out that would have been less embarrassing than being part of Great Britain's worst-ever defeat.

I think somebody must have been playing a practical joke on Paul King, the then-Hull prop. He's scared of flying but he was named in the squad, made the trip and then didn't get picked for the game. He was not happy about it, I can tell you. When the French team Catalan Dragons came into Super League, he had to have hypnotherapy to get over his phobia, so he could travel to Hull's away games in Perpignan. Still, at least he came home from the Australia trip with his reputation intact, unlike the rest of us.

The Kangaroos are formidable opposition at the best of times but against a team who had been together for less than a week, they were just about unstoppable. It was a rout, 64-10. Leeds boys scored both our tries, Karl Pratt – on his Test debut - and Kev Sinfield getting over in quick succession after we had been 40-0 down, which is a pretty routine score against Australia, but nobody came off the field feeling like they could be satisfied with their own performance. Australia scored 11 tries and to rub salt into our wounds, Andrew Johns kicked 10 goals, so he must have been on a high. It was a disaster, no other word for it. The game had far-reaching consequences for me and the rest of the Rhinos lads. Chris McKenna played in the centres for Australia and he scored a couple of tries, going round me for one of them. That is one of my claims to fame, as probably the only player ever to get stepped by Frigger. It proved very embarrassing when he signed for us the following year.

As usual, after we got thrashed in Sydney, everyone said international rugby league was dead. Obviously Australia were streets ahead of us on that day, but we had been competitive against them the previous autumn and, without making excuses, the one-off Test was always going to be mission impossible. We shouldn't have been put in that position because it was obvious to anyone what would happen. We didn't go in with a defeatist attitude but with so little preparation time, everything was stacked against us.

After that fiasco everyone connected with the GB team was desperate for international success and we were even willing to claim a Test trophy when we hadn't actually won the series. At the end of 2002, the Kiwis came over for three games, which gave us chance to prove we were better than we had shown against Australia that July.

We didn't do that in the first game, which was played at Blackburn Rovers' ground, Ewood Park. I was in the left centre with Karl Pratt as my wingman. He had been axed by Leeds a few weeks earlier because Daryl Powell didn't think his attitude was professional enough, so he had a lot to prove. We were 10-6 up at half-time, but the second 40 was a nightmare, particularly for Pratty. He couldn't cope with their kicks to the corner and they scored three tries through that route, so he got all the blame in the press afterwards and he didn't play again in the series. Internally we all supported him because most of us have been in a similar situation at some time or another. I know it's a bit of a cliché, but it is a team game and everyone has to take responsibility.

After that defeat, most people probably expected us to lose the series 3-0. We stuck to our guns, though, and restored a bit of self-belief the following week at Huddersfield where we came from 10-0 down to draw 14-14 – and we would have won if Paul Deacon's last-gasp drop goal attempt had drifted an inch or two to the right.

Barrie McDermott was dropped for that game. David Waite never seemed convinced about Barrie who became a scapegoat after the Blackburn Test because he dropped the ball in the opening tackle of the second half and they scored in the next set.

I was pleased to keep my place and I enjoyed the game because of the way we fought back. After they went 10-0 up we could have chucked in the towel, but we stuck to our guns and Andy Farrell salvaged a draw for us late on with a penalty goal.

That meant we went into the final Test 1-0 down and the best we could hope for was to draw the series, but either the Kiwis were over-confident or they felt sorry for us. They decided that the third game, at Wigan, would be winner-takes-all, so whoever got the victory would lift the trophy.

We played well that day and beat them 16-10, so after six years in the Great Britain set-up, I finally got to do some celebrating. We hadn't won anything for so long – 1993 was the last time – that we really pushed the boat out, even though the series was actually drawn 1-1. Maybe it was a hollow victory, but we were happy to take it.

Like I usually do, I had a good game at the JJB, scoring our first try. Barrie was recalled and it was nice for him to be part of the celebrations, though I was disappointed that Kev Sinfield got dropped. He was one of our better players in the opening couple of games and I thought it was a harsh decision. The Kiwis' squad for that series included two future Leeds players, Ali Lauitiiti and Clinton Toopi. Toops had a big game at Huddersfield, but he missed the decider with a broken hand which he suffered in a fight with his team-mate Nigel Vagana after the second Test.

The first match of that series was the last time I played with Pratty. He spent the whole time trying to avoid Adrian Morley, because he owed him money from when Moz played at Leeds. He was okay while Moz was away in Australia, playing for Sydney City, but things got a bit tense when Adrian came back to join the Great Britain camp. Moz is a top fella, but not somebody you'd want to get on the wrong side of. I think that was one of the reasons Pratty didn't play against the Aussies when they came over in 2003.

Moz was in the thick of things in that series, which was lost 3-0. Looking back, that was one of the biggest disappointments of my career because we had a real opportunity to win the Ashes and we blew it. They were under-strength and we were as good as them, if not better, in all three games. There was only one score in it in each one, but somehow they found a way to win.

The first Test, at Wigan, is famous because Moz got sent-off after just 12 seconds, which takes some doing, even for a hot-head like Adrian! Robbie Kearns caught the kick-off and got smashed by Moz's forearm. He must have thought the Eiffel Tower had fallen on him. Steve Ganson was the referee and he has never been one to duck a big decision. Out came the red card and off went Moz, so we were a man down before we had even touched the ball.

I don't know whether we would have won the game if we'd had 13 players, but we gave it a really good go with 12. Things like that often pull you together as a team. You get a bit of a siege mentality and everybody works a bit harder for each other. I got Man of the Match for the third successive time in a Test at Wigan, so I was pretty pleased with my own contribution, though that never matters much when you lose. I scored our second try soon after half-time and we were leading 18-16 with five minutes to go, but Darren Lockyer got over for the winning try to leave us shattered.

After that we knew we had the measure of them, so what happened in the rest of the series was extra-disappointing. The second Test was at Hull and if we had won that, which we should have done, I am sure we'd have gone on to lift the Ashes for the first time since 1970. Sadly, ifs, buts and maybes don't mean anything; the fact is we blew it. We were 20-8 ahead after 23 minutes and 20-12 up at half-time but we got a bit giddy. We went away from what we had been doing and they took advantage to win 23-20. We weren't in the habit of winning Test matches and we weren't able to close the game out, so that was it, the series was gone.

We played very well in the early stages of the game and our defence was solid throughout, but that wasn't much consolation. I am always going to look back on that match as a missed opportunity and a case of "what if?" It was 20-20 going into the final few minutes and we should have knocked over a drop goal, but we didn't get set for one and when they got to the other end the Aussies took their chance.

After Steve Ganson had refereed the first game – and sent Moz off – an Australian, Tim Mander, got the job for the match at Hull. He gave us only two penalties in the entire game – to Australia's eight - and both of those were in the first quarter, so we weren't happy with that, but we should have been able to cope, especially after making such a good start. Afterwards questions were asked about our tactics, particularly David Waite's decision not to use Sean Long, who was one of the substitutes. We needed something to spark us up in the second half and Sean might have been able to do that, so it was a strange option by the coach.

I was injured in the Test at Hull and missed the third game, which was played at Huddersfield. I broke and dislocated my right thumb, trying to fend off Luke Ricketson, the Aussie loose-forward. Normally I would have been devastated; if you are young and good enough, you always want to play for your country, but I wasn't too bothered about having to sit that one out because it was such an anti-climax after we'd gone so close in the previous game. Losing that Test at Hull was one of the lowest points I have experienced in rugby league because it was a chance to do something really special and we let it slip through our fingers. Even though we lost a decider in 2001, 2003 was worse because we were better prepared, we arguably had better players available and the Aussies were there for the taking.

Great Britain only had pride to play for in the final game, but that turned into a case of déjà vu all over again, as the saying goes. For the third time in as many weeks, we were in front going into the final quarter, but yet again Australia somehow managed to get back to their feet to pull off a last-gasp win with two tries in the final four minutes.

That was the last time I played against Australia in a Test series. From 2004 onwards, the Tri-Nations was introduced, which was later expanded to four teams. And after 2007, Great Britain was split up into England, Ireland, Scotland and Wales, which is something else I don't agree with.

I think proper Test series are a great concept and they should be brought back. I would have loved to do one of the old-style Lions tours, playing club sides as well as the Aussie team, but that went out of the window when Super League came in. Because Super League and the NRL now play at the same time, it would be too difficult to organise. That's a real shame and I don't think the Four Nations is as good a concept as a three-match Test series.

CHAPTER 7

THE BEST – AND BUSTED

Any sportsman who has a long career is going to experience ups and downs, highs and lows. You have indifferent years, bad years and good ones. How many of each depends on how good you are, how good your team is and a bit of luck as well.

My time at Sheffield probably falls into the first category. We had one major success, that fantastic afternoon at Wembley, but to be honest, for most of the time we were an average team and our results and performances reflected that. We tended to finish around mid-table and we usually lost about as many games as we won.

Going to Leeds was supposedly a step up, but the first five seasons I had there were bad. We won more games than when I was at Sheffield and we finished higher up the league table, but expectations at the Rhinos were much greater and generally we under-achieved.

There were reasons for that. We had a lot of injuries and some disruption behind the scenes with a couple of changes of coach and two players locked up. Some, probably most, of the signings the club made didn't come up to scratch and we had a lot of young players in the team who were still learning the game and didn't have the experience to be consistent at top level.

Since then, the good times have rolled and 2004 was my first really successful year, though it ended on a disastrous, career-threatening low. In terms of what happened at Leeds, it was one of those rare seasons when everything falls into place. Looking back it was probably not the most enjoyable season I've had, but it was definitely the most successful.

We finished as league leaders, nine points clear. We wrapped that up with three games still to go and we lost only twice in the league all campaign. We scored more than a thousand points – 1,037 – and had the competition's best defence, with only 443 conceded. That's an average score per game of 38-16, which is good going in anybody's book.

Most importantly we capped the year by going on to win the Grand Final at Old Trafford, beating our arch-rivals Bradford Bulls. That made Leeds champions for the first time since 1972, four years before I was born.

It wasn't a perfect season: we didn't manage a clean sweep of trophies because we lost at St Helens early on in the Challenge Cup, but apart from that we were dominant and just about everything went right for us from start to finish.

After the near-miss in 2003 there wasn't a massive turnover of players, but Tony Smith coming in as coach made a serious difference. No disrespect to Daryl Powell, but Smithy's arrival was just what we needed to transform us from a team of nearly-men into champions.

Tony can be one of the most sarcastic people I have ever met, but he is also probably the most technically gifted coach I have come across. He concentrates on getting the little things right and he came in and took us straight back to basics. We were a team of full-time Super League professionals, who had reached the Challenge Cup final and finished second in the league the previous year, yet Tony spent his first few weeks in charge teaching us how to catch and pass a ball.

I don't know about anyone else, but once I had got over the initial shock I wasn't embarrassed about effectively being shown how to play. Rugby league is a very simple game, but you are always learning and picking up new things. People take the fundamentals for granted, but if you don't get them right you won't win many games. You get taught how to pass and catch at eight years old, so you don't expect a top Super League club to devote whole training sessions to that aspect of the game, but it is the bread and butter. It doesn't get much more basic than that and it is where games can be won and lost.

It was constructive, Tony didn't come in and tell us we were all rubbish, he just expanded the core skills we all had. It was about fine-tuning the way we did things. For an example, if you watch one of Tony's teams in action, you'll never see a player put the ball down one handed over the line. You clamp the ball in both hands and dive over, so there's no danger of dropping it. Mark Calderwood forgot that in one game at Salford and bombed a couple of tries as a result. We won 44-0, but Calders didn't play in the next game.

Tony likes a work ethic and he wants everyone to do the little extra things. With me he spent a lot of time concentrating on the defensive line and what to do when the ball moves away. His philosophy was, you always keep working and plugging a gap.

In training, again it was all about work ethic. You weren't allowed to look tired, even when you were blowing out of your backside. It was all about deception, not showing any signs of weakness. He would have us all jogging from one drill to another. He took us all and expanded each of our individual games and by doing that, he created a work-hard mentality in the team. We all had to be prepared to work for one another, which is a huge thing in a team sport.

The technical side is only one part of being a coach. Tony wasn't the best motivator and his man management wasn't the greatest. You had to know what he was like. For young kids coming through, he could be quite intimidating because he was so sarcastic. If you didn't know how to take that you could be insulted by some of the things he said, but his coaching ability was never in doubt and he spoke a lot of sense, so he commanded immense respect. He came up with good game plans and definitely improved me as a player and the team as well.

Tony is a disciplinarian. He is a bit like a school teacher at times. He came into a club which didn't exactly have a drinking culture, but where players were known to enjoy going out and having a few beers and two of the club's star men had been locked up for violence following a night on the town just a few months earlier.

Tony put a stop to that. The Dews Fests got knocked on the head for one. I didn't see eye-to-eye with him about that because he admitted he had made lots of errors, going out on the drink and carrying on, when he was a young kid. He would say that he'd had to learn the hard way and he didn't want us doing the same. From my point of view, a bit of that is part of growing up. Everybody has to be allowed to make the odd mistake; it's only the stupid ones who keep doing them. That's how you gain experience and learn things. Tony wanted everyone to be squeaky clean and I don't think the world works like that.

In Tony's ideal world, there would be no alcohol at all in rugby league. He used to say: "In 10 years' time alcohol won't have any part in this sport." We're over half way there now and I don't think that prediction is going to come true. Alcohol detracts from some players' performance, but not everybody's. Obviously, you couldn't have a few beers and then go out and play, but for some players it helps the night before a game. Tonie Carroll would do that, to help him sleep or whatever - and he played for Leeds, Brisbane Broncos, New Zealand and Australia. Some people might say "I'll have whatever he's having!" I have also seen Adrian Morley have a skin full and then go and train the house down the following morning.

There aren't many coaches in the modern game who would accept a player turning up to training if it was obvious he had been drunk the night before. Some do drink through the week, but I couldn't get topped up and then train the next day - my body just wouldn't let me. However, I am of the opinion that each player knows his own body. It has to be in moderation, but if you can handle it and it doesn't affect the way you play or train, then what's the harm? In my view, a few drinks are okay as long as you respect your schedule, turn up on time and do your job.

Smithy was of the opinion that alcohol affected performance and hindered recovery, so it got to the stage when we weren't allowed beer after a game or if we were training the next day. In theory, if you stuck to the rules you'd only be allowed to drink in the off-season. I don't suppose everybody obeyed that, but it obviously worked because of the success we had.

We also had a curfew. We weren't allowed out after midnight. Tony wanted to know if we were planning an evening socialising and we were not supposed to go into nightclubs. There were exceptions, but if you were planning to stay out after midnight you were supposed to ask permission. It was a bit like being a 16-year-old kid at boarding school. I did find it a bit embarrassing having to go to Tony and say "It's Saturday night and I want to stay out past 12." To be fair, he never said no. I think it was just a case of wanting to know what was going on, so he could be prepared if something went wrong.

Bother does happen every now and then. I suppose if you had a group of office workers in their 20s and early 30s, some of them would get into trouble occasionally, though rugby players seem to attract more than their fair share. I have got into a scrape or two, like the time I tangled with Joe Naidole in Huddersfield.

Big Joe was a Fijian forward who had played professionally for a few clubs, including Huddersfield and Batley. That particular night I had asked for permission to go out, but I wasn't expecting to run into Joe. I had coached him at an amateur club, Huddersfield Sharks, and he wasn't my biggest fan. I made training quite tough and after a spell Joe stopped coming. For some reason he got the idea I was telling people that was because he couldn't hack it and it was too hard for him. I didn't say that, but the rumours had got his back up and he wanted to teach me a lesson.

We bumped into each other in a club called Livingstone's. Joe came over and offered me outside. I wasn't looking for trouble, so I said "What's the problem?" and his reply was "No problem, but I want you outside." Things got heated and the bouncers came over. Joe went out a lot and he was well known in Huddersfield, so the bouncers took his side. They went for me and it kicked off. My mates were there and they backed me up, but Joe simply walked away. I cracked one of the bouncers and cut his head open. The police turned up, sirens wailing, so I scarpered. One of my mates, Lee Mallinson, wasn't so fleet-footed and he got locked up for the night. After I had got away from the scene I went to a police van that was parked around the corner, told the coppers what had happened and asked if they could help Lee out. I explained that the fight had been over me, I hadn't started it, but Lee had got caught up in it. They said it was too late because he had already been nicked. I was going to go back but they said if I did, I'd be arrested too.

The following morning I confessed to Tony what had happened. He was okay about it because I had told him in advance that I would be going out. I explained the situation, said it wasn't my fault and he let it go. If I hadn't told him and he had heard about it from someone else, which he probably would as he lived in the Huddersfield area, there would have been dire consequences.

I didn't agree with everything Tony did, but he was a big influence on us that year, as was his assistant Brian McDermott. Brian is a former Marine and ex-professional boxer who was a prop for Bradford Bulls in his playing days, one of their Awesome Foursome at the time they were winning everything going. Brian's a real character and he was an excellent assistant-coach under Tony. He was a tough task master as well and he and Tony worked well as a team. He returned to Leeds later on, as head coach.

Probably to show he meant business, one of the first things Tony did was drop Francis Cummins for our opening game of the 2004 season. Franny had made 182 consecutive appearances, stretching back to 1998, so that was a big decision. Franny began to get involved in the coaching side of things that season as well and he is another one who did a good job.

We had a good team that year, with a lot of quality leaders. Kevin Sinfield was fantastic as captain and he got a lot of support from Dave Furner, who joined us the year before from Wigan. Dave had decided to hang up his boots at the end of 2004, so he was desperate to go out with a Grand Final winner's ring. As it turned out, the victory over Bradford was his final game and the perfect finale for him.

Dave had played for Australia and he had a big career with Canberra before coming to England. He was in great shape and he was a top trainer. He was a big inspiration to a lot of young kids in the side. You always need a player or two like that in your team. There's only so much the coaching staff can do, so you have to have older heads leading people in the right direction on the field. He wasn't a big talker, though he did make quite an emotional speech in the changing room after the Grand Final, but he definitely led by example. He has gone on to coach Canberra in the NRL and is a future national team boss, in my opinion.

Another of the characters in the team that season was Liam Botham, son of Sir Ian. He's one of those irritating people who are good at absolutely everything. He has played county cricket, Premiership rugby union and Super League and he's a pretty good golfer. He wasn't an exceptional rugby league player but he had a good engine and he was another good trainer – a very useful squad man. Because he has such a famous dad it was a bit surreal having him train with us. He got plenty of abuse, but he definitely wasn't a big time Charlie. He is a really nice bloke and he was a pleasure to have around the place, even if we could have happily strangled him on one occasion.

He got loaned out to London – to gain some first team experience - and when we played them in the capital, Tony said Liam could play for them against us. Most other coaches wouldn't have allowed that, but Tony likes to do things his own way. On that occasion it backfired. Liam had a brilliant game, scoring a try and kicking four goals including a last-gasp conversion to salvage a draw for them in a match we should have won.

That was a setback, but we had plenty of highlights. We won our first eight games, until we ran into St Helens at Knowsley Road and they caned us 56-10. I remember their fans singing "top of the league, you're having a laugh" at us at the end. Our supporters adopted that as a bit of an anthem, changing the word "you're" for "we're". The only other defeat was by four points at Wigan, who we also drew with late in the year. We led the table from start to finish and celebrated receiving the league leaders' shield by hammering Castleford 64-12 at Headingley in August, the week after we'd beaten Bradford 40-12 to virtually wrap it up.

To go a whole league season - 28 games in those days - and lose only twice is a massive achievement and something I am proud to have been a part of. But though you do get a trophy for finishing top of the table – everybody calls it the hubcap – winning the league counts for nothing: to be crowned champions you have to go on and win the Grand Final. In 2004 it was a top-six play-offs system and finishing top meant we would have a week off before the series started. It also guaranteed us a home game against the second-placed team in our opening tie. The winners of that would go straight through to Old Trafford and the beaten side got another chance, at home, against the play-offs' other survivors.

Having been unbeaten at home in the league all year we were confident we'd get past Bradford Bulls in the qualifying semi-final, but we got our backsides kicked. They beat us easily, 26-12, which was a huge shock. Yet looking back, it was probably the best thing that could have happened. It meant they had a weekend off before the Grand Final while we had to slug it out with Wigan, but playing an extra game suited us. It wiped away any complacency and it meant we weren't going into the final with as much expectation on our shoulders.

A lot of people thought we were going to choke and that we would slip up against Wigan. They had taken three points off us that year, out of the six we dropped, but we got our game spot on for the must-win final eliminator and we hammered them 40-12, with Marcus Bai scoring a hat-trick. We were so good that night, even Ryan Bailey scored. His tries come around about as often as Halley's Comet.

Tony swapped things around a bit that year, but Marcus, who joined us at the start of the season from Melbourne Storm, was my winger for most of the campaign and he was a terrific fella to have at your side. For a start, he is built like a tank, but he could run like a greyhound when he had to. He is from Papua New Guinea and he struggled with the language at times, but he's a top bloke and someone I have a massive amount of time for.

Marcus wasn't the fittest of players. We used to do a lot of work on the hills in Roundhay Park, which is really tough. You'd expect the wingers to be up at the front, but Marcus always used to run alongside big Barrie McDermott, right at the back. He was woeful on the hills, but he had a tremendous attitude and whenever he stepped on the field he was devastating. He was a punishing runner, his first carry was exceptional and his defence was cruel. He could cut players in half. We gelled really well and I think he always had a soft spot for me after I managed to get him a genuine police helmet. For some reason he had always wanted one. One of the lads I coached was a copper and he managed to get hold of a hat for Marcus, who was chuffed to bits.

Marcus was great for us that season, touching down 26 times. He would usually have been top try scorer with a tally like that, but Danny McGuire had a sensational campaign and got an extra 12. I got 13 and it would have been more but I wanted to help Marcus out!

After beating Wigan we overcame Bradford in the Grand Final, my first, so all in all, 2004 was one of my best years as a player, but it finished on a sour note which came close to ending my career and left me officially labelled a drugs cheat.

In the autumn of 2004, while I was in camp with Great Britain, I tested positive for ephedrine. I copped a massive fine and it is there as a blot on my record and something I am deeply ashamed of. Now I want to tell you the full story of exactly what happened in the most painful episode of my playing career.

I started taking the tablets that caused all the trouble during that year's Super League season. They were called sida cordifolia. One of the boys was taking them for weight loss, but they were also a cold and flu cure. He reckoned they made him feel better and he said they were legal because they weren't on the banned list.

A few of the Leeds lads started taking them, but only on a matchday. Just after they had started, we played a game on a Friday and one of the boys was drug tested the following Monday. He was given the all-clear, so it seemed like there was nothing to worry about. After that I started taking them and continued for a few months, up to the end of the league season and when I linked up with Great Britain.

Ryan Bailey was taking them as well. He got drugs tested after our Grand Final win over Bradford. I played in the first Test against Australia and got tested immediately following that. You have to fill in a form to declare if you are taking any medication and both Bails and I declared the tablets, so that shows we felt we had nothing to hide. I had also showed the packaging to someone with a medical background and had been told the pills were fine.

I played in the second Test and then in the build-up to the third game I had a phone call from the GB team doctor, Chris Brookes. I was at home at the time. He told me the sample I had given had tested positive for ephedrine and another member of the squad was in the same situation. What he said didn't sink in. I thanked him for the call and carried on doing what I was doing.

A few hours later he rang me back to ask how I was coping with the news and that's when it hit me, like a tonne of bricks. I asked him exactly what the situation was and he said "You're getting done for taking banned drugs." That was probably the worst single moment of my entire career.

Now, you can believe me or not – and I know some people don't - but I had absolutely no idea there was any problem with what I was taking. I was aware of at least one player who had used the tablets and had passed a doping test without any issues - and anyway, I didn't feel like they were doing me any good. I was only really taking them out of habit.

I know ignorance is no defence, but that's basically what it was down to. I was daft and naive, but at no stage was I trying to cheat in any way, shape or form. After the phone call from the Doc, I typed the name of the tablets into Google and they came up as containing ephedrine, which is on the banned list. Clearly, I should have done that before I started taking them.

I went into a panic and I could see my career and my good name collapsing in front of my eyes. I had no idea what I was going to do or what would happen, but I knew I could be facing a two-year ban, which was a terrifying prospect. Once I had been told about the initial failed test it was just a matter of waiting for the result of the B sample, which of course came back positive as well.

I didn't know that ephedrine was in the tablets, though I hadn't made any secret of the fact I was taking sida cordifolia, which is freely available for anybody to buy. I later found out that ephedrine passes out of your system in 24 hours, which is why the other player's test had come back negative. He had taken the pills before a game on a Friday and been tested three days later, by which time he was clean.

Both my case and Bailey's eventually went before the RFL. I pleaded guilty and got a hefty fine; basically my match fees for the Tri-Nations went straight back. I got one cheque from the RFL and wrote the governing body another for the same amount, so it was a fairly costly experience. But the big thing was, I didn't get banned and neither did Bails. There was a lot of controversy about that at the time and Bradford, who we'd beaten in the Grand Final that year, were particularly upset, which I can understand.

I am not so sure I would be as lucky if something similar happened now. In those days there was no automatic ban and I think with me being a high-profile player I got looked after a little bit. The hearing was held on December 23, so obviously it didn't get the publicity it might have done. And on the same day, the Rhinos announced that they were trying to sign Jamie Langley from Bradford Bulls, so that deflected some of the attention as well.

I regret the whole business. If I had my time again, there's no way I would ever have taken the tablets in the first place. It came about by changing room talk; someone said these things were good so I decided I would try them. I know that sounds dodgy, but there are a lot of supplements and so forth that you can take which are perfectly legal. A lot of it's psychological. If you give someone a water tablet and tell him it'll make him feel better, it probably will. There are things out there that are legal and do improve your performance, like creatine or gorana, which has caffeine in it. Whether that's a loophole or not, everybody is always looking for an extra edge, no matter how small. If you can get that edge legally, then fair enough.

It turned into a routine, something I did on match days. There wasn't a massive amount of ephedrine in the tablets and I honestly don't think they did anything to improve or alter the way I played or my performance. Cold and flu remedies have enough ephedrine in them to get you banned, but if you take one of those before a game it is not going to improve your performance that much. It is not like taking human growth hormone or steroids. A lot of amateur players take ephedrine in some form or another and it doesn't do them any good.

It is hurtful when people accuse me of being a drugs cheat, though technically that was the case. Without being big headed, I have achieved a lot in the game and I'm aware that what happened in 2004 does bring some of that into question. I've played for a lot of years and hardly picked up a serious injury. Inevitably some people are going to put two and two together and get five, but the fact is, I have never deliberately taken any illegal or banned substance in an attempt to improve my performance or to keep me fit.

Because two Rhinos players tested positive, that cast a shadow over our 2004 Grand Final win, which I regret. We were totally dominant that year and it will be put forward as a reason. The fact is the two things weren't connected in any way. We were the best team that year, because we had the best players, the best coach, the best game plan and we worked the hardest. It had nothing to do with drugs, but the scandal that followed definitely took some of the shine off.

I learned my lesson. Since those dark days I don't take anything other than multivitamins and protein and I make sure I get those checked out first. I don't feel, even coming towards the end of my career, that I need anything. That was the most disappointing aspect of the whole business, I came close to getting a ban and I have been classed as a drugs cheat because of some pills which didn't have any real effect on me and could be bought by anybody in a high street chemist.

For what it is worth, I have been tested loads of times before and since 2004 and I have never given another positive sample. That's not through lack of trying on the doping agency's part. After Bailey and I were done, they came down on Leeds hard. They dropped in on training and tested everybody - and nobody failed. Testing after matches is supposed to be random; the players are chosen by drawing lots, but my name seemed to be pulled out on a regular basis in 2005 and 2006, which I suppose is understandable and I don't have a problem with that.

The issue of drugs use is a big controversy in the game. It is a sport based on speed, strength and fitness and, as I have already mentioned, everyone is looking for an advantage, something that will give them that extra 10 per cent which might make all the difference between winning and losing. Some critics don't believe anybody can get to be as big or as strong as Super League players are naturally. Obviously some players do use illegal means to get that edge. We know that, because every season there are a few failed tests.

But hand on heart, I can say that I am not aware of anybody, team-mate or opponent, who is or has been using performance-enhancing drugs. I have heard through the grapevine of people taking recreational drugs, though I've never actually seen it. There are also rumours about players who suddenly seem to get bigger or stronger over an off-season, but I have got no evidence to say that's down to anything other than hard work. Maybe I am being naive again, but I've no reason to believe it is rife in the game, as some people claim. Clearly it does happen, but as far as I am aware, those are isolated cases, very much the exception rather than the rule. The unfortunate thing is that if one player tests positive, everybody else gets tarred with the same brush. That's what happened to Leeds in 2004.

So what about players who do test positive for steroids or human growth hormone, as Terry Newton - someone I knew quite well and who I played with and against - did in 2010? Do I understand why they do it? Yes. Do I condone it? No, not at all. Because it's such a physical game, rugby league does take its toll on your body and anyone in his early 30s is coming towards the end of his career. I suppose for some people there must be a temptation to take something to prolong that career and to keep the income coming in. I can understand that, but taking illegal substances isn't the right way to go about it. They are illegal because they have a detrimental effect on your health further down the line and, as far as I am concerned, it is simply not worth the risk. At some stage you are going to get caught and nowadays that means a two-year ban.

Terry's two-year suspension had a tragic outcome. He seemed to have coped quite well; he had his autobiography published, he was running a pub in Wigan and – after admitting his guilt – he took a strong anti-drug stance. The entire sport, me included, was left reeling when he was found hanged at his home in Orrell, near Wigan, in September, 2010, six months after his ban. Other factors played a part, but I am sure the shame of being labelled a drug cheat took its toll.

Terry's death was an absolute tragedy and it only underlines the dangers of getting involved with illegal substances. Prevention is better than cure and the RFL goes to great lengths to discourage players from taking the risk – and make sure the ones who do actually get caught.

At one stage, we were all on the whereabouts system. That meant that in the off-season you had to notify the drugs agency where you would be for an hour per day, six days a week, even if you were away on holiday. Now only the elite Great Britain players are on that, which is a bit strange. It was a pain having to fill in the paperwork and then remembering to be where you had said you would be, because a missed test is taken as seriously as a failed one and you could get banned for it. I know one or two players who put on their form that they would be at home in bed between 4-5am - and sure enough, at some stage there'd be a knock on the door. I used to say they could find me at home between 6-7am and they did turn up a couple of times.

When we were in Florida on a pre-season camp in 2009, the drugs testers dropped into a training session. They were Americans, but they had been contracted by the doping agency in this country. That proves the RFL takes drugs use very seriously and that's a good thing. It is annoying having to give a test sometimes, especially after a tough game when you are dehydrated and it's not easy to provide a sample, but it is something the game needs to clamp down on. The bottom line is, I couldn't look myself in the mirror if I knew that the caps and medals and trophies I have won – including the 2004 Grand Final - had been achieved through cheating. People can believe me or not, but my conscience is clear.

CHAPTER 8

WORLD CLUB CHUMPS

Of the near 600 games I've taken part in during my career, there's only one I really regret playing – and that was a Cup final. After the success we had in 2004 we expected to kick on to more glory the following year. We started off with another trophy and for a while we were just about unstoppable, but then the wheels came off and we were back to being the nearly-men, on three different fronts.

By winning the Super League Grand Final in 2004 we qualified for the following year's World Club Challenge against the Australian champions, Canterbury Bulldogs. The game was played at Elland Road, Leeds United's ground, in front of a full house of nearly 40,000. In those days the World Club was played as a curtain-raiser to the season, so it was both teams' first competitive match. It has now been put back a month to the end of February/start of March, so the Super League team get a few games under their belt, but it's still the season opener for the Aussies.

The thing I remember most about the Canterbury game, which we won 39-32, was not scoring the first try! We shuffled things around at the start of the match in an attempt to confuse the enemy. Chev Walker began in the left-centre with me on the other side for the first 10 minutes – and during that time Danny McGuire put Chev over to open the scoring. It should have been me; I was devastated. I don't have a good scoring record in finals – I've only managed one try and that was in a later World Club game which we lost. On the other hand, bearing my record in mind, if I had touched down instead of Chev maybe we wouldn't have won.

Another thing that sticks in my mind from that game is Sonny Bill Williams, an absolutely enormous Kiwi back-rower who played for Canterbury despite only being about 12 years old. He was a sensational player and could have been an all-time great in rugby league, but he got seduced by money and went off for an easy life in French rugby union, which was a real waste, though he did go on to win caps for the All Blacks.

He was Canterbury's best player against us. He smacked Ryan Bailey and then pulverised Marcus Bai, which is no mean feat. I dropped off a pass to Marcus, who could have stepped round Sonny Bill if he had wanted to, but that wasn't his style. He ran straight at him at about 100 miles an hour and got absolutely cleaned out. That's something I have done to every one of my wingers at least once a year. To his credit, Marcus got up – like Bambi on ice – and managed to totter back to his wing. The rest of us were all thinking 'thank goodness that wasn't me'. It still brings a smile to my face now.

We made a cracking start, tore them apart for 50 minutes and went 38-12 up, then either we took our foot off the gas, they improved or – more likely – some combination of the two. They got back to 38-32 and it actually looked like we might get turned over until Kev Sinfield banged over a late drop goal to put the game beyond them.

I absolutely love beating Australians, any Aussie team, in any game at any time, so I really enjoyed the match and the celebrations afterwards. They moaned a bit but that only showed how seriously they were taking it. Bulldogs had a few players missing but they definitely wanted to win. At the end, a few of them said "you've only beaten our second team". We told them "Don't be so hard on yourselves – anyway who cares, we're world champions and you're not." When you lose, you look for excuses or ways of putting a positive spin on it. That's all part of the sport.

Australians don't respect our game. They are very dismissive of English rugby league and I suppose in some respects they have every right to be, but that just makes it sweeter when we do beat them, once in a blue moon. Winning a World Club Challenge, which involves the two best teams from either competition, is a massive feat. It is a shame that the English side never get the credit they deserve when they win. I've played in four now, won two and lost two. When we have won, the media here and Down Under have said it is because the Aussies were under-strength, not well enough prepared or weren't interested. When we lose they claim it proves we're not fit to be on the same pitch as the NRL's best.

The Aussies like the World Club when one of their teams wins it. I think it's a good concept, but it has a lot of faults. If those could be ironed out it might become something really special. For a start, it is always played in England. We do have an advantage now that it comes a month into our season, because we are battle hardened, but that also means the British champions' league campaign begins as early as at the end of January, which is far too soon. Another problem is that the players who take part aren't necessarily the ones who qualified for it, as it happens in a new season. Gareth Ellis actually made his debut for us in the win over Canterbury, after signing from Wakefield in the off-season.

I would love to see it played on neutral ground: somewhere like Dubai

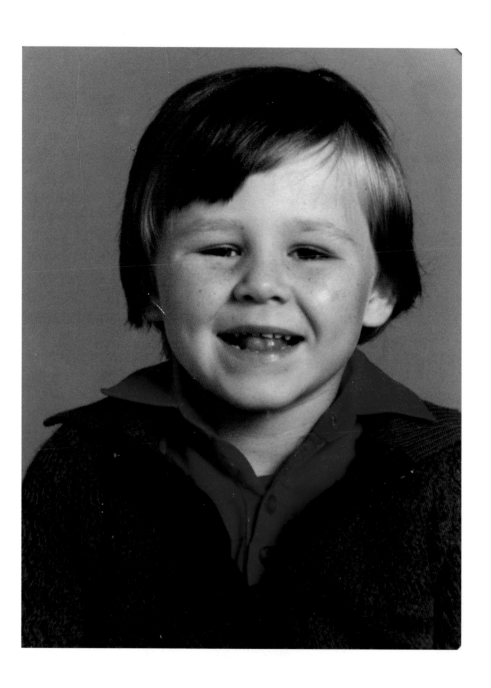

GUESS WHO?: This is me aged about four.

HAPPY DAYS: With my dad and brother on a family holiday at the East Coast.

OH BROTHER!:
John and I on a rare
occasion when we
weren't fighting.

HAIR TODAY: A rare shot of me in my hirsute days, before I had my head shaved.
Picture: Steve Riding, Yorkshire Evening Post.

NEARLY THERE: The tension shows on my face as the clock ticks down in the 1998 Challenge Cup final and Sheffield Eagles close in on an epic win over Wigan Warriors. Picture: Dave Williams (RLphotos.com).

GROUNDED: Here I am being tackled in the 1998 Challenge Cup final at Wembley. Picture: Dave Williams (RLphotos.com).

WHEN EAGLES DARED: Celebrations begin on the Wembley pitch after the 1998 Challenge Cup final triumph. The party went on for days. Picture: Dave Williams (RLphotos.com).

CUP KINGS: Matty Crowther and I show off our new toy, following the 1998 Challenge Cup final victory against Wigan Warriors at Wembley. Picture: Dave Williams (RLphotos.com).

NOT YET A RHINO:
Leeds are the opposition in
one of my 140 games for
Sheffield Eagles. The
tackler is Marvin Golden.
Picture: Dave Williams
(RLphotos.com).

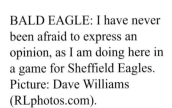

BALD EAGLE: I have never
been afraid to express an
opinion, as I am doing here in
a game for Sheffield Eagles.
Picture: Dave Williams
(RLphotos.com).

A YORKSHIREMAN BORN:
I scored four tries in four
appearances for Yorkshire and
here I am in action against
Lancashire at Headingley.
Picture: Dave Williams
(RLphotos.com).

NICE TACKLE: In
action against Hull,
along with Ali Lauitiiti
and Rob Burrow.
Picture: James Hardisty,
Yorkshire Evening Post.

CALENDAR BOYS: I'm happy to get my kit off for a good cause, in this case a charity calendar. I was Mr March.

THE WORLD AT OUR FEET: Leeds Rhinos' England contingent (back row) Adrian Morley, Andy Hay, me, Francis Cummins, (front) Chev Walker, Kevin Sinfield and Darren Fleary get together before the 2000 World Cup. It wasn't a happy experience. Picture: Steve Riding, Yorkshire Evening Post.

MASTER AND PUPIL: At Sheffield I was known as the 'new Daryl
Powell'. We played together there and at Leeds and he eventually became
my respected Rhinos coach, though we didn't always see eye to eye.
Picture: Steve Riding, Yorkshire Evening Post.

THE BIG STAGE: With Kevin Sinfield and Francis Cummins on the traditional eve-of-final walkabout at Cardiff's Millennium Stadium, before the 2003 Challenge Cup decider against Bradford. It was the first time I'd played indoors.
Picture: Steve Riding, Yorkshire Evening Post.

GUTTED: The final hooter has just gone in Cardiff and we've lost the 2003 Challenge Cup final by two points to Bradford Bulls. It was one of the low points of my career. Picture: Steve Riding, Yorkshire Evening Post.

DYNAMIC DUO: Willie Poching and Francis Cummins were two great servants to Leeds as players and on the coaching staff and we missed them when they left the club in 2010. Pictures: Steve Riding, Yorkshire Evening Post.

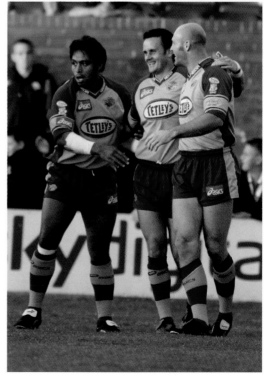

JUST CHAMPION: Showing off the Super League trophy in the changing room at Old Trafford, immediately after the 2004 Grand Final. It was Leeds' first title in 32 years and a great moment for me and the club. Picture: Steve Riding, Yorkshire Evening Post.

TOUCHING MOMENT: One of my team-mates rubs the lucky bald head, at a Rhinos pre-season photo shoot. Picture: Steve Riding, Yorkshire Evening Post.

GIZZA KISS: Chev Walker and I were close mates, as you can tell from our reaction to yet another Rhinos try. Picture: Steve Riding, Yorkshire Evening Post.

FLASH POINT: Wigan Warriors' Stuart Fielden and Iafeta Paleaaesina seem to be upset at something I've said or done. Picture: Steve Riding, Yorkshire Evening Post.

MONEY MAKER: I got into all sorts of bother for selling my World Cup medal on eBay - and made a packet from it!

YANKS FOR THE MEMORIES: Rugby league has taken me all over the world, including several trips to the United States. Here I am with wing partner Ryan Hall at the University of North Florida, in Jacksonville, where we trained before the 2008/9 seasons. Picture: Phil Daly.

THE THINGS I'LL DO FOR MONEY:
I know I look ridiculous, but I grew the
beard for a bet. Pictures: Steve Riding,
Yorkshire Evening Post.

would be ideal. That's half way between England and Australia and it would be a chance to showcase our sport to the world. Attempts are being made to get rugby league off the ground in the Middle East, so having the planet's best two teams on show there would give it a real boost. I also think it would be better to play it at the end of the season, though logistically that would be very difficult. As it is, there's not enough time between the end of the domestic season and the start of international matches to chuck another big game in there.

After the win over Canterbury we played some of the best rugby of my time at the club. In all competitions, we won our first eight, 16 of the opening 17 and all but two of our first 23. We didn't maintain it, though, and the first real signs of a wobble came when we played London on neutral ground at Perpignan in the south of France. That was the year before the French team, Catalan Dragons, came into Super League. London Broncos decided to play one of their scheduled 'home' games there, to help stir up a bit of interest and they chose us as their opponents.

Kev was missing after he dislocated a thumb playing against Bradford the previous week, so I was made captain for the day. It wasn't a happy experience. We had beaten London 64-6 at home earlier in the season and when we scored in the opening set it looked like being another easy afternoon. We built up a big lead and I can remember seeing our fans doing a conga in the stands, but the wheels came off, we collapsed and London won the game 32-24. It was a bad defeat and everybody in the camp was pretty fed up afterwards. The game was played at Stade Aime Giral, which is the home of Perpignan's rugby union team, USAP. They saw Catalan as competition and they were very anti-rugby league, so it wasn't a welcoming place to play. They put a lot of obstacles in our way, like shifting the coaching staff from the seats they'd taken in the stand just as the game started, so that left a sour taste, as did the result.

To make matters worse, the club had arranged for us to have most of the following day at the beach before flying home in the late afternoon. As I have already mentioned, the best drinking sessions tend to come after a defeat because you are a bit down and you need something to lift your spirits. Some of the players had their partner there, me included, so we were on our best behaviour. But the singletons separated off in a beach bar and got stuck into the beer. It was drinking weather as well - it was July so it was hot. The management had said we could have a few beers if we wanted, but one or two of the boys went too far, which is always a danger.

That's the problem once you start drinking. It is very difficult to have three or four beers because you get the taste for it and begin to lose your inhibitions. The booze was going down well and by the time to leave for the airport came around, several of the lads were totally scattered. At one stage Nick Scruton shoved his face in a melon and almost drowned. Tony wasn't very happy about this and he had a bit of trouble getting everybody on to the bus. When we arrived at the airport, which is basically a tin shed on a strip of tarmac at the edge of the town, some of the lads were feeling a bit worse for wear: Lee Smith spewed his guts up outside and Danny Ward fell asleep in the car park.

A lot of fans had made the trip and they were turning up for their flight back to England, so this drama was being played out in public. Tony was seething because some of the boys had taken liberties and he was still upset about us losing the game. He thought we should all be sulking, not making merry.

Not surprisingly, we were told not to have a drink at the airport. The Dutch courage – brave juice - had been flowing and Chris McKenna decided to stage a mutiny by getting himself a beer. Chris was an Aussie, whose nickname was Frigger. That was because he never swore; he would say "friggin" instead of anything stronger. We also used to jokingly call him Kilo. He had been signed as a centre and we enjoyed winding him up by saying he was half the player Tonie Carroll was. Kilo was half a Tonza.

Anyway, Frigger got into a barney with Smithy, who had said something to upset him. For a while it looked like it was really going to kick off because Frigger challenged him and asked him outside. To his credit, Tony handled it really well. He was calm and cool about it and he brushed it off, just saying "I'll see you tomorrow morning, if you want."

It wasn't a good situation and it hit me quite hard because I was captain that weekend and I felt like I had a responsibility to keep things on an even keel. The players had been given a bit of rope and some of them used it to hang themselves. No physical harm was done, there was no actual violence or damage, but it didn't look right turning up drunk at the airport and then a player and the coach having a bit of an argument. The fact our flight back to England was delayed several hours didn't help anybody's mood.

Some people have said that was a turning point in our season and things began to go wrong from there on. That may be the case but I think it was a coincidence rather than a consequence of what happened, off the field anyway, in France. There were no lasting grudges. Disciplinary action was taken and warnings were handed out but then everybody put it to one side and got on with things.

Looking back it was funny. Things were taken a bit too far but I think on occasions you have to let your hair down a bit. The bollockings were dispensed but that was the end of it. We are not like women, who brood for years on end. You know what a woman's like when she has got a problem with somebody, it carries on forever. With us, when something happens it is sorted out and forgotten about. That's a good thing about being in a male environment.

France had a big impact on our season that year. As well as the trip to Perpignan, we played their near neighbours Pia in the fifth round of the Challenge Cup at Headingley, a game we won 70-0. Then we faced Toulouse in the semi-final at Huddersfield. They were coached by Justin Morgan, who later went on to take charge at Hull KR, and their team included former Rhinos academy player Tommy Gallagher. They gave us a bit of trouble but we won easily enough, 56-18.

We knew we would beat Toulouse and we expected to play St Helens in the final, but Hull shocked them in the first semi-final the day before our game against the French team. There was a two-week gap between the semis and the Cup decider and eight days before the final we took on Bradford Bulls at home in a Super League game, which was when one of the worst weeks of my career began. Bradford beat us but the bad result was the last thing on my mind after the match.

Big Joe Vagana was the problem – 25 stone of a man, or that's what it felt like when he fell on top of me. Joe was a rough, tough Kiwi prop and a very good player. We'd had set-tos before at Test and club level, but this time what happened was a complete accident. I hit the ball up and somebody tackled me with a good shot. I went to ground but got back up. I should have stayed down and taken the tackle, but the fighting spirit came out so I regained my feet; then Joe came in and laid on me, my right ankle gave way and I heard a crack. I was in agony and I instantly thought I had broken something.

The medical staff came on and I had a big argument with them because they wanted to stretcher me off and I was adamant I was going to leave the pitch under my own steam. In the end the club doctor, Paul Lanfeer, strapped my legs together, so that ended the argument. I got carried off - which at the time upset me more than the injury did - and taken to hospital. I had a scan and I was told there was no break, but I had ruptured the ligaments to my tibia and fibula. I haven't had many serious injuries but when they do occur what happens is you get the initial pain, but then the endorphins start kicking in and you begin to feel better.

By the day after the game, which was exactly a week before the Challenge Cup final in Cardiff, I was walking. The ankle was swollen and I was limping badly but the scenario didn't seem so bleak, though the specialist basically told me I had no chance of facing Hull. As the week went on I began a bit of light jogging. It hurt like hell but at least I could move. Tony said he would give me until the last possible moment, which effectively was the night before the final, to see how things improved. Patrick Moran – known by the lads as Paddy – was our physio at the time. Normally it would be his call as to whether I was fit enough to make the team, but the decision was taken away from him. He made it very clear that I shouldn't even think about playing. Unfortunately, it was left to me and Tony – the last two people in the world who should have been making a decision like that. Naturally I wanted to play and Tony was keen to have me in the team.

It was the first time I had been in a situation like that and I didn't know how to deal with it. The build-up to the final was going on around me, we were massive favourites and after two defeats with Leeds it was a great opportunity for me to get another Challenge Cup medal.

We travelled to Cardiff on the Thursday, two days before the match. I didn't train with the team but I took part in some running on the treadmill, with Paddy. The pain was still really bad. The day before the final I trained in the morning with the team at Cardiff Arms Park where I had once played for Sheffield against St Helens in an on-the-road Super League game. I got through the team run, though not very convincingly. I did what I had to and then tried a few extras afterwards. I attempted a side-step and it was agony. Tony came over and asked me how it was. I told him it was killing me, but he questioned me – he said "Is it really painful, or is it in your head?"

To me, he was doubting my mental strength - my bottle - and that got my back up. By now it was getting to decision time: we had a team meeting that night and Tony wanted an answer 30 minutes before that began. That was when he planned to confirm his side to the players. I had a pain-killing injection and it was like a miracle. Within minutes I was running up and down a corridor in the hotel in no discomfort at all. I could run and step, no problem. I remember thinking 'how good is this? It is awesome, I am going to be all right'.

I went to Tony, told him the injection had worked and I would like to play. He was really pleased and his answer was "Good on you, well done." John Kear, who was in charge of Hull, had spoken to the media during the week and said "If Keith Senior plays, I'll play." That was a smart move on his part because he must have known I wasn't really fit enough, but his public doubts made me want to play even more.

On the day of the game I saw John at the ground and asked him if he had brought his boots. He just smiled and he must have known then he had won that particular psychological battle. John didn't keep his word and I am still disappointed about that.

As the clock ticked towards kick-off time I got ready, had injections all the way up to my knee and then went out to warm up - and I knew immediately the pain-killers hadn't worked. I was in agony again and I had no idea what to do. I was aware that I was putting myself at risk because the ligaments had gone and that meant I was in real danger of dislocating the ankle.

Somehow, I managed to survive the full first half, though I was no use to anyone. It is easily the worst pain I have ever played through and by the interval I couldn't take any more. I had to put my hand up and say "It's no good, I need to come off". I spent the second 40 sitting on the sidelines with my ankle swollen up to the size of a balloon.

We lost the game: it was a see-saw encounter and we led by five points going into the final few minutes, but Paul Cooke got over for a try with the clock running down, Danny Brough booted the conversion and Hull snatched it 25-24.

In hindsight I should never have played. Even now I feel like I let down the rest of the team and the Leeds fans who had expected us to win the game. I still feel bad for Paddy, who was placed in an impossible situation, and for Barrie McDermott, who was left out of the team. If I had pulled out, as I should have done, he would have played and maybe the result would have been different.

Some supporters blamed me for the loss but as far as I know, none of the players did. That's just not the way we do things at Leeds. Back in the 2003 final, when Kevin Sinfield opted to take a tap penalty rather than kick for goal to equalise against Bradford Bulls, we all stood by him. It was the same with me. I think everybody realised how tough a decision it was and I am sure they would all have been just as desperate to play if they had been in any sort of fitness doubt.

Whether the result would have been different if I had been fully fit or if someone else had played in my place is impossible to say.When I had to cry off at half-time that left us down to only 16 fit players. We had only three men available on the bench for the entire second half and obviously in an intense game like a Cup final you need all hands on deck.

I love him to bits but Marcus Bai made an horrendous error when he tried to pass the ball behind his own goal line, but messed up and simply handed a try to Richard Whiting. Perhaps if I had been on the field he wouldn't have done that. Who knows? But I took full responsibility for playing when I shouldn't have done and to this day I feel guilty about the result.

That's not to take anything away from Hull and John Kear, who is a master in situations like that. I was on the right side of his ability to get a team up for one-off games in 1998, so I know how he will have approached the match. They were the underdogs and all the pressure was on us. He will have built up the 'world's against us' scenario and really got them motivated. On top of a good game plan and some excellent individual performances that got them home, albeit by the slenderest of margins.

I didn't play another game for Leeds that season. The leg/ankle didn't heal until the internationals at the end of the campaign. We managed to recover from the Cup final defeat sufficiently to finish second in the table, behind St Helens – and we won at Knowsley Road in the Grand Final qualifier, which meant we went straight through to Old Trafford. Ali Lauitiiti scored a spectacular length of the field try and we held on as Saints came back at us late on, with Jamie Lyon almost snatching victory for them.

Saints had a lot of injuries by that stage and they lost the final eliminator as well, to Bradford Bulls, who had finished third. By the week before the final I was back in light training and there was some speculation in the media that I might be available for Old Trafford. Tony came over to me and asked how I was feeling. I got as far as saying "Well, erm…." and he came straight back with "You're not playing!" So I suppose that was a hard lesson learned.

Bradford won the Grand Final 15-6, becoming the first team to lift the trophy from outside the top-two. I think if we had maintained our early-season form we would have retained the championship, but they were better than us over the second half of the campaign and they deserved it for how strongly they finished, though it was a bitter pill to swallow.

I was back to full fitness for the start of the 2006 season, which began with the shock news that Danny Ward had been sacked for breaching club rules. We were never told exactly what had occurred, though obviously rumours went around the camp. Danny was a bit of a lad and he had fallen foul of the club's disciplinary regulations a few times, but I was sorry to see him go. He was a mate and a good fella and also a very good player. He wasn't a flashy type of prop, but he did the hard yards and the dirty stuff that maybe fans don't notice, but team-mates really appreciate and opponents respect.

Wardy's dad David is a Leeds legend who captained and coached the club and I know he must have taken it hard. Danny did too. He felt like he had let himself, his family and the rest of the team down, though he did get some revenge - of sorts - later in the season. He joined Castleford Tigers and scored a long-range try when they beat us by a point at the Jungle. I said to him afterwards: "You never did that when you played for us!"

While Wardy was on the way out, Jamie Peacock came in. He captained Bradford in the 2005 Grand Final against us and then joined Leeds for the start of pre-season a few months later. JP is probably the best signing the club has made, certainly in my time. He is a total one-off: in terms of talent a long way short of the best player in the world, but one of the fiercest and most determined competitors I have ever met.

On match days he is one of those players who bangs his head against a wall to get himself fired up. Johnny Lawless, at Sheffield, was another of those. JP has a pretty broad Leeds accent and people who don't really know him think he is a bit thick, but he is far from it. He is a smart bloke; a bit like a slightly less bonkers version of Jamie Jones-Buchanan, who hails from the same part of the city. He really thinks about the sport and he is very passionate. He is always looking for ways to improve his game and he is one of those who has had to work really hard because he doesn't have as much natural ability as a lot of other guys. He is highly motivated and he can be a pain to play with because he will run himself into the ground. If there's a hit-up to be made, he'll make it. Sometimes he does a bit too much work for his own good and he is the only player who has ever punched me for helping him up off a tackle. This was when we were on the same side. He made a tackle, I was at second marker and I lifted him off the ground. He was so into the game he turned round and walloped me. I lost it and I was standing there yelling "Don't you ever do that to me again".

He enjoys winding me up sometimes. When I make a tackle he likes to join in as third man so he can jump in at marker, just in front of the opponent who is playing the ball - and I have to retreat back 10 metres to get into the defensive line. We have had a bit of a competition over that, to see who can make the other retreat the most times during a match.

JP has an immense engine and sometimes he will pinch other people's hit-ups - he wants to be involved in every big play, every defence. He has been absolutely massive for us and I am not sure we would have won three consecutive Grand Finals if he had been playing for anyone else. When he missed the Challenge Cup final in 2010, after rupturing knee ligaments two weeks before the big game, everyone was absolutely gutted for him. We also felt sorry for ourselves, because it's going to be harder to win any game without JP in the team.

With JP, you know that if the going gets tough, when things are going wrong and you are out on your feet, he will come up with something special to get you back on the front foot. When you are attacking, everybody comes to life and the whole team wants the ball. But in yardage, which is when you are coming away from your own goal line, that's when you need the tough guys to help out because those are the worst hit-ups: the defence is set and every metre is tough. JP will always put his hand up because he likes getting stuck into that sort of situation; he sees it as a test of character and he doesn't like to give in.

It is tougher playing in the middle than it is out in the centre and sometimes I'll ask him if he wants to swap over for a spell, just to get a breather. He's as stubborn as hell and more often than not he won't do it. That's what has made him as great as he is, but it has also been a bit of his downfall because he doesn't know when to quit. At times you need a rest and if there's someone offering to help out, the smart thing to do is to accept the gift. If you do two hit-ups in a set of six, the second one isn't going to be as good as the first because you are doing it under fatigue. It's a better option to let someone take a fresh hit-up, but JP is the sort you would always want alongside you in the trenches and he is one of rugby league's ultimate warriors.

Even with him in the squad, the 2006 season was one of those indifferent ones with a few highs, a few lows, but mostly somewhere in between. Winning 30-0 at Bradford – when I was among the try scorers – was a highlight. We also had a couple of really big wins, against Castleford and Harlequins, and we hammered Catalan in Perpignan to atone a bit for the previous year's debacle there against London.

For me, the low point was losing to Huddersfield in the Challenge Cup semi-final at Odsal. We were massive favourites; everybody thought we had got a bye into the final and that was probably our downfall. Maybe we started to believe the publicity because - for whatever reason - we didn't turn up properly on the day and we got out-played and well-beaten 30-12. Losing a semi-final is bad enough, but for me the fact it was against the Giants made it worse. I always like to play well against my home town club because inevitably if I don't, all my mates will make sure I hear all about it.

After that game, one of them had a poster made up. It said in big red letters over a picture of me in Leeds kit: "Missing. Keith Senior. Last seen wandering aimlessly sometime between 3pm and 4.40pm on Sunday 30th July along with 16 of his friends in the Odsal Top area of Bradford. Answers to the name of Our Keith." My dad has kept that in his scrapbook for some reason.

Losing to Huddersfield was a big shock, as much to our supporters as anyone. About 12,000 people turned up for the semi and I reckon 11,000 of those were from Leeds. A lot of them had bought tickets for the final, at Twickenham, before we even played Huddersfield. People who went to the final told me there were more Leeds shirts on show in the crowd than Giants'.

We finished third in the table in 2006, behind St Helens and Hull. We had a strong start and were going pretty well until the Cup semi-final, but that was one of five straight defeats which knocked us off track. Our slump coincided with Brian McDermott, Tony Smith's assistant, leaving to take over at London Broncos.

He told us in the changing room after a last-minute 26-24 win over his old club Bradford, at Headingley. Brian Mac is a tough guy, but he was in tears and the lads were disappointed to see him go. We lost seven of our 10 games after he left so a lot of people began to wonder how much of an influence he had been on the team. The fact is, he was a big part of what we did, but that was in partnership with Tony. They were a strong coaching team and they worked well together. Tony, as I have mentioned, isn't the best at man-management. He has a sarcastic manner and that can be difficult for young players to cope with. Brian was able to be one of the lads, as well as a boss. He's a great character and a good person to have around and some of the less experienced boys found him easier to talk to than Tony.

He is also a very good coach with some terrific ideas of his own and I was pleased when he returned to Leeds and was appointed head coach at the end of 2010. Of course we missed him once he had gone south. I think Tony did as well, but to say he had been the one coaching the side during his first spell, rather than Smithy, isn't true.

Coming third on the ladder meant we had no margin for error in the play-offs. Sadly, our campaign lasted one game and we were out after Warrington Wolves beat us 18-17 at home, thanks to a late Lee Briers drop goal. That was a disappointing end to a season which promised a lot but delivered nothing.

Chapter 9

Blazing saddles

I am definitely not a typical equestrian. Before I met my partner Victoria, donkey rides on the beach as a kid were about the nearest I'd come to the horsey set - that and watching the Grand National on TV. But when you get into a relationship you share interests and with Vic, that meant learning one end of a horse from the other.

Vic has been riding since she was knee high and it is a passion of hers. When we got together she had her own horse and, being keen to show willing, I got dragged around various events with her. After a while, rather than standing around looking bored, I became an unofficial groom. While she got changed, I'd prepare the horse, brush it down, place the bridle on and that sort of thing. It might not sound like much fun but it's quite relaxing.

Obviously I used to watch Vic ride and it didn't look too tough. Being a sportsman, I'd rather be doing than watching, so I decided I'd have a go and booked myself a lesson at a riding centre near Halifax. Gilbert was my introduction to the equestrian world. He had been a riding school horse for many years and he was bored to death. I couldn't get him to do anything, other than plod around in circles. I had two lessons with Gilbert and then I decided I was ready to move on to something a bit more adventurous.

Vic is a solicitor and she got a circular e-mail from another lawyer who had a horse he was trying to sell. He had bought the horse for his girlfriend and he was saddled with it, if you'll pardon the pun, when they split up. He had also bought her a car and he let her keep that, but he decided he was hanging on to the horse. Unfortunately for him, he didn't know anything about them and all it was doing was standing in its stable, costing him money - £160 per week in stabling fees.

He was a good quality horse. He had been to HOYS – that's what we equestrian types call the Horse of the Year Show – about five times and had been reserve champion one year. Unlike me, he was very well bred. Vic looked his picture up on the internet and it was love at first sight. We were told he was 16.2 hands high, but when we went to look at him he was about 17.2. One hand is four inches, so he was a big horse and a thoroughbred. He had been passed from pillar to post, which is what happens with show horses. All we knew about him was his history. His owner didn't have a saddle or a bridle or any kit, so Vic couldn't ride him and we had no idea what his temperament was like. It was a bit similar to buying a car without having a test drive.

The initial plan was to buy him for Vic. She was keen, but knowing more about these things than I do, she realised he was just too big and powerful. Had we known he was 17.2, we wouldn't have gone to see him in the first place. After we got back from looking at the horse, I said to her "What about buying him for me?" She told me not to be so stupid. I was still a beginner and Vic knew what I really needed was an old cob, something like Gilbert. The horse we had seen was what you aspire to, not what you learn on. She was experienced enough to realise I needed the equivalent of an old Ford Fiesta - and he was a Porsche. If you tried to learn to drive in a Porsche, you'd crash it and kill yourself. She was absolutely right of course, but – flying in the face of good sense - my mind was made up.

I rang the owner back and - not knowing anything about the price of horses and being a tight wad anyway - offered £1,000. He was not amused - he had paid £11,000 for him a few months earlier - and Vic was livid when she found out. She knows the horsey world and she was aware that we would be laughed out of town if we went around offering £1,000 for a thoroughbred. I was guessing, but I thought it was a decent price, because we didn't know anything about him. Vic had been thinking about £5,000 and she reckoned that would have been a bargain.

We thought that would be the last we heard about it after the horse's owner practically slammed the phone down on me, but a week later he rang back. He said a dealer had come in and offered £2,500, but he was ours if we could match that. The owner knew we would be able to give him a better life. The dealer obviously would just sell him on again. The strange thing was, the owner really cared about the animal. When he got told off by his girlfriend, he used to go into the stable and talk to the horse. The fact we really wanted him and we were obviously going to care for him won the owner over. Vic told me to snatch his hand off so we agreed a deal. I had to rush off to training, so it was left to Vic to get him home where we've got stables and around 10 acres of land.

The horse's stable name was The Thatcher, or Tommy to his friends. He was in great physical condition but emotionally he was depressed. Show horses don't live like your average nag, running around in fields. They spend most of their time indoors because you can't risk them getting a cut on one of their legs or any sort of injury. If that happened they'd get marked down by the judges when they went to a show. Tommy was sick of being stuck inside so the first thing we did when we got him home was take him into one of our fields for a bit of a run around. He went absolutely crazy, bucking and kicking - and we are not talking about a small horse. Vic and I looked at each other and we were both thinking the same thing: 'what have we got ourselves into'? I'd had two lessons, remember, on a riding school horse which spent all his time plodding around in sedate circles. I said to Vic "If you think I'm getting on that thing, you've got another thing coming."

She felt like crying, because she'd fallen in love with this horse and it turned out he was an uncontrollable lunatic – and yes, I do realise the irony in that statement! We had no idea what to do, so we just left him out in the field for a week to allow him to play at being a horse. Eventually he calmed down and Vic took the bit between her teeth so to speak, and rode him out. The first ride was on a bridleway which runs past our house, with me walking alongside. Vic took a whip with her, but Tommy kicked off until she threw that away. He was still hard work, rearing up, backing into things and generally being tough to handle, but that was the first step negotiated.

After we'd had him for a few months I booked in for a lesson on him in a little turnout arena we have in the garden, opposite the stable. A local instructor, who specialises in problem horses, came down to show me the ropes. Once I had learned the basics with Tommy, I started hacking out with him, going for a ride in the local countryside along with Vic and her horse Apollo - show name Little Moss Easter Parade.

Once all that was sorted, we started taking him to shows. The first time, Vic wasn't confident about riding him - and I definitely wasn't up to it - so we got someone in to partner him and he won champion of the show. Then we decided to introduce him to jumping and that blew his mind. It was probably like showing Kevin Sinfield a rugby ball for the first time, he loved it. There's an indoor arena about a 10 minute hack from our house and I took him there. Until then he had never been allowed to gallop, let alone jump over anything, and given the chance he went totally bonkers. We practiced on poles which were laid flat on the ground. It was my first jumping lesson as well and Tommy was behaving crazy, he was so excited. He was cantering on the spot, his eyes were popping off his head and I couldn't do anything to calm him down. He had no idea how to jump, so he basically ran straight through the obstacles, knocking the poles everywhere like skittles. It was so bad we were effectively told to go away and not come back.

Anyway, we persisted, he calmed down and, though I say so myself, we started to get quite good. We moved on to doing a bit of cross-country and all the fun stuff as well, like rides on Blackpool beach. We still go to shows and we're still jumping. At the moment we are in the intermediate show jumping class, which is 85 centimetres, and at my last jumping lesson we got up to 1.3 metres. That's quite a good standard, so he has come on really well.

In addition to Tommy and Apollo, we've got a miniature Shetland pony, who is slightly bigger than our dog. We got him for my daughter Saskia to ride and for me to practice my horse care on. I am actually in the Shetland Stud Book as the registered owner. He is not a stallion any more - in other words, he has had his bits cut off - but the owner gets included in the book anyway. His show name is Parlington Rudy and his stable name is Rudolph, because we got him at Christmas time. He gets called Rude Man as well. We got him as a three-year-old and he's a companion for Vic's horse.

I like show jumping and cross country, but Vic is more into dressage, working hunter and that type of thing. Vic shows Rudy in hand, which basically means you walk him around a ring, showing him off. It's confirmation of the horse, how he moves, how he looks and so on. They have to be clean with no marks. It's easy with a Shetland because all you have to do is give him a good wash. With a show horse you have to plait the mane and all that sort of thing. It takes 30 minutes with Rudy but two hours with the big horse. When you are in the show ring at 9am, it means getting up at 5.30 to get him ready. After I've played a game the night before, that's not much fun.

We are out at horse events most weekends during the summer months but we rotate what we do each week, so all three horses get involved. Like anything, the more you do it the better you get. At the moment I am trying to get to affiliated standard for the jumping, which is 95 cms. It is a hobby, but it's nice to get involved in something which has nothing to do with rugby yet still has a competitive element to it.

They are two very different worlds but it's surprising how many horsey people are interested in rugby league. That definitely helps with the running costs because it's an expensive pastime. Vic is an expert blagger and she has used my name to get quite a lot of free stuff. I get all my gear from Caldene, who are based in Bradford. They are Rhinos fans and they provide me with jodhpurs, riding hats and so on. They sponsor Ellen Whitaker and I'm hoping to have a jumping lesson with her. I get saddles from Barnsby, who supply to riders like Mary King.

Horse riding might sound like quite a sedate hobby for a professional rugby player, but it isn't. I am a fair-weather rider. I like it on a nice warm sunny day, but if it's raining, forget it. The hard core horsey people - like Vic - love it when it's chucking it down, but I'd rather be inside with my feet up. Having said that, even in ideal conditions there is a lot of risk in the type of riding I do. Statistically, according to St John Ambulance, horse riding produces more injuries than any other sport. It's a big adrenaline rush. I have a good horse, a thoroughbred, and he's fast and exciting to ride. If he was a nag I'd probably get bored, but when you're hurtling through the countryside, trying to stay on, it's a big thrill.

That's what appeals to me; it's a bit like riding a motorbike. I like the excitement and the danger - and also it is a good way of showing off to women. The first time I had a proper lesson the instructor said to me: "This horse is far too good for you." I was really offended and that's what spurred me into taking riding - and competing - more seriously. I decided there and then that I was going to learn. She had given me a challenge - she basically said you are rubbish and the horse is really good - and a challenge is something I have never shied away from.

Tommy knows that when I turn up with the tack, he's in for a bit of fun. Vic shows him every now and then and she admits he doesn't get too excited about that, but he gets quite giddy when we partner up. We make a good team. I think when we first got him I would have been willing to sell him on if someone had come up with the right offer, but now I wouldn't part with him.

I do get some funny looks when I turn up at shows and riding events and not just from people who recognise me. I've been on equestrian weekends, when you get lessons every day for whatever type of riding you are into: cross-country, show jumping or dressage. The first one I attended was in October, 2009, just after Rhinos' third successive Grand Final win. There were 30 women, one gay guy and me. It is a very female-oriented sport and that's one of the reasons I don't really like doing shows, because I am competing against 15-year-old girls. All professional sports people are competitive by nature and we don't like to lose at anything. I am no different, but when you're being humiliated by teenagers it can get quite embarrassing.

The first cross-country I did was at a venue in Leeds. The daughter of one of Rhinos' sponsors - who runs LSS Waste Management - rides and she saw me. She was with all her friends, so they came over for a chat - or rather to take the mickey. They were all about 13 and they kept saying: "We're going to beat you". It was much worse than being sledged by the Aussie Test team. At least then you can answer back. When it came to my turn, I was terrified and the horse could tell I was nervous, so he was getting worked up. The obstacles were only a couple of feet high but when we got to the first jump - a log - he wouldn't go over. We must have been there five minutes. Normally you have three refusals then you are out, but because it was a beginner's day you could go round at your own pace. Eventually we had to miss that jump out and go on to the next one. I was totally embarrassed and angry. I ended up getting off Tommy and going home in a huff. It was a nightmare experience and I swore I was never going to do that again.

Another time, we did our first working hunter class. That's where you do a jumping course and then an individual show on the flat. The jumps were quite high, about 3ft 6in. One of the spectators recognised me and the video camera came out. I was nervous already and the attention made me even worse. I ended up doing about four jumps, then Tommy refused three times and I got eliminated. That was the second time I 'retired' from the sport. Now Tommy is getting a bit better, I can jump higher and I don't feel as bad because I am competing against a few more men.

People say horse riding is a posh sport. I don't think that's true - I am as un-posh as they come - but it can be expensive, so it does tend to attract people on higher incomes, which is a shame. To get a decent horse you are looking at spending £5-10,000. The really top horses are worth hundreds of thousands. If you haven't got your own land you have to pay livery, which is £100 per week. That's a hefty mortgage. A lot of people who ride horses are women who don't have children. They treat their horses like kids and Vic definitely falls into that category.

It's not just horses, she's keen on all sorts of animals and we had some trauma at the start of 2011 when her beloved Rottweiler Cleo died. They were inseparable and I was fond of Cleo as well because we were pretty much alike; towards the end she was old and miserable and she had arthritis in her shoulder and dodgy knees, just like me. The average age for a Rottie is eight or so and Cleo was 13 when she got cancer. Vic had had her since Cleo was six weeks old, so she was very much a member of the family and she really got pampered. She was more of a daughter than a dog and she got looked after better than I do. That's something I had to put up with, but she was a tough old thing. She was on all sorts of pills and potions which cost us a small fortune and she even went for physio, just like I do. We took her to the vets once a week for an injection in her shoulder and she used to go to water aerobics to help her walk properly and build up her muscles.

We even thought about getting a stairlift put in for her. She struggled to get up steps because of the arthritis, so Vic had the bright idea of having an elevator installed. We spoke to a stairlift company about redesigning one of their models, putting a cage in instead of a chair, but sadly Cleo died before the work could be done. At 13, she was one of the oldest Rotties in the world – the eldest is a dog in Germany, who is 16 or so.

We've also got three cats who came to us from the RSPCA and are basically feral. My favourite is Mae, who I have long meaningful chats to when I get in from training or after a game. As soon as I see her I say "hello" and she miaows back to me. The other two are a bit wilder and are real characters, Minnie and Mike. Minnie lives in the house but on her own terms. She can be quite cuddly at times, but she has a real mean streak. One minute she'll be lying next to you having her back rubbed, the next she'll go psycho and start ripping your hand to shreds. I've got the scars to prove it. A few years ago we had another feral cat, called Dave. Because we've got stables, the RSPCA asked us to take a feral cat as a mouser. They are hard to re-home because people tend to want cuddly kittens. Dave lived outside for a while and then moved indoors and he was one of the friendliest animals you could meet. We used to go for family walks together, me, Vic, the Shetland pony, Cleo the dog and Dave the cat. He was a kitten when we got him and Cleo helped us bring him up. I am sure he thought he was a dog. He was totally fearless and that was his downfall. He tried playing chicken with a car one day and came off worst. If you've got the space and the patience, I'd recommend taking in a feral cat because they can become really good company – and you won't be bothered by rodents. Minnie and Mike don't go outside but Mae is the scourge of the local mice population.

There are a few animal lovers in the Leeds Rhinos camp. Jamie Jones-Buchanan keeps chickens as a bit of a hobby and some fun for his three young boys. He was telling me that the other week one of the poultry was looking a bit off-colour, so he took it to the vet! The chicken cost him a fiver and the vet's fee was over £150. That's typical Jonesy.

Back to horses, and polo is the really posh arm of the sport. I have been to a few polo events and I've even had a lesson at a polo yard near our house. The woman who runs it, Rita, invited us to a match. There were some seriously posh people there and I was way out of my depth. There's a lot of money in that because you need two horses at least, plus a horse box and a groom.

Hunting is something Tommy and I have tried with Rockwood Harriers in Barnsley. That was drag hunting. A scent is put down and you follow it with a pack of hounds. It is organised mayhem; you go out for hours and you are jumping over anything in the way. That is really good fun. The first time I went out, about 60 of us set off and 20 or 30 came back - the rest fell off, or their horse bolted or one or both of them got injured. I was quite proud of the fact I survived the whole experience intact and so did Tommy.

Alex Caddick, wife of the Rhinos chairman Paul Caddick, is a member at Badsworth and Bramham and she has said she'll take me hunting, so that's something I am looking forward to. I know hunting is a controversial subject and it tends to divide opinion between people who live in the countryside and townies. For what it's worth, I do think it serves a useful purpose as pest control.

If you have a fully fit fox, a pack of hounds won't catch it. Since the hunting ban came in, the rule is that - to stop hounds chasing a fox - the hunt master has to shoot the fox. That means whether the animal is sick or fully fit, it is going to get killed. Hunting comes down to survival of the fittest. It takes out the old and sick animals, which would probably starve to death otherwise. When a pack of hounds gets hold of a fox, the end comes very quickly so I don't see it as being cruel. In the countryside, foxes are pests. The other day I found a dead lamb in my riding arena. A fox had killed it and dragged it down on to our land, then left it after it got spooked. Hunting keeps the fox population down and I don't think there's anything wrong with it.

Everyone at the Rhinos knows about my riding, but nobody has ever tried to talk me out of it, despite the danger involved. In fact nothing has ever been said. I don't suppose I'd be very popular with the coaching staff if I fell off and broke an arm. If I got injured I guess something might get written into my contract, but so far, touch wood, it hasn't been an issue. Various clubs have rules about riding motorbikes and that sort of thing, but I don't think horse riding has ever been an issue.

I am not aware of any other rugby players who ride, certainly not competitively, but one sport definitely helps with the other. Because of my leg strength and balance I have taken to riding like a duck to water. When I've had lessons, I've been told I have great seat position on the horse and my strong legs help immensely. So far, I've only fallen off three times. Once was when I was having a struggle with Tommy at Escrick, near York. I couldn't get him over a jump and it turned into a battle of wills. If I had let him walk past, he would have known that refusing was an easy way out. We were there for 15-20 minutes before I got him over it. The first time we tried he ducked out at the last moment and I went straight over his shoulder - and landed on my feet.

Another time was on a weekend away. He had been jumping really well, so I was a bit over-confident. We came up to a fence and he thought 'no I'm not doing that' and he ducked out again. I went head over heels and landed on my backside on the floor. A photographer happened to be watching and he captured the whole sequence. It looks really good, actually.

Vic reckons the third occasion is one of the funniest things she has ever seen. It was actually at the first show jumping competition I ever took part in. Everyone, including me, thought I was going to mess it up. It was a proper show jumping event, with commentary on the public address: "Now entering the ring is Keith Senior, on The Thatcher." Somehow, we managed to get a clear round, much to Vic's, mine, Tommy's and everybody else's amazement.

The problem was, everyone who completes a clear round goes into a jump-off against the clock. And we hadn't practiced that. Panic set in, but Vic did a bit of quick coaching. She said: "The aim is to get round as quickly as possible, so cut all the corners you can and take the shortest-possible route." The object is to leave all the fences up and the quickest time wins.

There were about 40 people in that class and six went clear. Vic was telling me I had done brilliantly to get into the jump-off, but having reached that stage I decided I might as well try and win it. And, deep down, I thought that was what I was going to do, win on my debut.

I decided to floor it, so we set off like a train. I tried cutting the corner to a jump – a big red wall - too much and Tommy obviously thought 'can't do that', so he slammed the anchors on. I went over his shoulder and fell on the jump. I was lying there wondering what had happened and all I could hear was the guy on the Tannoy saying: "Oh dear, that's an unfortunate elimination for Keith Senior." I had to get up and walk Tommy out of the ring with everyone watching. Vic was trying not to laugh because she thought if she did, I might pack in there and then. Once she realised I was all right about it she collapsed in hysterics.

Still, it was a lesson learned. The second time I show jumped I got a double clear, but I took it a bit more steadily. We were third out of 21. I was the only man in the class and at the end we, Tommy and I, had to go in the ring and do a lap of honour. That was quite cool, though I wasn't happy about two others beating me.

Around the time I first started riding, we played Hull in a televised game and one of Sky's presenters, Angela Powers, came to my house to film me and Tommy for a feature in the build-up to the match. Like an idiot, as we went past the camera, I said "trot on Tommy". You can imagine the response I received from the rest of the lads when I turned up at the next training session. I got totally abused. When we moved from one training drill to another, they all got together and trotted off - straight backs, hands pointed down in front of their chest, all chanting "trot on Tommy". Very amusing, not. Now, though, it is quite accepted and a lot of them have shown an interest. Rob Burrow has said he wants a lesson, so we're going to put him on the Shetland! Even then, his feet wouldn't touch the ground.

I have endured a few horse-related mishaps and the worst of them got me in the papers. That involved a bloke called Terry George, who is a businessman in West Yorkshire. He runs several night-clubs and was on TV in the series The Secret Millionaire. His big passion is photography and in 2007, when Tony Smith was Rhinos' coach, Terry spent the year filming us for a behind-the-scenes type book, which came out at the end of the season.

I got to know him through that and it turned out he lived only about a mile away from Vic and me, in a big house in Calderdale. Terry won Britain's Best Home and on the night that was televised he had a big party. Quite a few of the players got invited. Vic and I were going for a hack that evening, so we decided to combine the two. We got there, rode in through an open gate and shut it behind us. Terry lives with his civil partner Michael Rothwell and a lot of their friends were there. I made quite an impression on them, turning up in my jodhpurs. That was an experience in itself. When we went home, we left everything as we saw it. The gate was wide open, so we didn't touch it. It had been opened for us and we assumed somebody would lock it after we had gone. According to the Countryside Alliance, you should leave things as you find them, so that's what we did.

Terry has guard dogs and when the party was finished he let them out.

We had a match the following day and afterwards I got a message from Terry saying his dogs were missing because of the gate we'd left open. He couldn't find them and he was really upset about it. Unfortunately, the dogs attacked some sheep and a farmer shot them. It was reported in the papers that rugby player Keith Senior had been to Terry George's house, left the gate open and because of that, his dogs were killed. I do take some of the blame because we should have told someone we had left the gate open. But we thought whoever had opened it would close it and check the grounds. What people didn't know was the fact these weren't pets, they were guard dogs and they were attacking sheep at the time.

That was a distressing experience, especially as Vic is so fond of animals. But, generally, getting into equestrianism has opened up a whole new world for me. You should try it sometime.

CHAPTER 10

BRENT WEBB IS SUPERMAN

Early in 2007 Tony Smith dropped a bombshell when he announced he would leave Leeds at the end of the year to become full-time coach of Great Britain. After David Waite he was the second Aussie to get the international job, but Smithy had lived here quite a while, he had done his citizenship and he thinks of himself as English as much as Australian, so I had no quibble on that score.

All the players at Leeds understood his reasons for moving on. In professional sport you always want to better yourself. If you are playing amateur you would like to have a go at turning professional; players in the lower divisions always fancy a crack at Super League and when you get there you have an eye on an international cap.

When you are coaching Leeds there are not many jobs that would represent a step up, in this country anyway, but one that does is the Great Britain/England role, so nobody in our camp had any complaints about Tony's decision to leave.

I am not sure the international job is a bigger and better one, considering how few games England play, but I could understand the attraction for Tony. I think the fans sometimes wonder how anyone can leave a club like Leeds, but you have to remember that as far as players and coaches are concerned rugby league isn't a hobby, it is a living.

Tony is a smart bloke and he knows coaches have a shelf-life. He came in on a blaze of glory with all the success we had in 2004, but when we failed to win anything during the next two seasons, some people – though nobody who actually knew what they were talking about – began to say he was a flash in the pan.

That was complete rubbish. Tony is a superb coach and he made us into a better team, but he recognised that after a while the job gets harder. Four years is a long time to be a coach at one club and it is a great achievement when you consider how many get the boot each year. Yet you can get stale – like I did when I was playing at Sheffield – and sometimes you need a change, no matter how good you are.

It is difficult for any coach to keep introducing new ideas. As a player if you go through the same routines, day-in and day-out, it gets a bit monotonous; it becomes hard to keep yourself motivated and to maintain your enjoyment of the job. Equally, it's tough for a coach to keep players focused and interested. We love what we do but it can become a chore at times. Tony managed to keep things fresh and interesting throughout his time at the club, but if he had stayed on he would have found it more and more taxing.

Smithy achieved a lot at Leeds, but he needed a fresh challenge to excite him and with a World Cup coming up, there was a project he could really get his teeth into. I don't think anyone was particularly pleased when Tony called us all together and said he was leaving, but he went with our best wishes. He had done a lot for us and we were grateful for that.

In any walk of life it is important to leave on a good note, so I think Tony was pretty determined to bow out with a Grand Final win, but for a long time that didn't seem very likely. We had an okay-ish start to the year, went through our usual mid-season dip, but then finished really strongly. There was one particularly bad game towards the end of the campaign when we lost to Wakefield at Headingley. Tony got some terrible abuse from some of our fans who wanted him to resign there and then. I know he took that hard but he stuck to his guns and we timed our run to perfection, giving him the ideal send-off with a sparkling Grand Final win over St Helens.

Our last game in the league that year was a repeat fixture at home to Wakefield, which we won easily. That was my 300th game in the regular Super League rounds – not including play-offs – which made me the first player to achieve that particular milestone. Unfortunately we didn't quite manage to get on level terms with St Helens in the league table. They finished a point above us in first spot so we had to go to Knowsley Road in the opening round of the play-offs, with the winners of that game going straight through to the Grand Final.

It was one of the most brutal contests I have ever played in, with both teams bashing each other relentlessly - more or less within the rules – for 80 minutes. Though Saints won 10-8 it was one try each and we came out of that tie knowing we had the tools to beat them at Old Trafford, if we could overcome Wigan in the final eliminator at Headingley the following weekend – and that is exactly what happened.

Having already won two play-offs games, Wigan had the momentum and they went into the tie in confident mood, but we hammered them 36-6 and it was one of those nights when we came up with pretty much a perfect performance. We didn't drop the ball, hardly missed a tackle and scored some cracking tries. Late on, even though the game was won, Kev knocked over a couple of drop goals which I think shows what a smart player he is. You can practice all you like on the training ground, but it's different in a match situation and Kev knew a one-pointer might be crucial in the final.

Reaching Old Trafford for the third time in four years meant we had an opportunity to give Tony the perfect farewell. That is the sort of thing that gets built up by the media, but among the players themselves it wasn't really an issue. Yes, it would be great if Tony could go out as a two-time Grand Final winner; he deserved that for the impact he had on the team and the club, but it wasn't the reason we wanted to win that Grand Final.

In the build-up to games like that you have to say the right things. When you talk to the media it is always a case of wanting to win it for the coach, your family and the fans, but really it is all about doing it for yourself. It was very fitting, after all he had done for us, that Tony's last game was a Grand Final win, but his departure didn't affect the way I approached the game one bit and I am sure the other lads were the same.

I play rugby league because I want to achieve things: I want to reach finals and I want to win medals and trophies. It may be selfish, but that's just the way it is. I play the game for me. I am the one who gets the batterings and the beatings and has to put up with the injuries and the pain, as well as the abuse and the plaudits. I also do it for my immediate family and my friends and if anyone else gets enjoyment out of what I achieve that's great, but it's only a bonus, not the main motivation.

Though we finished strongly, the most games we won on the bounce in 2007 was four. We never really got into our stride until the end of the season and it wasn't the best of years for me as an individual because I only managed seven tries from 30 appearances. One of them – against Warrington, in April – was the 200th of my career, which was a good milestone. It was particularly pleasing because I had made a right mess of things in the previous game, at home to Wigan. We were leading going into the final few minutes and I threw an unnecessary pass into touch near our own line. Wigan got the ball from the scrum and Pat Richards scored the winning try on the final play of the game, which was a real sickener. As usual, nobody in the team blamed me, at least not to my face, because they knew how bad I felt. It was good to be able to put that behind me by scoring in the next game, which was a 50-point win. Rugby's like that, it is all about highs and lows.

In terms of getting over the whitewash, that season's was the poorest return of my entire career and I finished behind people like Clinton Toopi and Jordan Tansey on our try scoring chart. Not that any of that mattered at Old Trafford, but for a long time it looked like being one of those nearly-but-not-quite years. We had some really bad defeats, losing at Catalan and Hull KR as well as getting beaten at home by Wakefield.

That is one of the frustrating things about Leeds teams: throughout my time at the club we have been able to beat the top sides, but we've struggled against ones lower down the table. No disrespect but we should have been good enough to beat teams like Catalan and Hull KR, who had just come up from the first division. It is easy to get motivated to play sides like Wigan and Saints, but games in which we are massive favourites always give us problems. Even when we aren't the defending champions, teams always raise their game against Leeds. Even though Gary Hetherington is tighter than I am, Rhinos are regarded still as the big-spenders who are there to be shot at. In the seasons when we have been champions, games against us have been everybody's cup final. Obviously in an ideal world you should be professional and play at a high standard whatever the opposition, but players are only human and it simply isn't possible to do that. In the early years of Super League the best sides could get away with playing poorly in some games and still win. Nowadays, because of the salary cap, the playing field is much more level and if you are off your game, at best you're going to find yourself in a real battle and usually you will lose. It is good for the competition if sides like Catalan and Hull KR are beating big-guns such as Leeds, but obviously it put us under pressure and a lot of pundits wrote us off in 2007 because of those setbacks.

We always seem to have a mid-season wobble, even in the years when we have gone on and won the title. I don't think that's just us, though, because it is tough to be consistent all year round. It is a hard game and you can't play to the best of your ability every week. Everybody has off days, even the Mr Perfects like Kev Sinfield, though he doesn't have many. We have enough talent in our team to get away with it if it's just one or two of us, but if you have four or five playing below par, you are going to struggle. The key thing is the timing of when these ruts happen. Accepting that you are going to have a bad spell, the best time is at the beginning of the year or in mid-season, because then you still have an opportunity to recover. One of the good aspects of the Grand Final system is it means you don't have to win every week; you can go on and lift the title at the end of the year even if you haven't finished top of the table, so individual defeats aren't as costly as they would be under a first past the post system. Apart from 2004, we had bad spells in each of the years we won the title, but we got through them and came good at just the right time. It is about building form for the big games at the end of the year, though finishing the season with a clean bill of health is important as well. Sometimes losing to a team near the foot of the table can be a good thing in the long-run because it gives you a kick up the backside and shakes off any complacency if you're getting a bit carried away with how good you think you are.

The 2007 Catalan away game came early in the season and it was memorable for only one thing, Jamie Thackray's try. If you have ever met Thacks, he will have told you about it and, to be honest, it was worth the bragging. He got the ball about 40 metres from their line and, being a front-rower, should just have hit it up into the defensive line. Instead he chipped over, ran through, chipped over again, gathered, stepped round the full-back and went between the posts. I've never seen anything like it. That helped us into an 18-point lead late in the first half and we were 10 ahead at the break, but they came back and pipped us 30-22.

Thacks' score was voted our try of the season and rightly so; somebody like Danny McGuire would have been proud to get one like that. That was Thacks for you, he never did the expected. He has been around a bit, which says something about what sort of character he is. He started at Hunslet and played for Castleford, Halifax and Hull before joining Leeds in 2006. Since he left us, in 2008, he has been back to Hull and on to Crusaders in Wales and then out of Super League to Barrow. I was sorry to see him go when he rejoined Hull. He is one of those blokes who is good to have around the changing room because he's a bit of an idiot. He doesn't really care about anything. He had an argument with Tony Smith once after he had been given a rollicking for something. Thacks turned round to Tony and said: "How many caps have you got for your country?" Tony came back with: "We don't dish them out like sweets like they do over here," and it turned into a slagging match that went on for about 10 minutes. It was great entertainment for everyone watching.

Another time, Thacks turned up late for training. He was very apologetic and said it wouldn't happen again. Tony replied with: "No it won't, or you'll be on your way." So Thacks just told him: "I don't care, I'll just go and sign for Brisbane Broncos." That was in front of the whole squad and things like that were among the reasons he eventually got the boot, after being left out of the 2007 Grand Final, something he took very hard.

You could always have a laugh and a joke with Thacks. I could put up with him for about 30 minutes at a time before he got a bit too much for me, but it's good to have characters in the team. He didn't have the greatest of skill as a player but he was very off-the-cuff. He doesn't look like a rugby player, he is a bit porky, but his ability to pull something out of the bag really helped him along. He also tended to do something really awful at least once in a game; he had a loose carry which meant he dropped the ball a lot, but he was fun to play with.

Apart from the Grand Final, the highlight of the 2007 season was the first Magic Weekend, in Cardiff. That year the RFL decided to stage a whole round of six matches at one venue on the same weekend. For us that meant a return trip to Millennium Stadium, which was where we lost the 2003 and 2005 Challenge Cup finals. This time there were only two league points at stake, but because of the venue it felt like the game was more important than that. We played Bradford in the final fixture on the Sunday night, which closed the whole event. It turned out to be probably the most controversial game in Super League's history. It was a bizarre enough encounter anyway, but the way it ended – and what happened afterwards – was a complete farce.

We won 42-38, thanks to Jordan Tansey's try on the final play of the game, but the score should never have been awarded. With seconds to go Gaz Ellis dropped the ball, but video referee Ashley Klein told man in the middle Steve Ganson to give us a penalty because Matt Cook had picked up the ball in an offside position. That was a wrong call for a start, because the ball had come off one of our players, so Cook hadn't been offside. Anyway, video refs aren't supposed to interfere in things like that.

Time was up, so Kev had a shot at goal even though it was about 40 metres out to the left of the posts. The ball hit the crossbar and Jordan ran through, collected the rebound and touched down. Tansey was way in front of Kev when the kick was taken and just about everyone in the stadium knew the try should have been disallowed for offside, but Ganson awarded the touchdown straight away and we won the game.

That sparked absolute chaos. We all went well over the top celebrating – as did the Leeds fans - and the Bradford players were furious, which is probably where they went wrong. As soon as Tansey put the ball down they were in Ganson's face, telling him to go to the screen. If he had handed the decision on to Klein, it would have been 'no try', because it was crystal clear Tansey had been in front of the kicker.

But I have learned through years of bitter experience that if you tell a referee to do anything he will do exactly the opposite. As soon as a player gets in the ref's face like that, it gets his back up. If you confront a referee his reaction is 'I am in control of this game, not you'. Iestyn Harris and Terry Newton were both at him, shouting and carrying on and telling him to put the square in the air and it backfired. You will probably have a bit of a laugh when you read this and the words pot and kettle might spring to mind, but it is all about respect. Sometimes it is hard to control your emotions and naturally players do get carried away in the heat of the moment because rugby is our job and our livelihood. I have conceded some costly penalties for dissent in my time – for example in the 2010 World Club Challenge - and I have regretted it on every occasion. If you get in a row with a ref there'll only ever be one winner and it won't be the player. Ganson's attitude was 'don't you dare talk to me like that – it's a try'. If the Bradford boys had let Ganson do his job he would probably have gone to the video official just to check everything was in order and they would have won the game, because they'd have got a penalty and the hooter would have gone as soon as they had taken it. If that had happened we could have had no complaints because we hadn't really deserved to win.

Bradford should have taken it on the chin, but they didn't and the way they reacted after the match made them look silly. Steve McNamara, their coach, kicked off big style in the post-game press conference, describing the whole situation as "ridiculous" and "ludicrous", which was true. Their board then got in on the act, claiming we should concede the game and hand the points back, which is even more ridiculous and ludicrous. At one stage they were even talking about legal action. Gary Hetherington must have been rubbing his hands together, because we were due to play them again at Headingley a few weeks later. Gary's response was: "If you want the points, come and get them next time we play you." That game drew a packed house, 22,000, and they beat us 38-14. And yes, every 50-50 decision went their way.

That's the thing: referees make mistakes, just like players do. You get angry at the time and understandably so, but you have to get on with it and hope those things even themselves out over the course of the season. Bradford should have cast their minds back to a game against Harlequins at Odsal the previous year. They were trailing by two points with a few seconds to go when they were awarded a penalty for the Quins marker, Danny Williams, not standing square. Paul Deacon kicked the goal and the game finished as a draw. Looking at a TV replay it was clear that Shontayne

Hape had moved off the mark as he played the ball, so he should have been the one who was penalised, in which case Harlequins would have bagged the victory. I don't remember Bradford offering to donate their unfairly-gained point to the Londoners that time. Incidentally, the referee that day was Ashley Klein.

Things like that add a bit of spice to the sport, in my opinion. It is a talking point and it gets people interested. The Gansongate row gave Super League and the Magic Weekend loads of extra publicity. Obviously you want referees to get decisions right all the time and nobody likes winning a game on the back of a mistake by an official, but they are only human – apparently – and they do make errors, so you have to live with that. There were decisions awarded against us earlier in that Cardiff fixture which should have gone the other way. If you looked at the tape closely enough you would spot dropped balls and missed tackles that were just as costly from Bradford's point of view, but the decision at the end grabbed all the headlines because it came at such a key moment in the match.

Brent Webb scored a hat-trick for us that evening and he finished the year with 24 tries from 27 appearances, which is good going by anyone's standard. He would have played – and probably scored – more, but he got a four match ban after the RFL disciplinary panel threw the book at him for two separate high tackles in the same game, away to Quins in August. We were losing 16-6 at half-time but clicked into gear in the second period and scored 48 points to win 54-20. We had lost three of our four games before that and I think the win at the Stoop was a turning point in the season.

Webby's ban was harsh and he got it reduced by one on appeal, but it worked out well for us. He struggles a bit with various ailments so the enforced rest did him good and he was fresh and raring to go when he came back for the play-offs. I think Webby has revolutionised full-back play in Super League, he is that good. With Webby in the team it is like having a third half-back on the field. He has silky skills and he would get in any Super League team playing stand-off, scrum-half or even hooker. He has played in the halves for us a time or two and been outstanding. Before he got over here, full-backs were runners, but now – because of Webby's influence – they are being used as extra ball-players. Webby's pass is exactly the same, whether it's a short one or a 30 metre ball; it always comes at identical pace. My only beef with Webby is those cut-out passes he throws to the wing! If he started hitting me a bit more I would be a lot happier. Eight times out of 10 it's the right decision, but he is putting Ryan

Hall over when he should be giving me a few more tries. Hally, incidentally, made his debut in that Cardiff clash with Bradford.

Our other major signing that season was Kylie Leuluai, who's a slightly smaller version of the Incredible Hulk. I first came across him during a tour to Australia when we were staying in the Manly area and he played for the local Sea Eagles club. It was a lovely, sunny day and I remember seeing this brute of a man walking towards us. He is raw-boned and as strong as an ox, probably the strongest bloke I have ever played with. He is a ridiculous bench-presser, he has no neck and he is as hard as nails. He is a Samoan international and I've never met a small Islander. Players from the Pacific tend to fall into two categories: the wild sort, who like a drink and a party, and religious types, like Kylie. He's a bit of a beast on the field, but he is very into his religion and he is one of the most decent people you could meet. He tries to be a bit of a trickster, but he always ends up second best because he is not devious enough. He was one of the players who didn't come over with a particularly big reputation, but he proved to be worth his weight in gold.

Chapter 11

Wizards of Aus

The Australia team who won the 2004 Tri-Nations were fantastic to watch – and I should know. Along with the rest of the Great Britain side, I watched them power to victory in that year's final in front of a mesmerised Elland Road crowd. As proud Brits, that would have been a painful experience if we had been sitting in the stands. The fact we were out on the Elland Road pitch with them made it almost unbearable.

We went into that series with a new coach, Brian Noble, and high hopes after the near-miss in all three Tests in the previous Ashes series. The internationals came at the end of a title-winning campaign for the Leeds boys and there were six of us in the GB squad: myself, Ryan Bailey, Matt Diskin, Danny McGuire, Chev Walker and Danny Ward. The shock was who wasn't included. Kev Sinfield had enjoyed a great year and he deserved to play in the Tri-Nations, but I don't think Brian Noble ever really rated him as a world class player and he was left out. That was the wrong decision in my opinion.

Team selection only really gets criticised if things go wrong and for most of that series it looked like Nobby was pretty much spot on. We lost 12-8 to Australia in our opening game, at City of Manchester Stadium, but only after they scored the winning try in the final minute. That was a disappointing result but an encouraging performance and we backed it up the following week by beating the Kiwis 22-12 at Huddersfield. Stuart Reardon scored a couple of tries and I put him over for one of them.

Then we went to Wigan and beat Australia 24-12. That was a weird evening for me because I hardly saw the ball all game and when I finally did get a decent pass, it was from one of the Aussies, Scott Hill. I intercepted and went 60 metres for the final try, late on. I was delighted with the win but disappointed not to have been more involved. Other than get the try, I did next to nothing. That happens a lot in Test matches if you're a British outside-back. We tend to play through the forwards too much and I have had quite a few boring afternoons watching from the edges. Obviously that's where successive coaches have felt our strength lies, but maybe if we had been more expansive we would have fared a bit better over the years.

The final group match was a 26-24 win over New Zealand at Hull. I scored a try but it was a costly afternoon for Leeds because Disko – who was sensational for us that year - ruptured his knee ligaments on his Test debut. He was out of action for around six months and I think it took him a few years to get back to his best.

That victory set up a final against Australia, which quite a lot of people thought we might win. Fat chance. We were 38-0 down at half-time and ended up losing 44-4. It could have been even worse, but they basically stopped playing with about half an hour left. We were poor that day, but not as bad as the scoreline suggests. The fact was, they were absolutely outstanding. It was the best performance – in the first half anyway - I have ever seen from an Australian team, and there have been a lot of good ones. Darren Lockyer ran the show and everything they did turned to gold. We just couldn't get near them and they were on fire. Nothing we tried to do came off and in a game of rugby league, once a team gets on a roll it's very difficult to stop. It was like trying to turn back the tide.

The Aussies and Kiwis were back the following year for another Tri-Nations. Before that one we went on a warm weather training camp to Marbella, in Spain. That's a good venue. We stayed in a really nice hotel with excellent rooms and the most comfortable beds I've ever slept in. I had the bright idea of inviting Vic, who is now my partner, along. To be honest, I didn't think she would go, but the next thing I knew she turned up in the hotel. She had booked flights three days apart, but only one night's accommodation, so that left us with a bit of an issue. I was rooming with Kev and as much as I like him and value his company, I'd rather spend a night with Vic. I had to ask him if it was all right if she moved in. Fortunately he didn't get jealous and agreed to swap rooms.

Chev Walker had a spare bed in his room because Iestyn Harris hadn't made the trip, as his wife Becky was expecting a baby any day. Chev was on his own so Kev moved out of my room and in with him. I was the only one who'd invited his partner and that didn't go down too well with some of the other lads, especially Adrian Morley, whose other half is best friends with my ex-wife. That has made things interesting at times.

Towards the end of the camp we were unleashed for a night out on the beer, which turned into one of the heaviest sessions I have ever had. I was totally comatose by the end of it, as was more or less everybody else in the squad. I was recovering from the ankle injury I aggravated in the Challenge Cup final a couple of months earlier, so I didn't really train with the rest of the players; I spent most of the week working on re-hab with the physio Rob Harris. That didn't stop me going out on the lash, unfortunately. I was with Vic, plus a former player Paul Rowley and his wife, who just happened to be there on holiday. Apparently we ended up in a lap dancing club to prolong the drinking. I don't actually remember being there but Vic tells me I threw up in an ashtray and that got us thrown out. Vic had to get me back to the hotel, which had a tiled floor. She literally had to drag me across that to the lift, shovel me in and then manoeuvre me into our room. I was throwing up on a regular basis and then Vic almost drowned me by pouring water down my throat. But the important thing is, I managed to report for training the next day. So did everyone else, apart from Gareth Raynor, the Hull winger who had been called into the international squad for the first time. He was too blathered to make it and he could hardly walk. There was a health scare about bird flu at the time and he claimed he had got that!

It almost cost him his place in the squad because Nobby was furious. He was thinking about sending Gaz home. Everybody knows if you go out drinking during a camp like that you have to be able to train the next day. It was a big black mark next to his name but he was quite a young kid at the time and he was a bit naïve. A few of the boys spoke to Nobby and we managed to persuade him to give Gaz another chance.

Nobby was a good coach and someone I like as a person, but – and I think this will surprise a few people – he was quite easily swayed by player-power. Raynor's reprieve was one example; another was what happened to Kev Sinfield that year. He got selected in the squad this time and played in the first couple of games but then got dropped. What happened was Nobby had been planning to leave Iestyn Harris out of the team for the third game, against New Zealand, which we had to win to have any chance of reaching the final. But Iestyn wasn't happy with that. He went to see the coach and Nobby – who was his club boss at Bradford - changed his mind, so Iestyn was in and Kev got the Spanish archer (elbow). With Nobby, senior players tended to get treated differently, better than young kids just coming through.

Nobby had his favourite sayings and phrases, which used to cause a bit of amusement in the camp. 'In relation to' was one of his catch-phrases. If we were in a meeting, we'd all be counting how many times he said that. Coming up against the Kiwis, he would always tell us we'd need our baseball bats. Another choice phrase, when he wanted an aggressive performance, was: "You're going to need your horns, teeth and testicles today." The day before a Test we would have the shirt presentation, when each player would be handed his game jersey. "We're coming to the exciting part of the week again," was how Nobby introduced that. In team meetings we'd all sit there trying not to laugh.

As a coach, Nobby was a good operator. He was very passionate and he knew his stuff, as you'd expect from someone who had also been Great Britain captain and had a great record at club level. He has certainly known how to beat Leeds over the years. His problem was he spent too much time trying to improve us as players. I know that sounds a bit ridiculous because that's what coaching is all about. But that's a club-coaching thing and, in my opinion, at Test level you don't need to do that. Any player who has got that far in the game should be able to do the basics. We spent far too long working on things like tackle technique. What we should have been doing, with only limited preparation time, was getting a game-plan together. Basic skills should have been dealt with over the previous few months, during the domestic campaign. The GB coaching staff did have an opportunity to tell an individual's club that this or that needed working on, but the end of the year was too late to be worrying about that sort of thing. We only had 10 or 15 minutes in GB training sessions to sort out our game plan, which I didn't think was nearly enough.

During the 2005 series itself we were based in the Worsley Marriot, near Manchester. It was a decent hotel but, like all camps, there was nothing much to do and we had to make our own entertainment. Kev Sinfield and I spent hours playing one-touch football with a rolled up sock in our room. The ice machines were another source of amusement. We'd spend a good 10 minutes each morning lobbing ice cubes at each other in the corridor. One time Kev caught me smack on the forehead and drew blood.

Things on the field were pretty bloody as well as we failed to reach the final, which – considering we had home advantage – was a bit of a disaster. We managed just one win from our four games, hammering the Kiwis at Huddersfield after losing to them and Australia in the opening two weeks. For some reason our first match – against New Zealand – was played at Loftus Road, QPR's soccer ground in London. That area is a bit of a ghetto for Aussie and Kiwi back-packers, so they had massive support on what was supposed to be our home turf. It probably didn't make any real difference, but I am not sure why the RFL decided to give the opposition a possible advantage in such a big match.

Anyway, we got thumped 42-26. It was my first game since I hurt my ankle in the Cup final in August and to be honest, I didn't really want to play. I wasn't 100 per cent after what had happened at Cardiff. I was seriously concerned about coming back too early, but the physio staff gave me the all-clear, I got through it okay and didn't give the injury a second thought after that. The game went okay for me and I managed to score our second try. Kev put up a high kick, Clinton Toopi - who signed for Leeds less than a year later - fumbled and Chev Walker gathered to send me over. That was a good moment but we were seriously out-played.

We did a bit better in the second game, even though the scoreline doesn't suggest it. Australia won 20-6 but we were well in the game until they scored a couple of late tries. That gave us a bit of confidence and we got right back on the horse in week three when we thrashed New Zealand 38-12 at Huddersfield. That was the game when Paul Deacon suffered a facial injury which almost killed him. I scored our final try and the result meant any of the three teams could go through to the final, depending on the result of our final group game, against the Aussies.

The maths was pretty complicated but the bottom line was we needed to win and, if we did it by nine points or more, it would be a GB v Kiwis final. Yeah, right – we lost 26-14, even though they had stand-off Trent Barrett sin-binned twice! New Zealand played Australia in the final and beat them 24-0 at Elland Road. It was the first time anyone in this country had really heard of their coach, Brian McClennan.

The 2006 series was fairly similar. We won one of our four games and New Zealand played Australia in the final again, though the Kangaroos managed to win that one in golden point extra-time. The only real difference was the competition was staged Down Under.

That tournament is famous for three things: Willie Mason punching Stuart Fielden, Leon Pryce upsetting the Aussies by having the nerve to say he preferred England and Sean Long flying home early.

We played New Zealand in our opening game and lost 18-14. Brent Webb was their man of the match, which was a sort of good-news/bad-news scenario, as he had signed for Leeds for the following season. I had played against him before but it was the first time I'd really paid him any attention. My first introduction to Webby – who scored an absolutely belting long-range try early in the game - was the sight of him hiding behind one of their back-rowers, Frank Pritchard, and hurling insults at me. I wasn't very impressed at the time - in fact I told him "Wait until you get over to Leeds next year, then I'll sort you out." Actually, I never did get my revenge, until now. Webby's a great player but did you know he has little legs like a girl's and he shaves them? He is a weird shape, like a triangle. That's why he has so many problems with his back. He is as strong as an ox, with the biggest upper body you have ever seen and the smallest legs.

After being beaten by the Kiwis in Christchurch we took on Australia in Sydney and beat them 23-12. That's probably one of the highlights of my whole career. I played in the right centre, so Kirk Yeaman could partner his Hull club mate Gaz Raynor on the left. Raynor scored the winning try from Yeaman's pass, so that worked. It was a superb team effort from start to finish and Big Willie's assault on Stu Fielden really got us fired up for a big game. The punch-up happened early on, after Stu had got a bit upset at a tackle from Mason and Nathan Hindmarsh. Stu can get a bit mouthy at times and he has a habit of cocking his arm, as if he's about to throw a punch, whenever an argument starts. Usually nothing happens, but on this occasion Mason decided to get his retaliation in first.

He landed a beauty right on Stu's chin, knocking him over. Mason got a one-match ban for that, but it had a long-term impact on Stu. Up to that point he had an aura and he was regarded as being a bit untouchable. He was – no question – one of the best front-rowers in the world and he had come out on top, more times than not, in his long-running feud with Barrie McDermott, which is no mean feat. But when Mason floored him, that took away some of his invincibility. His bubble was burst and young kids who wouldn't have tangled with him before that, started thinking they would have a go. He became a bit of a target. A while later he got pounded in a charity boxing match with Hull's Lee Radford and that was another big blow. He was having a difficult time of things then anyway, because of the death of his mother, and a bit of a decline set in. It took him until 2010 to get his international place back, after he played in Wigan's title-winning side.

That was a shame because the game needs people like Stu. His spats with Barrie always used to make me laugh. Fielden was one of the best props in the game at the time when Barrie was at his peak. When Stu was the main man for Bradford, they used to come up against each other on a regular basis and something always seemed to kick off. Barrie was an established hard-man when Fielden burst on to the scene and it was a bit like in one of those nature programmes, when the old lion has to defend his place in the pride from a young upstart. It led to fireworks and they had some great contests. I think it was good for both of them. They needed that competition and it brought the best out of both of them. Stu was never the same after Baz retired.

We all enjoyed the win over Australia but it was especially sweet for

Leon Pryce. He copped unbelievable stick from the Aussie media after saying he preferred Blackpool beach to Bondi. It was a tongue in cheek remark but the papers over there went completely crazy in reaction to it. I've mentioned earlier that being in camp – particularly on tour – gets mind-numbingly boring after a while, even when you're based somewhere as nice as Manly. We were all pretty bored and Leon made a jokey comment which got blown out of all proportion. All Leon did was say he liked England better than Australia. What else did they expect? I would have said the same thing if anyone had asked me.

If an Australian had said something similar to the press over here, nobody would have taken much notice, but rugby league is much bigger news Down Under. Leon had photographers following him everywhere. They were even hiding in bushes to catch him unawares and there were pressmen trying to set him up all the time. On a couple of occasions they sent a woman to chat him up, trying to trap him into saying or doing something they could use against him. They even got the mayor of Manly to come out and say what a fabulous place it is. It was completely ridiculous. The rest of the squad got dragged into it and it's the only time I've experienced what a Premiership footballer's life must be like. It was a distraction but we were all totally on Leon's side; we just thought it was funny, even though all the fuss got a bit annoying as the tour went on.

We were on top of the world following the win over the Aussies, but it was a case of after the Lord Mayor's Show when we got hammered 34-4 by New Zealand in Wellington exactly a week later. I got sin-binned early on in the game, after a bit of a set-to with their centre Steve Matai and that incident is one of my biggest regrets. If I had my time all over again I'd make sure I actually got a punch or two in! Matai is one of those players who has a bit of an attitude, the sort who thinks nobody has a right to tackle him. He took offence when Danny Mags had the nerve to do just that. Danny had his back turned and Matai threw the ball at him. There was no need for it and I went in to have a quiet word and to help out Danny, who isn't one of the sport's natural brawlers. There was some pushing and shoving and basically we ended up having a bit of a cuddle. It was no more than that and looking back, I am devastated I didn't knock Matai on his backside. The Kiwi water carrier tried to get involved as well; he came on and squirted some water at me, so I wish I'd flattened him also. Referee Paul Simpkins showed both me and Matai the yellow card and they scored back-to-back tries while I was off the field.

Losing that game was a big setback to our chances of reaching the final because it meant we would have to beat Australia in our final group game. Considering that hasn't happened twice in one series since 1970, nobody was holding their breath. That said, after the earlier result we knew we could do it, so it wasn't all doom and gloom. Not until the flight home anyway. One of the problems with that trip was the amount of travelling we had to do. We were based in Manly, a suburb of Sydney, and our games were staged at Christchurch, Sydney, Wellington and Brisbane in that order. That's not like playing Test matches in Wigan, Hull, Huddersfield and Bolton; there is a lot of flying involved.

After the second Kiwi game we were allowed to have a few beers, with a warning not to go overboard. Most of us listened to that advice but a few of the lads didn't and the main offender was Sean Long. We flew back to Sydney the day after the game and Sean, who is a bit of a law unto himself, began to get a bit rowdy at the airport. Sean's one of the game's rebels and that is what has made him the player he is, which is one of the best and most successful scrum-halves this country has produced for a long time. But he is the sort who, if you tell him not to do something, will do it. He began drinking in the hotel, along with his mate Martin Gleeson. Basically, they got blathered in the hotel and when it came to checking out the following day, they filled their water bottles with spirits and carried on drinking.

When we boarded the flight they were in a pretty bad state. Things like that can be funny for a while but you always get to a tipping point after which is just gets to be annoying. I was sitting behind Sean on the flight and he had a man and a woman in the row in front of him. He was knocking the seat in front and after a while the guy took offence, turned round and told Sean to pack it in, at which point Sean decided he wanted a fight. He was totally out of order, the guy wasn't doing anything wrong and an aircraft is not the best place to be kicking off anyway. A few of the other players, me included, had to have a word with Sean to try and calm him down. When someone's that drunk it's not easy to reason with him, but we managed to get things sorted out, apologised to the bloke and the rest of the flight passed without incident. The damage had been done, though, because it was a scheduled flight, full of the general public, fans and members of the media. That sort of thing sets a bad example for rugby league and Sean realised he had messed up.

Once he had sobered up he decided he wanted to go home, so he quit the tour a few days before our most important match. As far as I know it was his decision. The management were angry over the way he had behaved but they didn't send him packing, he had just had enough. It was a long tour, we weren't doing very well and he got fed up. It was a shame, but Sean shot himself in the foot.

All the fuss that caused wasn't exactly ideal preparation to be taking on an Australia team who were all fired up for revenge after the previous meeting. I scored a try but they hammered us 33-10 and that was a miserable end to another disappointing experience.

It was also the end for Nobby as coach, with Tony Smith taking over for the following year's home Test series against the Kiwis. It was the final time we played as Great Britain, before the split into England, Wales, Scotland and Ireland. Tony's spell as national coach started a bit like his reign at Leeds, in a blaze of glory. New Zealand weren't at full strength and they played pretty poorly overall. We beat them 3-0, I scored in a couple of games and after 11 years I had finally managed to play in a winning Test series. And yes, I have still got the medal.

Tony was smart, he tried to recreate some of the conditions he knew we'd be facing in the next year's World Cup in Australia, moving us around different hotels and exposing us to the media – literally, because he allowed them into the changing room straight after matches.

That was a good series, for once, and I really enjoyed myself. All the Leeds boys played well and we felt we had a team that was good enough at least to reach the World Cup final and maybe even win it. For me the only thing that put a bit of a downer on that series was Tony's decision to include Maurie Fa'asavalu, the St Helens forward, in the GB squad. I have absolutely nothing against Maurie, who is a good player and a really tough impact man off the bench. But he is Samoan. He had played for his country in the rugby union World Cup before switching codes and in my opinion he had no business playing for Great Britain just because he had lived here for a few years.

He did nothing wrong and under the rules, neither did Tony. Maurie qualified under residency, but I believe you should only play for the country where you are born, where you've lived most of your life or maybe where your parents are from. Similar things happen in most sports. Lesley Vainikolo, Henry Paul and Shontayne Hape have all played for England rugby union after being capped by New Zealand in league. In cricket there's a joke about it: Where do the England team stay when they are touring

South Africa? With their parents. But just because other games do it doesn't make it right. To me it devalued Great Britain's victory in that series a little because it gave the impression we could only win if we brought ringers in. It's the same with Brent Webb. He is an Aussie, but he played for New Zealand because he qualified on residency, after playing for the Warriors in Auckland. I'm sure he would rather have got caps for the Kangaroos but he had players like Darren Lockyer and then Billy Slater in front of him. He wanted to play Test rugby and I don't blame him, but I think the regulations should be changed.

It is open to abuse anyway. In the 2006 Tri Nations, New Zealand had the two points they got for beating us in the opening game taken away when somebody discovered that Nathan Fien, their hooker, didn't actually qualify as a Kiwi. He was born in Queensland and played for the Maroons in State of Origin, but was selected for New Zealand on the basis that his grandmother came from there. It turned out, when a newspaper reporter bothered to check, that it wasn't his granny who was a Kiwi but his great grandmother. I think if anybody dug deep enough, they'd probably find other players in the same boat.

Fa'asavalu played pretty well in 2007 and he kept his place in the squad for the following year's World Cup, which was the next big international event and a return to business as usual. We travelled to Australia with high hopes but the competition was a massive let-down from an England point of view. We played four matches, lost three of them and were back home watching on TV when New Zealand beat Australia in the final.

There have been a lot of inquests into why we did so poorly. As far as I am concerned, we had a bad month, we didn't play well and Australia and New Zealand were better than us, full stop. You can look at other issues, like the number of overseas players in our game, but the bottom line is we had a squad that was good enough to go all the way, if we had got our game together.

There were eight Leeds players and seven from St Helens in a 24-man squad and a lot of people have blamed our poor performance on that. The World Cup started less than a month after we had beaten Saints in the Grand Final for a second successive year, but claims there was a massive split in the camp and that the Leeds and Saints players didn't get on simply aren't true.

Yes you do get cliques on tour and yes, the Leeds and Saints boys did tend to hang around in their own groups, but that's human nature.

Obviously, on days off the Leeds and Saints lads tended to stick together, with others from different clubs joining either group. You go with what you know. It is natural to spend time with your mates and the people you are most comfortable with. I spend most of my life in the company of Rhinos players, so if they are heading for a coffee or to the cinema, of course I'm going to go with them, rather than with a bunch of Saints boys, who I don't really know.

But when it came to getting down to work, we all mucked in together. You'll either believe this or you won't, but I can honestly say that there was no rift in the group, we all got on pretty well and suggestions the Leeds and Saints lads hated each other are complete rubbish. For a few years Leeds and Saints was the biggest rivalry in rugby league, but as far as I am concerned there's no animosity, just a healthy respect. That doesn't make for good copy in the newspapers but it's true. Maybe it would have been better to mix things around and have Leeds lads sharing a room with Saints players, so we did get to know one another. In hindsight, I can see that would have been a good idea. But could it have made enough difference to get us through to the final? I doubt it.

It was the first World Cup since 2000, when there had been a lot of one-sided matches. To avoid that, the organisers designed the format to virtually guarantee that Australia, New Zealand and England would reach the semi-finals. We were all in one 'super group', along with Papua New Guinea. The top-trio in that pool went through to the competition's last four, with one team from the other six also qualifying.

In other words, if we beat PNG in our opening match, we'd more or less be one win away from the final. We managed that, but lost all the rest. I thought we played quite well against Papua, though we got a lot of criticism in the press. What people don't realise is they are a tough team to play against, mainly because all their players are completely mad! Rugby league is the national sport in Papua New Guinea and it is like a religion to them. They are brought up on rugby league, they love the game and when they get out on the field they never take a backward step. They are like brick walls and they are totally fearless. Every tackle you go into, you end up getting hurt. They can be a bit raw, but however many times you knock them down, they always get up again. They are tough players and when you add some skill into the mix, it is always going to be a ferocious battle.

We certainly got that, but we did enough to win and, to put the icing on the cake, Lee Smith scored a hat-trick on his debut. I put him over for his final try when I could have scored myself and that earned me a rollicking from Tony Smith. He said: "Fair enough, you are club-mates and you want him to get a hat-trick, but if he had dropped the ball or not scored, it could have changed the game." We won 32-22 and that was a reasonable result in the circumstances. A 10-point winning margin wasn't an embarrassment at all but things went rapidly downhill after that. We got belted 52-4 by Australia in our second game and then blew a 24-8 lead to lose 36-24 to the Kiwis. We played them again in the semi-final and came off second best, 32-22. That was my final game as an international, though not entirely by choice.

At the final whistle we were all devastated. We'd had a bad tour, copped a lot of stick and totally under-performed. For me, it was a tough time because of things happening away from rugby – which I talk about elsewhere in this book. I was tired and fed up, my home life was in turmoil and I'd had enough. In the changing room after the game I went round all the players shaking hands and Adrian Morley asked me if that was it? I just told him I had come to the end, because I was at a low point in my life and I was utterly depressed. I had reached the stage where I hated rugby and I was ready to walk away.

Word got round that I had retired from the international game, but sometimes in the heat of the moment you say or do things you regret. Thankfully, there was light at the end of the tunnel, things got back on an even keel at home and after the World Cup debacle, 2009 was one of my best seasons for Leeds. I was named in the Super League Dream Team and picked up another Grand Final winner's ring. With the Four Nations – France were included this time – just around the corner, I had got my appetite back, plus, to be honest, I would rather have played for England than gone through a full pre-season with Leeds. Jason Davidson, the Rhinos conditioner, had a similar role with England and towards the end of the season I had a word with him and asked him to let Tony know I had made a hasty decision and I was keen to come back into the fold.

Jason went away, spoke to Tony and came back with the message that I wasn't in his plans. I wasn't totally surprised, because Tony is a stubborn sort and once he has got something in his head, he very rarely changes his mind. He had got used to the idea that I wasn't going to be available and obviously he had got thoughts of his own about who he was going to pick instead. I threw a bit of fuel on to the fire by telling the press I would be willing to play, if Tony wanted to pick me. His response to that was to confirm I hadn't spoken to him and to state that as far as he was concerned I had retired and he wasn't going to do business through the media. Technically, that was true. I hadn't rung him up and I wasn't going to beg for my place back, but he knew full well that I wanted to play because I'd told Jason that and made it clear in several interviews. If Jason had come back to me and said "have a word with Tony" I would have done, but he made it clear he didn't want to do that. In my eyes, Tony took the easy option by claiming I hadn't been in touch. I would have had a lot more respect for him if he had said that I was no longer in his plans, things had moved on and he had other ideas about who he wanted in the centre. It's a shame because I could still have done a job, but as far as I am concerned, it was his loss.

CHAPTER 12

LOVE RAT

You will find this hard to believe, especially if you have a look at the fine features staring out from the cover of this book, but I haven't always been the best looking of blokes. In fact when I was a teenager I was a bit of a geek. I was thin and spotty and I wasn't really one for the ladies. Going through school I didn't really have girlfriends - my first was Kathryn Commons, who I met when I was 18.

As a youngster I was very insecure with the opposite sex, so it was a massive shock to the system when they began to find me attractive. That coincided with when I started playing rugby. I got rid of the acne, began working out, put on some size and weight and all of a sudden I went from being a bit of a turn-off to girls, to someone they were throwing themselves at. It went from being just about impossible to far too easy.

That was something I didn't cope with very well and haven't done for most of my rugby league career. I enjoyed the attention because I never had it as a kid. I went from one extreme to another and I took advantage. In fact I abused the situation I was in and did so for a long time, right until I met my current partner Victoria and, to my shame, beyond that.

That's not an excuse for what you're about to read but it's an explanation of sorts. I am not proud of the way I have behaved towards the various women in my life and I know I have caused a lot of upset to myself and others but, being honest, most of it has been my fault.

As I mentioned earlier, Kathryn was my first real girlfriend and we were living together within months of meeting. I used to see her at the Corn Mill, a pub in Huddersfield, which had a nightclub attached. Eventually I got hold of her phone number, we went out on a date and it progressed from there. Before either of us really knew what we were doing we had moved in together and were sharing a flat near where my mum and dad lived in Longwood.

My parents were going through a rough divorce at the time and home life wasn't very good. It was a bad time to be in the household so I took the first available opportunity to get out. I was 18 and I jumped straight into my first serious relationship, which eventually produced my daughter Saskia.

Kathryn was a few years older than me and early on, when she asked how old I was, she said: "Please tell me you're not 18." So I obliged and told her I was 20. I was playing in the first team at Sheffield at the time and she came to watch a game. Afterwards, Gary and Kath Hetherington were talking to Kathryn and my dad in the Cocked Hat pub near the ground. Gary and Kath told her they thought I had great promise for an 18-year-old. My father had to come clean and admit I had been lying about my age. By that time we had been seeing each other for a few months so she was aware of what a mature, sophisticated fella I was and she forgave me.

The best thing to come out of our relationship was Saskia, who was born three months after I joined Leeds, on December 29, 1999, when I was 23. She was eight weeks premature and weighed only 2lb13oz when she was born. She spent the first four weeks of her life in an incubator, so it was a really worrying time. Saskia has S11Q deletion syndrome. It is a mild form of Down's and can lead to a lot of problems. Fortunately, Saskia is fine, apart from the fact she was born with a sub-mucus cleft palate which affects her speech. The syndrome is hereditary and that is why it caught the doctors unawares. Kathryn and I have had tests and we were both negative so it's something that came out of the blue. Unfortunately, if Saskia has kids they could be affected.

People say playing rugby league is tough. From what I have seen it's a picnic compared to giving birth. Kathryn was in labour for 40 hours before Saskia was born at Dewsbury Hospital. I was at the birth and when Saskia finally came out, for a few seconds – though it seemed much longer at the time – she didn't make a sound. That was probably the worst moment, then she started crying and we could all breathe again.

It was a surreal experience. More or less as soon as she was born, Saskia was rushed off for some special care, which was a bad situation after such a long labour. Apparently it was touch and go for a while. She was being monitored and fed through her nose via a syringe. It was tough for both parents seeing her like that. For the month she was in an incubator we visited her every day but at least it gave Kathryn chance to get over the labour and birth.

It was a very stressful time, particularly for Kathryn, and our relationship never really recovered. About a year later, in December 2000, we split up. Around that time a lot of the lads who had played for England in the 2000 World Cup went out for a few beers at a nightclub in Leeds. Adrian Morley was there with his girlfriend Claire Richards. She had a friend with her, Beverley Lupton, and we got talking.

We were attracted to each other, one thing led to another and eventually we ended up in a relationship which progressed to an ill-fated marriage and more trauma all round. Bev, who had two kids, lived in Normanton. For a while after Kathryn and I split up I crashed with Neil Law, who played for Sheffield when I was there. He's one of my best mates and it seemed like a perfect solution, but he only had a small two-bedroomed house and with him having a girlfriend I soon felt like a spare part.

It wasn't much fun being a gooseberry so I moved out of Neil's and in with Bev. Kathryn and I put our house, which I had left her in, up for sale and we sorted out bank accounts and that sort of thing. Obviously at the time it was a bad situation but it was reasonably amicable. After about 18 months I bought a house in Huddersfield and Bev upped sticks and came to live with me there.

One of the worst things about splitting up with Kathryn was I didn't get to see her step-dad any more. We were really good friends – I'd have described him as one of my best mates - and we spent a lot of time together. Understandably when I fell out with Kathryn it changed his opinion of me and brought that friendship to an end.

I went from one long-term relationship with Kathryn straight into another with Bev. That turned out to be a case of out of the frying pan into the fire. We got married in 2003 and split up a couple of years later, after I had an affair.

My marriage ended in an acrimonious divorce which earned me some unwanted and pretty embarrassing publicity in the national press. It all began around Christmas, 2004, when I saw Victoria Greetham, my current partner, for the first time. I was smitten. Our eyes met over the Aspirin and make-up in Boots the chemists. It was proper romantic. We got chatting and she made quite an impression on me.

Vic is probably as well-known as I am, certainly in the Huddersfield area. She is a former model and has done a lot of TV appearances on things like Emmerdale and Coronation Street. She was in an exercise video produced by Peter Kay and caused uproar at Channel Four when she hoaxed one of their documentary makers by fooling them into thinking her boyfriend at the time was her father!

The pair of them were going to feature in a programme called Daddy's Girl, but her real dad, Geoff, found out and tipped off the TV company. The documentary got cancelled and the story featured in the national media, so that's something we have got in common for a start. She's also a smart cookie with a law degree from Huddersfield University, which means in our relationship she is both the beauty and the brains.

The summer after we first met, Rhinos played Toulouse in a Challenge Cup semi-final at Galpharm Stadium, in Huddersfield. Our game was on a Sunday and the previous afternoon St Helens took on Hull in the first semi. With it being in Huddersfield I went along to that game. Toulouse were a French league side and we were pretty confident we would beat them, even though they had defeated Widnes – then a Super League club – in the quarter-finals. I thought I would pop along to the other game to have a look at who we'd be playing in the final. Coincidentally, Vic was there doing some work for Powergen, the competition sponsors. After a few minutes of exchanging glances she came over and asked if I was the man from Boot's a few months earlier. We got chatting and as I was leaving she sent a friend over to ask me for my phone number.

I was walking out of the ground and I got a tap on the shoulder. Honestly, I did try to do the right thing. I told her friend: "Sorry, I can't do that, I'm married". My dad was with me and, this is perfectly true, he gave her my number. So much for attempting to be good. We started exchanging text messages and that's how our relationship began.

Vic was different to my previous partners. She was educated and successful in her own right with a great job, home and car. That was new to me and I suppose I knew that because she was financially secure herself she wasn't dating me for access to a walking cash machine. I knew she wanted to be with me for the right reasons and we clicked immediately. The result of all that was divorce from Bev, who got a measure of revenge by slagging me off in the national tabloids. The story was that love rat Keith Senior had kicked his ex-wife out of the marital home and I had called in the cops to back me up. That's not exactly what happened.

The relationship with Vic was serious from the start and as time went on she decided she couldn't cope with me going back to my wife every night. She told me she needed a break from me and went travelling around Australia with a friend. The separation was a tough time for me and it was then I realised I wanted to be with Vic on a permanent basis. When she came back I went to Manchester Airport to pick her up and we had a long talk. The following day the end came for Bev and me after I'd been on a trip with my amateur team, St Joseph's, to a game in Cumbria. They are always good days out because it's at least a three hour journey back and you can get stuck into the booze on the coach trip home. That day I met up with Vic in Huddersfield when we got back and then I went home and had an argument with Bev, one of those 'what time do you call this?' kind of discussions. It was late - 3 in the morning or something like that - and Bev, understandably I suppose, wasn't best pleased. I had been out all day, I'd had a skin full of beer and I didn't like the earache I got when I arrived home, so I just left and didn't go back.

I'd just had enough. I went to Vic's and stopped there. The following morning Bev rang and asked where I was and I lied and said I'd slept in my car at St Joseph's. She told me: "No you didn't – I've already checked." She had got on the phone, asked whoever answered at the club to have a look in my car and he'd said I wasn't there. I had my back to the wall again so I did what any gutless man does, I hid. I stayed away rather than facing the music.

Because we were living in my house, that caused a major rumpus. When it was clear I wasn't going to get back with Bev I began divorce proceedings. Solicitors got involved, we went to court and Bev agreed that she would move out of the house in Huddersfield, which was in my name and had solely been paid for by me. I'd agreed to pay her £38,000 so she would leave. The plan was I would move back in and put the property on the market. When I turned up to resume living there, with the funds already in Bev's account, she refused to go. As far as I knew she had found a house of her own and everything was sorted. For some reason that fell through and when I arrived at the door she said she was staying put because she had nowhere else to go. We got into a big row and the police turned up. I think Bev called them because I was refusing to go away. But as it was my house, the cops' view of the situation was that I hadn't done anything wrong and she would have to leave, as we had agreed. Conveniently a press reporter and photographer just happened to be there hiding in the bushes when all this was going on and that produced the best part of a whole page's coverage in *The Sun* the following day, along with three pictures of me and Bev rowing outside the house. I spoke to one of the neighbours afterwards and he said the press had knocked on his door before I turned up, asking if they could take shots from inside his house. He told them to stick their camera where *The Sun* doesn't shine – pardon the pun - so they scuttled off and hid somewhere else. Obviously they knew exactly when I was going to be arriving, so I must have been set up. Bev denies that she contacted them but somebody did.

Bev's son's grandma was there and she was hurling abuse, which added to the drama. Eventually they left and, though I had won that particular battle, there was an emergency court case and I knew the judge would say she could stay put. To add insult to injury, Bev managed to get a court injunction preventing me going within 500 metres of my own home. In situations like that the law stinks. Married or not, how can it be right for a woman to move into your own home with you and then get an injunction to keep you away from it while you are still legally obliged to pay all the mortgage and costs?

In the end I actually found myself living at Headingley Carnegie Stadium for a few months, which was another bizarre twist. There's a hotel at the ground called the Lodge, and Gary Hetherington arranged for me to stay there, so I had no excuse for being late to training.

All that is sorted now but the aftermath has caused a bit of tension for me every time I have been into camp with England or Great Britain. Claire, Moz's partner, is still best friends with Bev who, as you can imagine, isn't my biggest fan. Claire says she feels a bit awkward because she introduced me to Bev. She hasn't forgiven me for what happened. She remains angry about it, which I can understand, even though it's a long time ago.

While my marriage to Bev is now water under the bridge, unfortunately Kathryn has come back into my life in the last few years, which has caused me no end of problems. We tried to remain on good terms for the sake of our daughter, but things have gone sour because of money. I have been paying child support to her for Saskia ever since we split up, which I have no qualms about and is the right thing to do. A while ago I was negotiating with Leeds over a new contract. When you get to the later stage of your career the money doesn't necessarily go up and that was the situation I was in. I mentioned to Kathryn that I might have to take a pay cut and asked her if I did, would she be prepared to accept a bit less money in child support? At that stage I was paying her a fixed amount on a regular basis, £650 per month. That more than paid her mortgage. By then I was living with Vic in a nice house with its own land and Kathryn told me: "If you can afford to live there you can afford to pay me more money, not less." I thought she was bluffing and I didn't spend much time worrying about it.

About six months after that I got a solicitor's letter demanding an £80,000 lump sum. I had already paid her near enough £100,000 in maintenance over the previous 10 years or so. She refused to talk to me about it and told me I would have to deal with her through the lawyer, which was when things started getting a bit heated between us. Every time I picked

Saskia up it was a struggle to stay calm. I didn't – and still can't – see what gave Kathryn the right to start demanding more money from me just because I was coming to the end of my career. She knew my income would dry up when I finally stopped playing, so I suppose she wanted to get what she could out of me while the going was good. That made it hard when I saw Saskia, because of the bitterness between me and Kathryn.

The row over money went to court and the case was unbelievable. Kathryn and I were never married but because I'd had a child with her several years earlier that apparently entitled her to see all my wage slips, contracts, investments, property details and pensions. I had to disclose everything to the court despite the lawyers being warned that this sensitive information could end up finding its way into the tabloids.

It is a mystery to me why a former partner can turn up several years down the line and be entitled to turn her ex's life upside down. Kathryn and her lawyers even got hold of information about Vic's company and her financial assets, which – as you can imagine – did not please her one bit.

That situation has dragged on ever since and is still continuing. I have lost count of the number of times I have had to go to court over it and it has wrecked my relationship with Saskia, which is the worst aspect of the whole sorry saga. One of the last times I picked my daughter up was in January, 2010. For a birthday present I took her to see Disney on Ice, in Sheffield. I took my dad and his wife as well, but I have only seen Saskia once since then, which was under sad circumstances eight months later, when I took her to visit my gran, who was terminally ill. After that day out I agreed, through court, to pay Kathryn's legal costs of £10,750 and a lump sum, £16,800, plus child support of £650 per month and my own legal costs. It came to more than £40,000. The court case happened during the week and I was told I could collect Saskia on the Sunday. I arrived as arranged, but because Vic was with me, Kathryn said she wasn't going to let Saskia come with us and she more or less slammed the door in my face. That is the last bit of contact I have had.

At one time I bought Saskia a mobile phone so I could speak to her directly rather than having to do everything through Kathryn. Unfortunately, that didn't work out as the phone was permanently switched off. I have also tried to go through my solicitor and that didn't succeed either because Kathryn wouldn't agree to allow me to collect my daughter at a reasonable time. It was 10 years since we had split up and she was still dictating what I could and couldn't do. In the end, for the good of everybody concerned, all contact stopped.

I will be honest, it hurts. Saskia is my daughter and I would like to be part of her life. She is at the stage now when she's going through an important time at school, she has to make decisions about her future and I want to be able to contribute to that. I have made mistakes in my relationships and I didn't behave very well at the end of my time with Kathryn, but I don't want Saskia to suffer because of that and I wouldn't want it to affect how she feels about me in the long-term, though obviously I think it will. That is one of my biggest regrets.

It has been a bitter experience and one I have learned from. I do now warn young players about the repercussions of getting someone pregnant. Even if it is only a one-night stand, the woman is entitled to unbelievable access to your personal finances and your bank balance for the next 18 years of your life. Sportsmen seem particularly susceptible to that sort of situation because of their perceived large pay packets. I don't regret having my daughter and I love her dearly, but it is sad that, in my opinion, greed seems to have reared its ugly head. It cost me £8,000 in solicitors' fees to defend myself against a claim for £80,000, something I did not think I should have to face in the first place.

Looking back, I will admit I am ashamed of the way I have treated some of the women in my life. Though I have tried to do the right thing by Saskia, what happened with Kathryn and Bev has shaped the way some people I was close to feel about me. It has cost me important friendships and a lot of money, plus a great deal of emotional pain. I deserve everything I have got but you live and learn. I have made decisions and I have to deal with the consequences.

I think a lot of the mistakes I've made have been down to youth and inexperience and hopefully I am a better person because of them, but sometimes you don't always take lessons on board. I hope and believe I have met my life partner in Victoria, but I almost chucked that away because of one silly mistake. This is something I have never spoken publicly about and when I first started planning this book I wasn't going to mention it. But it is something that, because it was reported in the media, a lot of people are aware of, so here's what really happened.

It began when I was part of the England squad for the 2008 World Cup, which was staged in Australia. On that particular camp I roomed with my Leeds team-mate Lee Smith, who had a Facebook account. Through that he met an Aussie woman, who I'll call Carol. That's not her real name but she's had enough publicity and done quite well financially out of me, so I don't want to give her the satisfaction.

She was a Facebook friend of quite a few of the players involved in the tournament and when we got out to Aus, Lee kept in touch with her. Just for the sake of something to do I jumped into their conversation a few times. We had a bit of a laugh and a joke but I had no intention of taking it any further than that.

Unfortunately, it turned out she was from Townsville, which is in north Queensland, and by an unhappy coincidence we were based there for our opening game, against Papua New Guinea. One day she came round to the hotel and Lee and I met up with her in the car park. After that, Carol invited a few players round to her house. She was employed at the airport and had some young girls working for her. She said: "We're having a bit of a party, do you want to come over?" When we got to where she lived it was a strange situation to be in because her two kids were there. We didn't know what to make of that but she basically said they met all the blokes she brought home.

A few drinks were had, though being professional athletes Smithy and I stuck to coffee and pop. Anyway, without going into the gory details because this isn't that sort of book, one thing led to another and we ended up in bed together. Carol drove us back to the hotel and we moved on to the next base for our second game. The next thing I knew, stories about me and her were all over Facebook. She played me a bit; she would ring me up saying she didn't know what to do. She claimed she had the press wanting to come and see her and she wasn't sure what to say to them. I told her to say nothing but I don't think that was in the plan.

What I was telling her she was passing on to Vic via email. She had already been in contact with Vic, telling her what had happened. Everything I said to Carol was being reported back to Victoria. She was telling me 'I won't talk to the press, I won't do this and I won't do that', when she was doing the exact opposite. She was milking the situation to suit herself.

I had made a bad mistake and then the whole thing escalated out of control. To make things worse, she had done this more than once before. She had been involved in kiss and tell situations with some of Australia's top rugby league players. She knew how to make the best of it and I was totally out of my depth.

I am not sure if that was her intention from the start, but if I hadn't been so slack it wouldn't have mattered what she was hoping to achieve.

Honestly I don't blame her for what happened. It was all my own stupid fault. She has her own lifestyle but I made a decision to get involved when I should have stayed well clear. I am a big boy now, I am not the kid I was when I met Kathryn or Bev and I ought to have had more sense.

It was a foolish thing to do and it had serious repercussions. I have made a lot of mistakes throughout my life, I am no saint and I would never pretend to be, but this was probably the biggest let-down to my family and the people I care for the most. At one stage Vic was threatening to come out to Australia and Carol was planning to meet her. That didn't happen, thank goodness, but it was a tough time for Victoria through no fault of her own. She had press camped outside her house back in West Yorkshire, harassing her for a story, so she was having to cope with that as well as with what I had done. Eventually she did an interview for one of the British Sunday papers, which didn't show me in a good light.

When the news broke, the reaction from the rest of the England squad was fairly sympathetic because it's not nice being on the end of a kiss and tell exposé. But after a few days, normality set in and the rest of the lads just took the mickey out of me as you'd expect. That tour wasn't a happy one but I don't think my off-field indiscretions had any bearing on the way the team played on it, though perhaps it did affect my relationship with the coach Tony Smith. It happened during a major tournament when he was in charge so I don't suppose he was too pleased. Obviously he was keen for everything to go smoothly and didn't want his players appearing in the newspapers for anything other than winning rugby matches. I have never really spoken to him since the World Cup and I don't know whether he believes what happened had a bearing on the team in some way.

It certainly didn't harm the way I played. Rugby league has always been a release for me. I have been through a lot of strife in my life but I have always been able to put that behind me when I have stepped on to the field. Once you get out there into the heat of battle it's one of the few times when you can forget what's going on in your life. If you have any troubles you can vent your aggression and your anger in a focused and hopefully controlled manner, on the opposition. If I have had a bad week I can go out and knock seven bells out of someone on the rival team. I think playing rugby has got me through all the various problems I have had – including with the women in my life – because it has given me something else to concentrate on.

However, after the tour I had to come home to face the music. Vic booted me out, as she had told the Sunday newspaper she would, so I moved into my dad's house, camping down in his loft conversion. That led to the lowest point of my adult life – the day I came home from training and he told me: "I hope you're going to tidy your bedroom tonight!"

There I was, a 32-year-old England international and my dad was treating me like a naughty schoolboy. Staying with my father worked out well in the end. I could have moved in with one of my team-mates - Biff Burgess and Ian Kirke both offered me a place to say – but Vic made it clear if I did that, there'd be no chance of us getting back together. She was wise enough to realise if I got myself into that situation I would soon fall back into the bachelor lifestyle.

I was at my dad's for a good few months but eventually, after a lot of pleading and grovelling, Vic took me back. I had to grin and bear it and keep my head down. I didn't go out, do anything or see anyone. I even submitted to relationship counselling, which is basically two women ganging up on one man! I am not the best when it comes to talking about relationships. I like to keep everything bottled up, so that was hard. It has been a big problem throughout my relationships - whenever I have had an issue I have basically tried to run away and avoid it.

It took a long time for Vic and me to get over what happened and, to be honest, it is still there. It is something I am going to have to live with and I know it won't go away. What occurred with Carol has changed me. Now I don't go out, I don't drink – other than maybe three or four times a year – and all my spare time is spent at home. We have the horses, so that's a shared hobby, and socialising with the lads is something I only do very rarely. I have had to make sacrifices but I am prepared to do that because I want to be with Vic and I'll do whatever it takes to make it work.

CHAPTER 13

THE NAKED TRUTH

If it hadn't been for my old Sheffield Eagles team-mate Johnny Lawless I would have had to call this book something else. I may be as bald as a coot now, but in my younger days I had flowing locks with a trendy side-parting. I was very thorough with my hair; the parting was dead straight and I used a lot of gel and spray. It was rock solid and I looked pretty good, though I say so myself.

I certainly looked a lot better than Johnny, who resembled Yul Brynner and used to shave his head like I do now. At Sheffield in those days we would review every game and, unfortunately, things always appear 10 times worse on TV than they actually are. Even at that tender age I was starting to get a bit thin on top and every time we watched one of our games, Johnny would point out the growing circle on the crown of my head. He was into me constantly about it, calling me a bald git and telling me to have it all chopped off.

I tried shaving my hair shorter, with a little quiff at the front. That was quite 'with it' at the time and another of my team-mates Matty Crowther was the same. We thought we looked the bee's knees but I was fighting a losing battle. I was desperately trying to avoid the bald truth that my hair was on its way out. My Rhinos team-mate Carl Ablett is going through something similar now. He's trying the comb-over, just like I did, but he's not fooling anyone and I know from experience he is just delaying the inevitable.

So eventually I got sick of all the abuse Johnny was giving me and I bit the bullet; I got it all shaved off and I've been bald ever since. It was probably the best thing I ever did. It has become a trademark and it makes me instantly recognisable. Without being big-headed – I'll leave that to Jamie Jones-Buchanan - I am probably one of the most recognisable people playing rugby league and that's all down to the shaved bonce. At least my tries never get credited to anyone else.

I am fortunate that I suit a bald head. And since I've started shaving my scalp I've developed a hatred for hair anywhere above the waist. I step into the shower, get the Bic out and shave my head, do my face and then work my way down to my chest, which is pretty hairy if I let it be. I'm probably the only rugby league player who has had his chest waxed, for vanity rather than charity. God, that was painful! It was one of the worst things I've ever done.

I went to a beauty salon in Halifax where the staff were very surprised to see me and basically I paid to get tortured. It cost me £18, which was bad enough for a tight wad like me, but the actual process was agony. After a game if you've had your ankle strapped you pull the tape off and that rips the hairs out. I thought that was bad until I got my chest done. It was excruciating. I was lying on the bed and laughing to get myself through the pain. Otherwise I'd have been in tears. It was awful and to make things worse I came out in a massive rash afterwards. It's not something I'm looking to do again. Instead I am considering having laser treatment now.

Being bald has earned me my own song from the Rhinos fans – 'We love you Senior because you've got no hair….' Secretly I love that and it's something else most players can't boast about. I consider it a great honour and it's fantastic to hear the South Stand in full voice, though I do wonder sometimes how they came up with it. Does someone sit down and write these songs – and if so, how do they get everyone else to join in? It gets a bit embarrassing when you're in the park or walking down the street and you hear kids singing it, but to be honest I quite enjoy that as well.

I am definitely not the only player in Super League to be famous for his hairstyle, or lack of it. My old Great Britain team-mate Sean Long, of St Helens and now Hull, has had loads of ridiculous haircuts, each one as bad as the rest. Ali Lauitiiti and Chev Walker had big Afros at one time or another and as I write this, another of my Leeds colleagues, Ryan Bailey, is going through a bit of a David Haye phase; his latest hairstyle makes him the spitting image of the world heavyweight champion. The Sideshow Bob look Warrington's Matt King used to sport was pretty impressive until he had it shaved off. Big Les Vainikolo – the Bradford Bulls winger who is now at Gloucester RU - had braids in his hair and that certainly made him stand out. The South Sea Islanders can carry it off, but when Sean Long tried it he looked a bit of a berk.

While I am famous for being bald, there was a spell a season or two back when I started to grow a bit of a thatch. Fortunately not many people noticed because I had a beard as well. Like a lot of things, that was due to a bet. I may hate hair but I love money! Danny McGuire and Rob Burrow bet me £100 - 50 quid each – that I couldn't grow my hair for eight weeks. With that sort of dosh riding on it I took the whole thing very seriously. But rather than just growing my hair I thought I'd sprout a beard as well because I knew that would take attention away from what was going on up top. It certainly worked because that was all people talked about. Jamie Jones-Buchanan grew a beard at the same time for a similar reason but he carried on a lot longer than I did. By the time he finished he was practically falling over it; he looked like someone out of ZZ Top. Jonesy's next fad was to grow sideboards. He saw the musical Oliver and liked the way the character Fagin looked, so he decided to follow suit. That's Jonesy all over, as mad as a box of frogs.

There's a picture of me – with Tommy at a horse show - in a tweed jacket, wearing a flat cap and with the beard. I look like a proper North Yorkshire farmer. Changing your appearance is a bit of banter that most rugby league squads indulge in. Every now and then you'll see teams all wearing beards or with shaved heads. Wigan did it a few years ago: they grew moustaches until they got knocked out of the play-offs. It usually starts either as a bet or with someone deciding they aren't going to shave until they've won so many games in a row or reached a certain points tally. It's a bit of fun and it gives everyone something to talk about. Sometimes it gets done just to be awkward – you might grow a beard or get your head shaved before the pre-season photo-call, then go back to your old look straight afterwards.

A while ago Jamie Peacock and Rob Burrow had a contest to see who could go the longest without drinking caffeine. Rob's a big caffeine man, he's into Coca-Cola and Red Bull and JP likes a coffee; he has an espresso every morning to pick him up.

It's quite childish but that sort of thing creates a bit of banter and makes turning up for training a bit more interesting. It actually gets quite competitive because that's our nature. We are professional sportsmen and we don't like to fail at anything. As far as I'm concerned if there's money involved I'm not going to get beaten.

Occasionally hairstyles come about as a result of punishments, though that usually involves having your head dyed blond. Jamie Thackray and JP both sported blond mops at the end of the 2006 season, but that was just the pair of them being weird and trying to look a bit different.

For some reason most in-house punishments seem to involve getting naked. The most famous one is the nude run, which players have to do if they go through a whole season without scoring a try. At Leeds that usually happens at a pub in Headingley on our end-of-season Mad Monday night out, but naked runs take place for a variety of reasons.

The naked truth is, most players enjoy getting their kit off. I certainly haven't got a problem with it; it's only the fat lads who don't enjoy it. Barrie McDermott was never very keen and Luke Burgess is the same. But ask someone like Ryan Bailey to get naked and run around the streets and he would do it at the drop of a hat and everything else come to think of it.

I've only actually done a naked run once. That was on a social night when we went out in 1970s fancy dress, complete with Afro wigs. We started off in Headingley and worked our way into the centre of Leeds. One of the rules of the evening was that if your wig came off you had to go on a nude jog.

Tonie Carroll and I ended up having to do it in a pub in Headingley. It was absolutely packed. We nipped into the toilets and I spent a while getting some blood into my manhood just to spare my blushes. We both put sunglasses on - so nobody would recognise us - but apart from that and the wigs we were stark naked.

We dashed out of the toilets into the main bar and I wasn't hanging about, even though I'd done a bit of preparation and I was quite an impressive sight. I got round the bar and back into the toilets in about four seconds flat. Tonie, being a show-off, came out skipping and prancing around like a total idiot. He hadn't bothered to get himself ready, so I think his reputation suffered a bit after everybody in the pub got a good look at him. I know it was pretty irresponsible behaviour, but we did check with certain people in the pub to make sure there were no kids about and we weren't going to offend anybody.

We ended that evening in a nightclub in full 70s gear, all apart from Kev Sinfield who proved why he's one of the organisers in the team. He arrived at the start of the evening in an ordinary shirt; he picked up some flowers from somewhere and safety pinned them to his chest and that was his 70s look. We wondered why he hadn't put in any effort but it made perfect sense when we got to the club. We were all there in flared jeans, tasteless shirts and ridiculous wigs, but Kev just unpinned the flowers and hit the dance floor in his civvies.

Nowadays there's a press conference after every Super League or Challenge Cup game and if the media want to talk to an individual player, they hang around in the tunnel outside the dressing rooms. But when Tony Smith was coach of the GB/England team he began inviting the press into the changing sheds. Most of the media are blokes, but there are one or two women and they'd be in there attempting to interview players wrapped only in a towel – the players that is, not the press girls, unfortunately.

I think they found it more embarrassing than the players, most of them anyway. I remember once Julie Stott, who then worked for *The Sun*, coming over after I had got dressed. She made some jokey remark about waiting until I was decent and I told her she needn't have bothered, I'd have done the interview naked. Naturally, she was quite upset she had missed out on such a spectacular sight and told me the next time she'd be a bit quicker off the mark.

Showing off my bits and pieces doesn't bother me. I did a Full Monty in front of 400 women and I can honestly say it was one of the biggest buzzes of my life. It was for my testimonial, so I was making money out of it as well, which was an added bonus.

The event was organised by Amy and Nicola, two of the Rhinos' cheerleaders. They were setting up their own entertainment company, Strawberry Split, and they offered to put on a gig for my benefit year. Knowing that I had done the famous Fully Monty photo shoot when I was at Sheffield, they came up with the idea of getting a group of players to strip off at a ladies' night.

Finding other lads who were willing to do it was the hard bit. As I've said, players don't mind getting naked, but it is persuading wives and girlfriends to give the okay which is the problem. In the end, Lee Smith, Luke Burgess, Ben Kaye and Ian Kirke all agreed to take part, so full credit to them.

We took it really seriously, but it was one of the funniest things I have ever done. Nicola choreographed the dance for us and she did a great job. The agreement was you didn't have to get fully naked if you didn't want to, though I was stuck with it because it was my Do. We got some comedy g-strings in the shape of an elephant's head and our conditioner Jason Davidson supplied the uniforms. His father-in-law used to run a security firm, so we were kitted out like the dancers are in the Full Monty film. We really looked the part, complete with trousers with Velcro down the side for ease of removal.

Ticket sales were slow at first and we nearly cancelled the show, but we got some publicity and in the end it was a complete sell-out. The closer we got to the event the more nervous we all became. I had to have a few drinks to calm myself down. Like that night in Headingley I had a reputation to protect, so I applied an elastic band which works a treat.

We did the dance and the idea was I would pull off my thong and a couple of the lads would cover me with their hats. They'd move and I would use my hat to protect my modesty – then the lights would dim. As I took my hat off, I dropped it – and the lights stayed up. I was really glad for the elastic band. Everybody got an eyeful for a couple of seconds before I managed to get off stage.

After that, all the lads were buzzing. It was like we'd won a Grand Final. It was awesome, definitely one of the best things I have ever done. When the Full Monty part of the evening was over, Nicola asked us if we'd go out in our undies and dance with some of the customers. I agreed as long as we could dance with people we knew. We got out there and it was like a cattle market. There were hands everywhere, women were trying to rip our pants off, someone tried pinching Ben Kaye's shoes and we all got thoroughly groped. Eventually we had to flee back into the dressing room for our own safety. Still, it was one of the best social nights I've ever been to.

Events like that are good for team morale and a bit of banter between the lads is essential to keep spirits up. The important thing is not to overdo it. Recently a couple of high-profile players have got the boot from clubs following drink-related matters. The drinking culture in rugby league has declined even in the time I've been playing the sport, but that's not to say the odd alcohol-fuelled incident doesn't take place. Different coaches and clubs probably have their own rules; at Leeds, nobody goes out boozing the night before training, but it's usually acceptable to have a drink after a match and events are laid on at certain times during the season when the boys can have a bit of a party.

Overnight away trips often lead to a good session after the game. Once, after we had beaten London Broncos in the capital, Kev Sinfield's throwing habit surfaced when he picked up a whole bowl of peanuts and chucked them at our chief executive Gary Hetherington, who was sitting on the other side of the hotel bar. As soon as he let fly, Kev realised what he had done and his whole career probably flashed before his eyes, but Gary just ducked, picked up another bowl and lobbed that straight back.

I went out to a nightclub later in the evening and when I got back to the hotel all the Kiwi boys were together in the bar, having a right old sing song. Andy Hay got absolutely ratted and while he was sleeping it off the following morning, somebody packed his bag for him. We had a set departure time and Gary Hetherington had to go round various rooms rounding up the stragglers. When Andy tried to pick up his bag he could hardly lift it – it was full of all sorts of rubbish from the room, including a toilet seat. I'm not sure who the culprit was, but the Dewsbury mafia of Matt Diskin, Francis Cummins and Ryan Sheridan had stayed up all night drinking shorts, so they were leading suspects.

Mad Mondays are one of the most enjoyable times of the season. It's the end of a long year and a chance for everyone to let their hair down, those who have hair anyway. Occasionally that sort of evening does end in tears. I've been on a few nights out which have culminated in punch-ups between players or heated arguments.

In 2003, after we were knocked out of the play-offs by Wigan, we had a big session in the famous Skyrack pub near the Headingley ground. Big Wayne McDonald was in the thick of things that night. Jamie Jones-Buchanan shook up a can of Coke and poured it down his back and then Macca had to do a naked run for some reason or other. He got his kit off and just as he was about to set off running Mark Calderwood tackled him round his ankles and he went down like a tree being felled. There was a huge crash and everyone in the pub turned round to look.

The same evening saw Calders and Daryl Powell go head to head. Calders didn't play in the game against Wigan, when Brian Carney – their Irish winger – scored a couple of spectacular tries. Mark made a comment to Daryl that Carney wouldn't have scored if he had been out there. Daryl came back with "no, but you'd have dropped the three bombs they put up". I think Daryl reckoned that would end it, but Calders hit back calling him a crap coach, then Daryl told Calders he would never play for England – and so it went on. We were all watching intently and it was like a tennis match, looking one way and then another as they served verbal insults at each other.

That didn't go any further but quite often nights out end up in wrestling matches which sometimes get a bit out of hand. One evening, Calders, Wayne McDonald, Matt Diskin and I had an enormous fight outside a club in Leeds. It started as a friendly-ish wrestle - me against Disko and Calders versus Macca - but developed into a full-on brawl. Eventually Disko and I called a halt because it was getting out of hand.

I managed to lose my car keys in the scuffle and had to go back for them the next day and to apologise. During the ruck a woman had been shouting out of the bar window, calling us a "bloody disgrace", so I don't think she was too happy when I turned up the following morning.

Another time, we had a mid-season trip to the races in Newcastle. We had a long turn-around between games, from Friday night to Sunday of the following week, so we were allowed to go on a team day out as guests of Tote.

We were in a box in the grandstand, right above the finish line. Someone had taken a stereo along and if you had been on the side of the track and looked up at the stand, you would have seen people fine dining quietly in all the boxes apart from one – which was full of rugby players all jumping up and down and waving their arms in the air. We looked like a load of monkeys hanging off the ceiling.

There was a free bar, courtesy of Tote, but they got all their money back from our losing bets. Jamie Thackray was the only one to come out on top. He backed a rank outsider and won a couple of grand – though I think most of that was back in the bookies' pockets by the end of the day.

It kicked off a bit on the coach on the way home. To start with, we nearly got arrested. A guy from Tote, Dave, travelled with us and he took his own till. Someone saw him carrying a cash register on to the bus and told the Old Bill, who arrived in numbers. They surrounded the coach and wouldn't let us leave until Dave managed to convince them we were legit and it was his money. We were there for about 25 minutes, surrounded by the Rozzers, with all the punters walking past wondering what was going on.

During the journey home Thacks was on the driver's microphone, taking the mickey out of Jordan Tansey and calling him Green Teeth. Tansey should not have got offended, because Thacks called everybody that, but he'd had a skin full so he got upset. Tansey and Danny Williams – an academy product who later joined Newcastle Rugby Union Club - are both from Whinmoor, in Leeds, so they joined forces. Tansey went up to the front of the coach and took a swing at Thacks. He fell on to the driver, the coach swerved and we were nearly off the road. A couple of the lads had to rush to the front and drag them off each other.

Then Jamie Peacock and Nick Scruton fell out. They started off messing about, pulling each other's tie, but something was said and that escalated. JP took a swing at Scroots and they had a proper full on fight. JP was roughed up a bit, but Scroots had his shirt ripped and a bit of blood on him.

I had to babysit Scroots at the back of the bus while somebody else looked after JP at the front. Scroots kept trying to get back up to have another go. I'd had a do with Scroots before on one of the Dews Fests, so I think he respected me. When we got back to Headingley I said I'd take him home because he had been in bother a few weeks earlier and nobody wanted to see him get in more trouble. On that earlier occasion he had put his foot through a car windscreen and cut his leg open. He wasn't in Gary Hetherington's good books because of that.

Anyway, on the night we got back from Newcastle, Tansey came over to try and persuade Scroots to go into town to carry on drinking. I told Tansey – who was never my favourite team-mate - to shove off, a few insults were exchanged and we ended up with my arm around Tansey's neck, with me saying I was going to kill him. Scroots had to drag me off, when I was supposed to be looking after him. Tansey's not a bad player. He left us to join Sydney City Roosters and actually played a few games in the NRL before returning to England and signing for Hull. After a couple of seasons they got rid of him for disciplinary reasons. He had to drop down a level to play for Dewsbury before Crusaders gave him another chance. If he could sort that side of his character out he could have a good career because he can play.

Reading this, you're probably going to get the idea that as a team we don't get on. That is not the case. I don't suppose anybody likes all the people they work with – do you? – but there is a strong comradeship in the Leeds camp and that was at the heart of our success from 2004-2009. It is an intense, high-pressure environment and yes there are fall-outs every now and then, but I can honestly say nobody bears grudges. The morning after, there's usually a handshake and it's all forgotten.

Scroots is a bit of a character and he was a loss to the team on and off the field when he moved to Bradford Bulls. For a start he was our karaoke king and he led the singing in the changing room after a win. He does have a bit of previous when it comes to breaking glass, though. On one of our pre-season training camps in Lanzarote he was wrestling with Wayne McDonald in their room and he managed to fall through a patio window, badly cutting one of his arms. He was lying there covered in blood and all Macca was worried about was his hair – he went through the glass as well and chopped off a bit of his mullet. Wayne was known as Tarzan: he used to train the house down, but unfortunately most of the time he played like Jane.

On that same trip, Jamie Jones-Buchanan nearly demolished the complex we were staying in. There were no kettles in the rooms but we did have glass coffee jugs. Jonesy fancied a cup of tea, so he filled the coffee jug with water and left it on the electric cooker to boil. His room-mate Willie Poching was lying on his bed reading when there was an enormous bang and all the lights went out. Luckily, neither of them was hit by the flying glass as the jug exploded.

We stayed at a place called Club La Santa, which a lot of Super League teams use for warm-weather training, along with various other football clubs, athletes and boxers. One year Warrington were due to move in the day we shipped out. Kev and few of the boys bought six cans of tuna from the hotel shop, opened them and left them hidden in one of the rooms – on top of wardrobes and places like that - so that would have been a nice surprise for the Wolves lads a few days later.

I got caught out that time by having to share a room with a player we called Boff. I won't name him, but he has been around a few clubs after not making it at Leeds. The living arrangements at Club La Santa are fairly basic: three sharing, with two in a bedroom and one on a camp bed in the living area. I was in with Boff – who I didn't know – and Matt Diskin. When we got there Disko said he would take one for the team and kip on the camper, so I got the room, with a proper bed. That seemed like a result but I soon discovered Disko had pulled a fast one. Boff had a serious problem with body odour and I ended up having to sleep with the door and windows wide open.

Inevitably when you get a bunch of blokes together there are practical jokes. Fortunately, I don't usually find myself as the victim. I would like to think that is because I have got the respect of my team-mates and as a – pardon the pun – senior player, I am above being part of things like that. Actually, the real reason is I have got the reputation of being a grumpy old man and it is well known that if anyone tries a prank on me there will be repercussions and retribution, which will be ten times worse.

Apologies if you are eating while you are reading this, but most practical jokes revolve around bodily functions. When I was with Great Britain, Brian Carney – the Irish winger – had a habit of sneaking into team mates' hotel rooms and having a reverse crap in the toilet – in other words he would do it facing the pot to cause maximum mess. He'd flush the toilet first and then leave it, so when you came in after training or following a night out, it would have been festering there for hours and the stench would be pretty revolting.

One time, when we were staying at the Worsley Marriott Hotel, near Manchester, Carney and Paul Johnson teamed up but they picked on the wrong victim when they targeted Rob Harris, the physio. They went into the medical room after we had finished for the day, so the dump was left

PRIZE GUY: Showing off the Baskerville Shield after Great Britain's 16-10 win over the Kiwis at Wigan in 2002. Both teams won one Test and the other was drawn, but we were declared series winners. Picture: Dave Williams (RLphotos.com).

MAN OF THE MATCH: The team comes first, but it's always nice to pick up the plaudits, such as this award after Great Britain beat New Zealand 16-10 at Wigan in the final match of the 2002 Test series.
Picture: Dave Williams (RLphotos.com).

A RARE SIGHT: This picture, taken during a Rhinos training session, must be unique. The world's two grumpiest men, Matt Diskin and myself, are smiling - at the same time! Picture: Steve Riding, Yorkshire Evening Post.

PARTY TIME: En-route to scoring a try in front of Leeds Rhinos' fanatical fans.
Picture: Dave Williams (RLphotos.com).

BIRD BRAIN: We get asked to do some strange things to promote matches. I
honestly can't remember what this was all about, but I look much more nervous than
the bird does! Picture: Dave Williams (RLphotos.com).

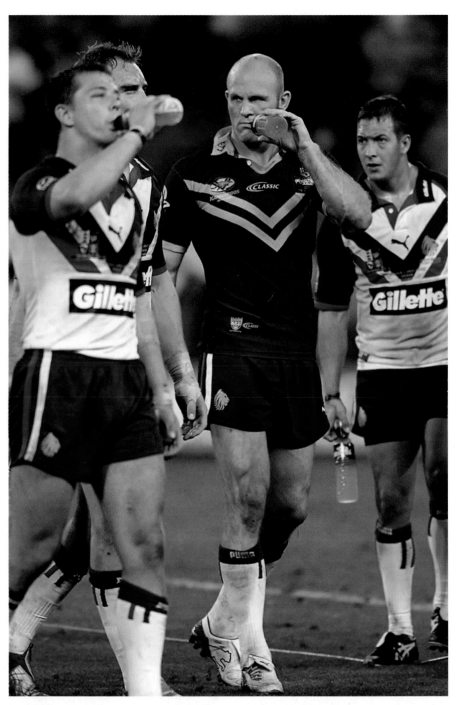

COLOUR CLASH: Do not adjust your set, this really is me in an
Australian Kangaroos shirt. I have just swapped jerseys with an opponent
following another series defeat. The expressions tell their own story.
Picture: Dave Williams (RLphotos.com).

BOWLED OVER: Trying my hand at a different sport, during a Super League promotional event. Picture: Dave Williams (RLphotos.com).

FULLY MONTY: Ben Kaye, Ian Kirke, myself and Luke Burgess get our kit off. That's something rugby players will do at the drop of a hat, on this occasion quite literally!

LONG SERVER: In 2007 I was granted a testimonial for services to the Rhinos, who produced a special shirt to mark the occasion.

FAMILY MAN: With my daugher Saskia at my testimonial game in 2007.

HAPPY DAYS:
Hull are one of
the teams I most
enjoy playing
against, because
they are always
good games. I'm
pictured here
(top) celebrating
the moment after
scoring against
the Black and
Whites in 2009
and taking on the
same team's
defence (below)
in a match the
previous year.
Pictures: Dave
Williams (RL
photos.com)

JUST CHAMPION: Here I am showing off the Super League trophy at a celebration party back at Headingley, hours after we clinched the title by beating St Helens at Old Trafford.

GRAND RIVAL: I always enjoyed facing St Helens' Matt Gidley (No 3), because he was such a tough opponent – as he shows here in the 2009 Grand Final. He later became chief executive at Australian club Newcastle Knights. Picture: Steve Riding, Yorkshire Evening Post.

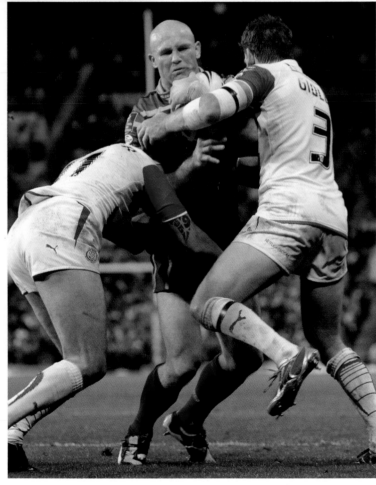

DREAM TEAM: Jamie Peacock, Kevin Sinfield, myself and Ryan Hall were all named in the 2009 engage Super League Dream Team - rugby league writers' choice of that season's form players.

GO WEST: Gareth Ellis and I at a Great Britain training session in Leeds. Gaz left Leeds to join Wests Tigers in Sydney and ripped it up in the Australian competition. Picture: Jonathan Gawthorpe, Yorkshire Evening Post.

TRY TIME: Going over to score Great Britain's first touchdown in a
26-24 win over New Zealand at Hull during the 2004 Tri-Nations.
Picture: Dave Williams (RLphotos.com).

HOMETOWN HERO: Being a Huddersfield lad, I always enjoy playing at Galpharm Stadium, as it is now. It was great to score in front of friends and family as Great Britain beat New Zealand 38-12 in the 2005 Tri-Nations. Picture: Dave Williams (RLphotos.com).

HOKEY COKEY: I put my right arm in, but it wasn't a case of best foot forward as Great Britain slump to a 33-10 defeat by Australia at Brisbane's Suncorp Stadium during the 2006 Tri-Nations. Picture: Dave Williams (RLphotos.com).

WHITEWASH: Scoring England's final try during a 44-0 rout of the Kiwis at Hull in 2007. We beat them in all three Tests, the only genuine series win I have played in. Picture: Dave Williams (RLphotos.com).

WORLD CUP WOE: Taking on New Zealand's Jeremy Smith during the 2008 World Cup semi-final. We lost 32-22 and went home - they went on to win the tournament. Picture: Dave Williams (RLphotos.com).

BLITZED: In action for England against Australia during the 2008 World Cup. I'd rather not mention the score of this game, played in Melbourne, but we didn't win! Picture: Dave Williams (RLphotos.com).

GOLDEN GIRL: My partner Victoria is the best thing in my life. We have been through some ups and downs, but she has been a tower of strength. Here we are en route to a typical night out at McDonalds.

JUMPING FOR JOY: Show jumping has become a major hobby of mine and I even had special fences designed to combine two of my passions. Picture: Matt Johnson Photography.

COUNTRY GENT: I have come a long way from my early days on a council estate in Huddersfield. Picture: Matt Johnson Photography.

WHY THE LONG FACE?: The good looking one is Tommy! Picture: Matt Johnson Photography.

TALLY HO: Tommy and I look the part, as we get ready to join the country set.
Picture: Matt Johnson Photography.

all night. Rob wasn't too happy when he rocked up the following morning, but he guessed straight away who the culprit was. To get his revenge, Rob crapped in a cloth and then left it in Johnson's bag. When he took it home he gave it to his wife to wash and she ended up pulling a turd out.

There's lots of similar stories. During the really cold winter in late 2010 Kev and I went to a dinner in Leeds along with the rest of the Rhinos team. When we came out everything was frozen over. We had been to the Comedy Club and being consummate professionals, we left a bit earlier than everybody else. When we got to where we were parked, Rob Burrow had left his car near-by.

It was too good an opportunity to miss. I peed in an empty bottle I'd got in the car and poured it all over Rob's windscreen and the locks. Kev had a load of protein shakes in his car, so he got those out and added them to the mix. It was about minus nine, so by the time Rob got back to his vehicle it was frozen solid. He couldn't drive anywhere because he couldn't see through the windscreen, so he had to sit there in the freezing cold, waiting for it to defrost. If you're reading this Rob, Kev made me do it!

CHAPTER 14

THE BLUEY YEARS

Tony Smith is a superb club coach who struggled at international level. His successor at Leeds, Brian McClennan, is the opposite. Bluey, as everyone calls him, came to us after a glittering spell in charge of New Zealand. He coached them when they won the 2004 Tri-Nations and was in charge of the Kiwis in the following year's tournament, which saw them beaten by Australia on the golden point rule.

He has a good pedigree. His dad Mike coached St Helens for a spell in the 1990s and we won two titles under Bluey, so he can hold his head up high whenever he recalls his time at Headingley, but I wouldn't rate him anywhere near the top of a list of the best coaches I've worked with. Don't get me wrong, I think he was a fantastic appointment for Leeds and he did some brilliant things as team boss, particularly in 2008 and 2009, but he is nowhere near as good a coach as Tony Smith and, technically, we went backwards as players during his time in charge.

I can genuinely say I like Bluey. He is a great bloke and personality-wise he is someone I have a lot of time for. You want to perform and do your best for people like that. John Kear was the same and that makes it harder when things go wrong.

Tony is one of the best technical coaches in the world. He can take your game apart, put it back together again and make you a better player. Bluey's strength is different - it is as a motivator. As a field coach he is no great shakes, but when it comes to the big games he can raise individuals and get them to produce something special.

Bluey inherited a very good team from Tony Smith and he had big boots to fill, a bit like Dean Lance did when he took over from Graham Murray back in 2000. With Tony's last game being a Grand Final win, there was only really one way we could go and that was down. To Bluey's huge credit he managed to continue our success for a couple of years but the wheels came off after that.

For the first couple of seasons under Bluey, when we won back-to-back titles, we were relying a lot on what Tony had taught us, as well as our natural ability and flair. I think Bluey was aware of that to a large extent. He used to say: "You get us to a final and I'll make sure we win it." Out on the training park he sometimes seemed to lose the plot but he could sit you down in a room, make you emotional and really give you a mental edge.

When he first arrived, Bluey told Kev Sinfield: "I guarantee this will be the best year of your playing career." For a new coach to come into the reigning champions and say that was a massive statement. He definitely delivered and we had two great seasons in 2008-9. The 2008 Grand Final was the best I played in, though our finest year under Bluey was 2009, his second in charge. We went into the campaign as back-to-back champions and that brings its own pressures. It is hard to maintain the hunger and at the same time you are up there to be shot at. Every game you play is the opposition's cup final. We struggled badly about a third of the way through the season. We were knocked out of the Challenge Cup by St Helens and suffered some really poor league defeats, especially at home to Salford and Harlequins. Everything seemed to be falling apart but Bluey kept the faith, we managed to turn things around and we went on to finish top of the table and win the Grand Final yet again.

Bluey likes to give each year a theme and that season's was 'three-peat', winning a hat-trick of titles. A lot of what we did was based on the LA Lakers basketball team, who are the only team to win a hat-trick of titles in America's NBA. He got medallions made up, which we wore during the campaign. It was all about unity in the team and having something to focus on when times were hard. The trinkets were designed around three triangles and at the start of the year three of the senior professionals – me, Kev and JP – talked about what it would mean to retain the championship for a second successive year.

I was pretty sceptical about it and a few of the other boys – fellow grumpy old man Matt Diskin for example - felt the same way. But we knew Bluey had done something similar with the Kiwis and it had worked for them, so we were willing to give it a try. How much of an effect it had I am not sure but we achieved our goals, so full credit to Bluey for coming up with the idea.

The 2008 Grand Final was Gareth Ellis' last game for Leeds, which was a big loss. Australians like nothing better than knocking the Poms, especially in rugby league. As far as they are concerned, Super League is a second-rate competition played by has-been Australians or never-will-be Brits. That's what they say, but clubs in the NRL are beginning to look at the British game as a source of good-quality players, especially in the forwards.

A lot of Brits, people like Ellery Hanley, Mike Stephenson, Garry Schofield and Malcolm Reilly, proved a big hit in the Australian domestic competition in the 1970s and 80s. In their day it was possible to play a season Down Under and then fly back to play for a club here because both leagues were staged in their respective winters.

When we switched to summer it became a lifestyle choice. Quite a few British players have tried to make it in the NRL, but haven't had the success they would have liked for one reason or another. But the two big achievers have been former team-mates of mine, Adrian Morley and Gaz.

Moz went over to the NRL and walked the walk, proving he was as tough as any forward out there. He went down a storm during his spell at Sydney Roosters and that paved the way for others to have a go. Gaz joined Leeds from Wakefield in 2005, making his debut in the World Club win over Canterbury. At the start of the 2007 season, NRL clubs began sniffing around and quite early the following year he announced he had signed a three-year deal with Wests Tigers.

Leeds wanted to keep him and I think he took a long time to make his mind up, but he made the right decision and he has been an out-and-out success, being named Wests' player of the year in his first two seasons there. That was no shock to anyone who had played with him at Leeds, though when Gaz first joined us I didn't necessarily think he was a great recruit. He played a lot in the centre at Wakefield and I used to enjoy going up against him because I didn't think he was much good. When he came to Leeds he made a permanent move into the pack and I realised I was wrong. By the end of his four years with us he was the best British back-rower in the game and one of the top players in that position in the world.

It is tough for any British player to make it in Australia because the Aussies have a set idea of how good we are – which is not very – and they are looking to put you down at every opportunity. You have to be something special just to be regarded as all right, but Gaz is exceptional and he made a massive impact.

Gaz has hands like shovels, which helps him, and he has a great all-round game. He has decent feet, he can offload and when he moved into the second-row his defensive game improved out of sight. He became a basher, one of those players like Moz who you don't run straight at. You have to have a bit of nous when you are playing against certain people and if you are up against Gaz you keep out of his way. He's not an enforcer, like a Barrie McDermott or an Adrian Morley, but he is very, very tough.

We were sorry to lose him but, like with Tony Smith, we all realised what a superb move it was for him. It was an opportunity to prove himself against the so-called best players in the world and he came up trumps. He fitted straight in and when he came back and linked up with the England national team it was obvious he had improved as a player. It is a shame Wests' coach Tim Sheens had to make the usual Aussie comments about having to teach him the basics of the game, but that's just what you come to expect.

I am not one of those people who thinks if someone or something is Australian, he or it is automatically better, but the NRL is an intense level of rugby and it is bound to improve the England team if we can select players who are playing at that level on a weekly basis – though as far as I am concerned, they should have to be born or raised here to qualify. The Aussie mentality is probably something we can learn from and lads like Gaz can pass that on when they are in camp with England. His attitude has always been spot-on and I think that is one of the reasons he has done so well over there.

I know Gaz had to think long and hard before he signed for Wests. Leeds were offering him a new deal on good money and it would have been easy for him to stay here, but it's not just a career choice, it is a lifestyle one as well. He was 27 when he went, so the opportunity might not have come up again and if he had turned it down he would have spent the rest of his career wondering what if?

When I played for England in the 2003 World Sevens in Sydney a few Aussie clubs showed a bit of an interest. We were coached by Mike Gregory and had a strong squad, which also included people like Marcus St Hilaire, Gaz Ellis, Lee Gilmour and Andy Farrell. For once, things went okay and we enjoyed a decent tournament. We beat Tonga, Australian Aboriginals, France and Manly, but then lost to Parramatta in the final. I really enjoyed it and the format suited me. I went over for eight tries in five games, which made me joint top try scorer and that stirred up a bit of contact from one or two Aussie sides.

Auckland Warriors, as they were then, were probably the keenest and I did give it a bit of thought, but I have never had a firm offer to play in the NRL. I would definitely have considered it, but I have always been under long-term contract, so the opportunity hasn't come up. If I'd been on a short-term deal and something could have been arranged, then maybe. But I like a bit of security and I'm always negotiating; even if I am on a three-year deal I am always talking about the next one.

It is not something I regret, because I have enjoyed my time in the

English game and I don't think I have anything to prove. I have competed against the Australians at Test level and done well and I feel I can justifiably say I have been one of the best British centres of the last few years. That is something I am proud of and I have been selected in the World XIII on a couple of occasions, so it's not just me saying that.

The 2008 season got off to a good start with a trip to Jacksonville in Florida for our warm-weather camp. At the time, the Rhinos had a link with South Sydney Rabbitohs, who are owned by the actor Russell Crowe. Both clubs went to Jacksonville for pre-season and we had a game against them at the end of it. That was supposed to be a 'friendly', but there was a bit of bad blood involved, at least on our part. Because Russell Crowe is such a big name, South Sydney got all the attention and we were ignored a bit. All the arrangements were made to suit them and we had to put up with it. A couple of times we had to change our plans to fit in with them, which we weren't very happy about. That gave us plenty of motivation for the match because we wanted to show what the Super League champions could do. We fielded a full-strength team at the start of the game and took them apart. It was a bit spicy and I got into a bit of a fight with their hooker Isaac Luke, which the American crowd enjoyed. I came off worst because Ian Kirke ran in and grabbed hold of me. That's the last thing you want when a fight breaks out. He had my arms pinned and I was getting battered by one of the smallest blokes on the field. When we got into a big lead, Bluey took a few of the senior players off and Souths came back at us, but we hung on at the end. It's always good to beat any Aussie team so I enjoyed that game even though it was only a friendly.

After the game the Souths players came into our changing room and presented each of us with a commemorative leather jacket, so we all felt a bit guilty about bad-mouthing them to ourselves earlier in the week, especially as we hadn't got them anything! Russell Crowe was among the crowd and he visited our sheds afterwards, which was quite a thrill for all concerned. He is a big rugby league fan and amazingly he was as excited about meeting us as we were about chatting to him. A lot of us had pictures taken with him and he couldn't have been friendlier. I shook his hand and I don't mind admitting I was totally star struck. I was going to introduce myself but he came over, said he was pleased to meet me and told me I was a player he enjoyed watching. I was quite taken aback because it's not every day an Oscar-winning movie star tells you he has followed your career. Russell Crowe is the most famous person I have met and I was quite chuffed he knew who I was.

The following year we went back to Jacksonville for another camp and played Salford at the end of it. That time we got all the publicity and Salford were the bit-part players, so I can imagine what they thought about that. We won that game as well, even though we had only 14 players because of people dropping out due to injury, me included, and they used a 26-man squad. I enjoyed watching how the young kids got on. They were 10-0 down after as many minutes, but really dug in, clawed their way back and won it 12-10 thanks to a late try by Ashley Gibson who signed for Salford at the end of the year.

Ryan Hall also scored in that game and for me, one of the best things that happened during Bluey's time as coach was his emergence as one of the game's top wingers. Hally made his debut in 2007 under Tony, but he really came into his own the following year when he was one of our Grand Final try scorers. In 2009 he scored 32 tries in 31 appearances and finished top of the charts. He also made his England debut and won accolades galore.

Ryan has been great for me. Originally I had Scott Donald on my side of the field but when Hally came through he was switched over to the left, so we were going with a mixture of youth and experience. With Lee Smith moving into the centre, Bluey didn't want him and Hally on the same flank, because they were both still quite green. Ryan is a deep kid. He's a maths whizz, he can do the Rubik's Cube, which he has taught a few of us, and he tries to play the piano, though he's not very good. He is big for a winger; he's actually heavier than me and if he had the hair to go with it he would be in the Lesley Vainikolo mould. But he is also deceptively quick, has good hands, is great under the high ball, is strong and is a top-class finisher.

We had a chat at the start of 2009 about his goals and targets and he told me he wanted to average a try a game, which would mean a minimum of 28 touchdowns over the year. That's a pretty big ask, especially for someone just coming through in his debut season as first-choice winger. It says a lot about him that he went on and did even better.

I think we were good for each other. I enjoy setting up tries as much as scoring them and if the people around me are getting over the whitewash I am happy with that. I like Ryan, he's a good kid and from the start I decided to look after him. If it came to a choice between me scoring or giving him the ball to go over, I would hand it on. I have been in the game a long time and tries don't mean that much to me personally any more. My goal was to help him achieve his. When he gets over the line he's so delighted that it rubs off on everyone else. I took great pleasure from the 32 touchdowns he got that year and I was like a proud father. It wasn't just me, he had a good team around him and he has fantastic ability, but over my career there have been numerous occasions when my winger has finished the season as the team's top try scorer and that gives me huge satisfaction. Karl Pratt became an international player; the first time Marcus Bai ever got top try scorer at a club was when he played alongside me; Scotty topped the charts and then Hally did it as well. He helped my game because he was relying on me to provide a bit of guidance and experience, so that gave me added responsibility. Like Jamie Jones-Buchanan he's super-smart, but he has absolutely no common sense. He acts like he needs looking after sometimes. I don't take a lot of the credit for what he has achieved, because he is a great professional - he works hard on his game and he enjoys scoring tries, but I hope I have helped a little bit.

Team-wise, after three great years things went wrong in 2010. We really found the going tough because we weren't coached and, in his third season in charge, the motivational side of Bluey's approach was wearing thin. He found it hard to come up with a successful game plan and there were a lot of cracks and breakdowns. It didn't help that his theme for the year was going to be based around Tiger Woods, who at the start of the off-season was head and shoulders above anyone else as the world's best golfer and maybe the finest sportsman on the planet. All that went pear-shaped when news broke about his affairs; he took some time off from playing golf and eventually his marriage fell apart and his game went off the boil. There was no Plan B and Bluey had to cobble together something based around Crazy Horse, the American Indian chief. Because there was no time to put any real thought into it, that angle completely fell flat.

To be honest we were all at sea. There wasn't much direction and we weren't really motivated. That's the thing about a motivational coach, it is hard to keep doing it year on year. I think that's probably why Bluey has a much more impressive record at Test level than Tony Smith. International rugby isn't about organising a great game plan or improving players technically. It is about pulling a group of lads together over a short space of time and getting them fired up for one-off games. Tony needs time to work on people's game, which he gets over the course of a 27-round league season, whereas Bluey is more about emotions. For that reason Bluey was the perfect choice as coach of the Exiles – the team of Aussie/Kiwi Super League imports put together to play England mid-way through the 2011 season.

In the third year of Bluey's coaching, people began to lose their way and there was a fair bit of unrest in the camp, which I think was reflected in the way we played. We produced some very good performances, but they were against the better teams. Throughout his time in charge we had some bad defeats against sides we should have beaten by 50, like Salford and Quins. Our reign as champions ended when we lost at home to Wigan in the play-offs, one game away from another return to Old Trafford. We finished fourth in the table and then won away at Wigan, the league leaders, in the opening round of the play-offs, before bowing out in the re-match.

The play-offs win at DW Stadium was one of the best results we had under Bluey, but it got overshadowed by a massive row. In the final seconds, with us leading by a point, Wigan's Pat Richards made a break with George Carmont in support. He got in a tangle – that's the diplomatic way of putting it - with Danny McGuire and Wigan were awarded a penalty which Richards missed.

Danny was hurt in the incident, had to be stretchered off and was diagnosed with an ACL injury, which meant he'd be out of action for up to eight months. What caused all the fury was some of the Wigan players' reaction and what pundit Phil Clarke said about it on Sky TV.

Danny was accused of "cheating", by holding Carmont back – and Clarke, who is a former Wigan player, later said that the injury might have been poetic justice. He suggested Danny had been punished by the "rugby gods".

To accuse anyone of cheating is a big statement. If you look at the video, maybe Danny was holding the Wigan man back, which is what the match officials decided, but equally you could argue that his knee went and he grabbed out in an instinctive reaction as he went down.

At worst, Danny was bending the rules and if everyone who did that got punished, the rugby gods would have a full time job dishing out the thunderbolts. There would be nobody left by the end of a season. In my view Danny was chasing back, trying to shepherd Carmont; he got tangled up in his boots and grabbed at the first thing to hand, which was the Wigan player.

For someone effectively to say Danny deserved his injury, even if he had been deliberately holding Carmont back, was disgraceful and I am sure Clarke has regretted it since. And this came from someone whose career was ended by a broken neck. Clarke's comments showed how biased he is towards Wigan and I lost a lot of respect for him, as did a lot of people at Leeds.

That furore came after the game, but there was a nasty incident on the pitch as Danny was being treated. He was obviously in a lot of pain, but a couple of the Wigan players – Thomas Leuluai and Mark Riddell - went way over the top, accusing him of cheating while he was lying on the ground. They actually got in the way of our physio David O'Sullivan as he tried to reach Danny, so that really wound the Leeds boys up.

Credit to Leuluai, he apologised afterwards when he realised how badly hurt Danny was. As far as I am aware, Riddell didn't, so it was probably a good job he went back to the NRL at the end of the season. I thought the way he behaved was disgusting.

Sadly, the second Wigan play-offs tie, which we lost, was the last time Franny Cummins and Willie Poching were involved in a game for Leeds. They announced mid-way through the year that they were leaving at the end of the campaign. Franny went to Bradford as assistant-coach and Willie took a similar job at Warrington, under Tony Smith. In Franny's case it was the end of an era because he had been with Leeds since he left school. Franny had been doing a lot of the actual coaching, particularly on defence. He played under Tony, who appointed him to the coaching staff, and that influence was crystal clear. Franny is going to be a very good coach. He is highly methodical and very thorough. He has picked up a lot of technical things from Tony and he has a big future. He didn't see eye-to-eye with Bluey during that 2010 campaign; they had different ideas and they didn't gel as well as they did in previous years, when we were successful. If things are going right it is quite easy because you can just carry on the way things are. When they start to go wrong you need to make changes and that leads to tension in the camp. There was a bit of a breakdown between Bluey, Franny and Willie and that showed. It was one of those years everyone found tough and heads dropped a bit because we had a lack of direction.

The Greg Eastwood situation didn't help. Rhinos originally signed Greg from Brisbane Broncos on a three-year deal mid-way through 2008. He was due to join us at the end of that season, after the World Cup. He was a member of the Kiwis' winning team and the club invested high hopes in him, especially as he was replacing Gaz Ellis. His application for a visa to play in this country was turned down and he went on loan to Canterbury Bulldogs for a season while an appeal was sorted out. Eventually he got the green light, but then he broke a hand playing for New Zealand in the Four Nations, so he was injured when he finally did get here. He played a few games, then fractured the other wrist. And after that healed up he did his knee. He was in one of those spells a lot of players get, suffering one injury after another. He played his final few games for the club wearing a skull cap after getting a nasty gash to the face. The official explanation was that he had been accidentally cut in a training ground clash of heads with Kylie Leuluai. Actually, he got the wound during an incident in a nightspot in Halifax.

Greg was single, it was his first time away from home and he found it very difficult to adapt to a new culture. Everyone at the club tried to help him settle in and make him feel welcome, but it got too much for him in the end and he asked to go on the transfer list. That was a huge shame because Greg is a fantastic player. He looks a bit like someone out of a pub team, but he is strong, has great footwork, can hit hard and has a good offload. I reckon he would have gone on to be a big hit in Super League and maybe even a Man of Steel contender, but he wasn't happy off the field and that homesickness led him to decide he should to go back to the NRL.

A lot of supporters seemed to think he was using being homesick as an excuse and actually he had been tapped up by the Bulldogs. That wasn't true; he genuinely was missing his friends and family back home. He was only a young kid who came over here with his dad originally and at that stage he was okay, but when his father went home Greg found it hard to cope. He was a big family person and it wasn't easy living on his own in a different culture. At Leeds we don't have a great social circle. A lot of it is family-oriented so it's tough for a young, single kid. The injuries added to it because they meant he wasn't involved for a lot of the year. Eventually he moved in with Luke Ambler, who is a bit of a character, and he settled in a lot more after that, starting to enjoy himself a bit, but by then he'd made his mind up about going home.

The fans weren't happy but as players we didn't really have an issue with Greg leaving two years early. When he played he did a job and he gave 100 per cent. Some of his performances that year, like in the play-offs at Wigan when we came from 14-0 down, were outstanding – and that was playing out of position in the front-row. It was his decision to go home. We could understand where he was coming from and we all respected that. If it had been a financial thing, if he had been offered more money somewhere else, we wouldn't have resented that either. Certain players play for certain things and you have to accept that. It is a short career and you have to make sure your family and your future are looked after. Also, it's important you enjoy it and if you don't there's no point carrying on.

The biggest disappointment of Bluey's time in charge was the Challenge Cup final in 2010. We set our stall out to win the competition, we got all the way to Wembley and then we came away with egg all over our faces. We had a fantastic run: we beat Hull away, Blackpool at home, Wigan at home – thanks to a last-minute Lee Smith try – and then Saints in the semi-final at the Galpharm, so nobody could say we didn't deserve to be there.

We played Tony Smith's Warrington Wolves in the final, a team we'd done the double over in the league season, but it was a complete and utter disaster. There is no other way to describe it, we got embarrassed. We lost 30-6 and, apart from the first few minutes, we weren't in the game. The worst part about it was that we didn't see it coming. Even after the problems we'd had that year we went into the game confident, but it was one of those days when everything went wrong. Warrington played at the top of their game and we didn't turn up. We had a few injuries – we lost Jamie Peacock and Luke Burgess in a game at Castleford two weeks before the final – and I think our lack of direction showed. We had got away with it to an extent that year, but the final exposed how disorganised we were. Up to then a bit of magic from special players had got us through. Against Wigan, Lee got over in the final seconds for the only try of the match. We were struggling against Saints in the semi before Danny McGuire grabbed a great try – off my offload as it happens – and then JP put him in for the winning touchdown. They were both tries nobody else could have scored.

There were occasions that year when we played really well, like Warrington away in the league, but then the game plan would get changed again and we would lose our way. We were trying to fine-tune things the day before a game, when training should be a short sharp run-through to top preparations off.

Against a side who had an effective game plan and stuck to it, all our problems showed. We weren't 100 per cent sure about what we were supposed to be doing in the first place and then we went away from that once the action began. We were at the stage where motivation alone wasn't enough. Being without JP was a massive blow because he is an inspirational part of the team and when he is not there it puts added pressure on other players, who have to take on roles that don't necessarily suit them. It meant there was more weight on Kylie Leuluai's shoulders, but he is a different sort of player to JP. He is a come on, do some damage and go off type of player, not an 80-minute man. When he has to operate over a 40-minute period he is not as effective as he is in short bursts.

Ryan Bailey had a good year and he almost got us off to a flying start in the final when he got over the line, but Richie Mathers stopped him putting the ball down. He tried to go over the full-back rather than round him and that cost us. Bails has a good engine and on his day he is a JP-type of prop, but he doesn't have that consistency yet. If he can develop that, he is going to be one of the best front-rowers in the game.

Bails is one of those Marmite type players; you either love him or hate him. Among other teams' fans he is probably the most disliked man in Super League, but I would far rather play with him than against him. He does a lot of work that from the stands does not get noticed and he has a bit of mongrel in him as well, which I think every team needs. He is a pantomime villain and that is something I can relate to. I get a lot of stick from spectators and many people think I'm a dirty player, but I reckon when you are getting abuse that means you are doing your job right. I take it as a compliment if rival clubs' supporters are trying to rattle me, because it proves they see me as a threat.

Anyone who thinks booing or jeering is going to put Bails off his game has got it wrong. He doesn't care what people think about him, he just goes out and does his job and a big part of what he is paid for is getting stuck in and shaking the opposition up a bit. He is a tough player; people accuse him of using cheap shots, but he plays the game hard. He is aggressive and sometimes he does some stupid things, but that's part of his game and you need people like that in your team. He is under-rated but a marked man. All the hard cases want to make a point when they come up against him, but after nearly a decade in the team he is still playing the game at the top level and that says a lot about his strength of character. He very rarely gets dropped - and that has been the case under a succession of coaches from Daryl Powell through to Brian McDermott, so he can't be that bad can he? And, despite all the allegations about his so-called dirty tactics, he has a pretty good disciplinary record.

One of the problems we had in 2010 was our early start to the season. We played Crusaders away in our opening game, in the snow at Wrexham, on January 29. So much for summer rugby. The reason for that was the World Club Challenge, which came a month later. That was slotted into a weekend when there was a full league programme, so we had to play the match originally scheduled for that date before the season-proper actually started. So our first match was in round four, then we played our week one fixture seven days later. I am sure that makes sense to someone, or maybe not because they changed the format the following year.

With going all the way through the Challenge Cup rounds, we didn't have a free weekend between mid-January and September. It wouldn't have been so bad if we had managed to get anything out of the World Club or the Challenge Cup, but we lost them both, so it was a lot of effort for no reward. The fact is, the way the competition is now, with the final in August a few weeks before the play-offs start, if you aren't going to win the Challenge Cup the best thing you can do is lose your first match, then you get four weekends off during the season to freshen up for the top-eight tournament. We had the worst of all worlds, no time off and nothing to show at the end of it.

We played in three World Club Challenge games under Bluey, winning in 2008 and losing the next two. The big one was the first, against Melbourne Storm, which we managed to win 11-4. That felt like a more important game than the others because it was Bluey's first big match in charge and he was desperate for a victory to get him off on the right foot. The most memorable thing about that game was the conditions. It absolutely siled it down all game and there was a gale-force wind blowing as well. It's always good to beat any Aussie team, so I enjoyed that one, which is more than can be said about the other two.

We were out-played by Manly Sea Eagles in 2009, then Melbourne beat us the following year. We were a bit unlucky in that one because we got over the line a few times but couldn't get the ball down and Kallum Watkins had a touchdown ruled out by the video ref with a few minutes to go, which would have edged us ahead. I think if we had scored then, we'd have won it. The fact Melbourne Storm were exposed for cheating a few weeks later didn't make us feel much better. It turned out they had been diddling the salary cap for a long-term period. They had all their points taken away for that year and the Grand Final wins they'd had were struck off their record. I did feel a bit sorry for their players because it wasn't their fault and they had earned those medals, whatever the club had done.

I got in trouble during the second Melbourne game for speaking my mind. We had an English referee, Richard Silverwood, which should have suited us, but he seemed scared of upsetting the Aussies. He made it hard for us all game. We were used to the way he refereed and we thought we knew what to expect, but he changed his style for that one-off match. We were expecting him to insist on quick play-the-balls and a clean ruck, but he let Melbourne lie on and slow things down, which suited their style perfectly and meant we couldn't play our natural game.

If it had been an Aussie referee in charge there is no way he would have changed his approach to suit the English team. It was a frustrating evening and my anger boiled over with about 20 minutes left. Silverwood penalised me for interference at a play-the-ball, which I wasn't happy about. I told him that - in no uncertain terms - and he marched the penalty 10 metres further down the field for dissent, which took it to within kicking distance. Cameron Smith kicked the goal and that gave them a two point lead. It looked like that penalty was going to cost us the game until they got a clinching try in the final minute. I was angry with myself because I lost my cool when I should have kept my mouth shut, but I also felt we hadn't been on a level playing field.

After the match the press were hanging around the changing room area and I was asked what had happened, so I told them and I made it clear what I thought about Silverwood. That made the headlines and I had to issue an apology, or rather the club did. They put out a statement retracting what I had said, but the first I knew about that was when they showed a draft of it to me on the coach leaving the ground. It was damage limitation and all I did was go along with it. I got charged by the RFL anyway and fined, which I wasn't happy about, but flogging my loser's medal paid for that.

I had no argument with the media over the way they reported what I said. They all had it on tape and they quoted me word for word. It was about 40 minutes after the game, so I'd had time to calm down and I knew what I was saying when I came out of the changing room. It wasn't really a heat of the moment thing, but I felt that a point had to be made. I do regret making it personal, but I didn't – and still don't – see why I couldn't express my personal view.

I managed to keep my nose clean with Silverwood right until what turned out to be our last game of the season, that play-off semi-final against Wigan. Late on we were chasing the game when he ruled I had knocked on after Sam Tomkins hacked the ball forward near the Wigan line. It went backwards so it should have been play-on, but Silverwood called for a scrum and then he penalised me when I hurled the ball down in anger. After Wigan kicked to touch he called me over for a ticking off and when he did that I am sure he was thinking about what I'd said seven months earlier.

I have no idea what Richard Silverwood thinks of me, but I don't like him as a person or referee. I know it is not a battle I am ever going to win, because he's the one with the power. All I can hope for is that we get a fair crack of the whip when he is in charge. Of all the referees I have played under, he is the one I dislike the most. In my opinion he is arrogant. He doesn't have a rapport with players, which I think is really important. Respect is a two-way street; referees expect it from players but I think with some of them you don't get it back. I also think they have to earn respect. The way things are in rugby league at the moment, nobody is allowed to criticise referees and I mean that literally – it's against the sport's bylaws to make any comment about a match official, which I think is ridiculous.

If I make a mistake in a match I am going to get criticised - by fans, by my coach and maybe by my team-mates. That doesn't happen with referees; if they mess up, everyone's supposed to ignore it and treat it as part of the game. That's pretty hard to do sometimes, when livelihoods are at stake. I think you need a bit of front to be a referee, you have to have an attitude, but it's also important to get on with players and to know how to talk to them. I've had a bit of craic with quite a few referees, like Steve Ganson for example. You can talk to Steve and have a bit of a joke as well. Steve is prepared to laugh at himself at times and I think that's a good thing. James Child is another one I get on with pretty well. He refereed a game at Harlequins in 2010 when I was captain for the day and I was impressed with the way he handled things. As captain you are allowed to talk to the referee during a game, to check the reason for decisions and so on. I had a bit of a laugh and a joke with him, I was sarcastic and he replied in kind. I like that and it was good to be dealing with someone who acted like a human being.

Karl Kirkpatrick, who packed in rugby league a few years ago and is now involved with union, was a difficult referee to deal with. You couldn't say boo to him. In one game, away to Salford, he threatened to red card me for looking happy, which isn't something I get accused of very often. He said to me – and honestly this is true – "You'd better stop smiling or I'm going to send you off." It shouldn't be like that. I do admit refereeing is a hard job and it's not something I'd do for a gold pig. Refs are in a no-win situation, but I think a lot of them operate in their own little bubble. I can accept referees making a mistake, but it would be nice if, once in a while, they admitted it. We have seven professional referees now and seven Super League matches every weekend, so no matter how badly they perform, they aren't going to get dropped. I don't think that does them or anyone else much good. You need competition for places to keep standards high and at the moment we haven't got that.

When Bluey signed a new one-year contract mid-way through the 2010 season, I was a bit disappointed and I know quite a few of the other boys felt the same. By that stage, I thought Bluey's time had been and gone. We were under-performing and he was no longer getting the best out of us, so as far as I was concerned the end of the year would be the right time for a change.

Franny and Willie both left and so did Matt Diskin and Scott Donald, who had both signed new one-year contracts, so it was obvious to everybody that all was not well. When Brian McDermott came back from Harlequins, as assistant-coach to replace Franny, I wondered how that was going to work. He was obviously being lined up to take over in 2012, but I had my doubts about whether, after four years in charge of his own team, he would be able to play second-fiddle to someone else. He is a strong character and so is Bluey, so it seemed like there might be a bit of a clash. My guess about what would probably happen was that Bluey would take more of a football manager role, with Brian Mac coaching the team, and that sort of arrangement rarely seems to work.

All the same it was a shock when Bluey departed and Brian Mac was promoted into the hot seat, about a month after the end of the 2010 season. I am not sure if player-power was involved, but everyone in the squad had the chance to give their views in the annual post-season review and I know not everybody was complimentary about what had gone on over the previous 12 months.

It had been a tough year, we had lost our direction and I think in the space of two campaigns we had seen the best and worst of Bluey. Everything fell into place in 2009 and it was a massive achievement to back up again after two successive Grand Final wins, but then the wheels came off and we lost our way a lot. Our game plan was changed too often and we didn't really know what we were supposed to be doing. Obviously the senior players – me included – could have done a bit more, but it is usually the coach who pays the price. That might not be fair, but it's the way it goes. As I've mentioned, it was a relief that the season was over when we lost to Wigan in the play-offs, rather than a feeling of disappointment. When that happens, something has gone badly wrong. If we had gone on to Old Trafford and won the title again, it would just have papered over the cracks.

I think in the end all parties, Bluey included, felt it was the right time for him to go. I spoke to him about it afterwards and he was pretty happy with the arrangement; he felt he had departed on his own terms, which was good. He is a decent bloke and he had two highly successful years before a disappointing one, so he deserves to be remembered fondly at Leeds and I'm sure he would be welcome back as a visitor any time. I have been critical of some of his coaching methods in this chapter and I stand by that, but I have a high regard for Bluey as a person and I think everyone else in the team felt the same way. But the fact is, coaches have a shelf life and you have to know when the time is right to call it a day. The eventual outcome suited everybody, Bluey went home with head held high, Brian Mac got the top job and – in terms of the team – we got a change of leadership just when we needed it.

CHAPTER 15

GRAND DAYS

I have been fortunate to play in four Grand Finals and we have won them all. After the first, the journalists' post-match questions have all been a bit similar and the one they always ask first is: "How does this compare to the others?"

The stock answer is that they are all special. That's true but I do have a favourite and it is probably not the game you'd be expecting. We were champions in 2004, against Bradford, then three years on the bounce from 2007-2009, beating St Helens in the final each time.

Of them all the one I enjoyed the most was the second game against Saints in 2008, which we won 24-16. Strangely enough three of the four finals we won were by an eight-point margin, but that 2008 match was probably the most competitive and that is why it's top of my list.

But to start at the beginning, the 2004 Grand Final was memorable mostly for being our first victory. Leeds had waited 32 years to be crowned champions, so it meant an awful lot to everybody at the club, not just the players and coaching staff but the backroom people and the fans as well. Afterwards supporters came up to me and said they had given up hope of ever seeing Leeds win the title, so that drove home what an achievement it was.

Beating Bradford made it a bit more special, especially after the 2000 and 2003 Challenge Cup finals. The Bulls finished second to us in the league table, nine points adrift, so it was the two best teams going head-to-head, which is how it should be in a Grand Final.

It was a tight game all the way through, though looking back not a particularly good one. It was tense rather than exciting. Kev Sinfield kicked an early goal but they gave us a shock by scoring the first try through big Lesley Vainikolo. That was a worrying moment but Matt Diskin, who eventually won the Harry Sunderland award as man of the match, plunged over soon afterwards and Kev added the conversion and then a penalty to make it 10-4 at half-time.

It was good to go in at the break with a six-point lead and we were confident and composed in the changing room, but the second half got off to the worst possible start for us when Shontayne Hape touched down for an unconverted try to make it 10-8. It stayed that way until five minutes from time when Robbie Paul knocked on near his own line.

You don't get many opportunities like that in a Grand Final and fortunately we took it. Danny McGuire worked the ball to me and I drew a couple of defenders and then gave him possession back. Danny's a fantastic finisher and he dived over in front of our own fans to spark some memorable celebrations. Kev kicked the goal and we held on quite comfortably to win 16-8.

It's hard to describe the emotion afterwards. Probably relief was the biggest sensation. We were the best team that year and if we'd messed up again when it really mattered, it would have been hard to take. But not everybody in the squad enjoyed the 2004 final. For the first time in the entire campaign Tony Smith picked the same team two weeks running, from the final eliminator to the title decider. He left out Matt Adamson and Andrew Dunemann, who had been regulars that year and had been in the team for the first play-offs game, which we lost to Bradford. Another one to miss out was Francis Cummins who had suffered a serious knee injury mid-way through the year.

Franny behaved perfectly before the game and after it. He was supportive to everybody in the build-up and he couldn't have been more delighted once we had actually won it. Dooners was the same. He must have been absolutely gutted not to play but he got behind everybody, stayed involved and was busy on the night running on with the water and delivering messages. You have to respect people who can react to adversity like that.

Matt was totally different. He had two personalities and his alter ego came out after he was told he wouldn't be playing. When things didn't go his way he could be really miserable and he just went into a sulk. He didn't get involved, he wasn't part of the squad and he didn't share in the delight afterwards. I could understand his disappointment; he was going home to Australia at the end of the season and he badly wanted to bow out with an Old Trafford appearance – he was a big Manchester United fan – and a winner's ring. But it was a shame he spat his dummy out.

It was a coaching decision not to select him. Matt was a good player but Tony felt there were better options and he wasn't the right person for that game. Coaches stand or fall on decisions like that and in that instance Tony was proved right because we won the match. It would have been better if Matt could have enjoyed the moment as he had played a part in us getting that far, but there wasn't any sympathy from the rest of the players afterwards because he had cast himself out of our environment.

I remember a discussion I once had with Kev Sinfield when I told him I thought it was better to have played and lost than to have missed out on a final. Kev had personal experience of that from Murrayfield in 2000, when Dean Lance dropped him for the Challenge Cup decider against Bradford.

In hindsight, I was wrong. I didn't play in the 2005 Grand Final because of the ankle injury which I suffered the week before the Challenge Cup showpiece. I made a mistake by playing at Millennium Stadium, I felt responsible for us losing that game and I didn't play again for Leeds that year. I had to watch the Grand Final from the sidelines so I was part of it but I wasn't directly involved. Having been through that I think it is probably better not to play than to go through the pain of losing, which has happened to me in four Challenge Cup finals.

After winning in 2004 and losing the following year we weren't involved in 2006, when St Helens beat Hull, but we were back at Old Trafford in 2007. Probably a lot of fans would pick that one out as their favourite final because of the manner of our victory. Saints were the defending champions, they had won the Challenge Cup final a couple of months earlier and they finished top of the table, a point ahead of us. They also beat us in the qualifying semi-final at Knowsley Road, but only 10-8 in a brutal game. We matched them blow for blow that night and after hammering Wigan, again, in the final eliminator, we went to Old Trafford full of confidence.

It was one of those evenings when just about everything went right. Saints had endured a long campaign, they were feeling the strain and we hit our peak at just the right time. It was Tony Smith's final game before he left to take over the England team, so it was an emotional occasion and we got practically everything spot on. The build-up was perfect and we carried out our game plan to the letter.

The first half was close but we knew it was going to be our day from the early moments of the game when Sean Long hit a penalty attempt off target. Kev kicked us ahead with a penalty soon after that and then Brent Webb scored the first try. I was involved in that one. Danny McGuire and Kev worked the ball to Webby, he passed to me, I handed on to Scotty Donald and his pass was finished off by Brent.

Kev made it 8-0 with his conversion but James Roby hit back with a try and Long's goal made it 8-6 at half-time. On the scoreboard it was anybody's game, but going off at the break we looked into their eyes and we could see they were finished. We still felt like we had plenty in the tank so we came out for the second period in confident mood and it went like a dream.

Ali Lauitiiti got over for a try from close range and then in the set from the restart I got Scotty away and he sprinted in for a superb long-range touchdown which Kev converted. That made it 18-6 after 52 minutes. Rob Burrow – the man of the match – kicked a drop goal and then with 10 to go Lee Smith went over from Danny's kick.

Kev booted the goal, we were 25-6 up and it was party time. Kev increased the lead with a penalty and Jamie Jones-Buchanan went in on the final play of the game, Kev kicked yet another two pointer and we had won 33-6.

That was as good a big-game performance as I have been involved in. We scored some superb tries, but our defence was rock solid and that's what really won it for us. Saints had been the leading team all year but we came good at just the right time, which was the most satisfying thing.

The following year was very different in virtually every respect, apart from the outcome. As I mentioned earlier, it is my favourite Grand Final win for a number of reasons. Saints came up with every excuse under the sun in 2007. They said they weren't prepared and we caught them off guard but they made it clear 12 months later that they were 100 per cent ready. They were even hotter favourites that year; they were unbeaten in 23 matches and had absolutely destroyed us 38-10 two weeks earlier in the Grand Final qualifier. All the media attention before the game was on Saints and how good a team they were. This time it was their coach Daniel Anderson's last game in charge and everyone seemed to think all they had to do was turn up and collect the trophy.

Even though we were the defending champions we were totally written off and on top of all that, we had a problem in the week leading into the game when Brent Webb injured his back in training. Webby has always had back problems, which is understandable if you look at his body. It is way too big for his frame! He could hardly move, so there was no way he was going to play. That was a big loss because Webby is a major influence for us. It is like playing with another half-back, as he has such good ball skills. In an ideal situation he would be one of the first names on the team sheet, so it was a blow to morale when he had to be ruled out. Bluey did the right thing, though, by announcing the injury to the media and making it clear that Brent wasn't available. It was like a vote of confidence in the rest of us. Lee Smith moved to full-back and Ryan Hall, who had only just come back from a long injury lay-off, started on the wing.

We were right up against it, but that brought the best out of us and Lee had the game of his life. His nickname is Smeagol, after the character from Lord of the Rings. If you want to know why, look at his teeth. He kicked a 40-20, scored a try, made some important tackles and got named man of the match. He transformed into Danny McGuire - everything he touched turned into gold.

The thing everyone remembers about that game is the weather. All the pundits said Saints would murder us on a dry track, which is very disrespectful to the quality of players we had in our side, but right on cue the heavens opened about an hour before kick-off and we definitely handled the conditions better than they did. It started badly when James Graham scored a converted try in the opening few minutes and at that stage I think everyone expected the pre-match predictions to come true.

They might have done if Matt Gidley had scored soon afterwards, but Matt Diskin and Scotty Donald got him into touch near the line and that was a big moment for us. Lee scored his try and Sinny converted to make it 6-6, then Ryan Hall touched down his own kick and a touchline goal sent us in 12-6 up at the break.

They levelled through a converted Gidley try, but Lee booted his 40-20 and we scored in the next set when Danny got over from Kev's grubber. The conversion made it 18-12 but they hit back again through an Ade Gardner try to leave us only two points ahead. With 18 minutes left Danny got hold of the ball after Francis Meli had knocked on from a kick and he swooped over for the winning try, with Kev's goal making it 24-16 at the end.

That game was even more enjoyable than when we hammered them the year before. One-sided encounters, even in finals, aren't that much fun; the best matches are always when it is close, or if there's a chance of losing at the back end and you hold on. You want intense matches and you don't get that if you are winning by 20 or 30 points. We had to play all the way to the final whistle – they got a few dubious decisions from referee Ashley Klein late on, but we kept them out – and it is always more satisfying when you do that.

The 2009 Grand Final was unique because we went into it as favourites. Saints led the table for much of the year but we overhauled them at the end, getting our necks in front in August and eventually finishing four points clear. It was a new top-eight system that year, which meant both finalists would have to win two games to get to Old Trafford and they'd each play the week before the title decider.

We beat Hull KR and Catalan Dragons and went into the big game on a long winning run, which included a victory over Saints in the league a few weeks earlier. That was quite a stormy game and I picked up a one-match ban for giving Jon Wilkin a bit of a slap off the ball.

That added some spice to the final and there was a lot of talk before the match about how Saints were going to get their revenge. As it turned out there wasn't much malice, though it was a close-fought game. We had to come from behind yet again after Kyle Eastmond scored a try, a conversion and a penalty. At 8-0 down in a final, which are usually tight affairs, you have a mountain to climb, but we kept our nerve and probably the experience of winning the previous two was what got us through.

Disko got us back into the game by burrowing over from acting-half and then Lee Smith scored a soft try after Francis Meli made an error. Surprisingly, Kev missed both kicks but he landed a drop goal right at the start of the second half. We had spoken during the break about getting something on the board early and that really gave us a lift even though it was only one point.

Eastmond kicked them in front with another penalty goal on the hour but we finished really strongly, which is a good achievement at the end of a long, hard season. Kev booted a penalty goal and then made a try-saving tackle on Eastmond. With seven minutes left Danny McGuire put a kick through and Lee ran in to touch down. We were all sure it was a try, but it went to video referee Phil Bentham and he took an age before giving the green light. People still say Lee was offside and to be honest I can see where they are coming from. But I've just had a look at the following day's paper and it definitely says Lee scored! Rob Burrow kicked a drop goal late on and that was it, 18-10, with Kev man of the match.

The most pleasing thing about that final was our defence. We were under pressure for a lot of the game but we dug deep. Kev's kicking game was top-class and we chased really well. It was also nice to go down in history as the first team to win three successive Grand Finals. Only Wigan have won more titles on the bounce, but that was in the days of first past the post when they could sign whoever they wanted. To do it when all clubs have to abide by the same salary cap is a special feat in my opinion.

It was nice to win the title as league leaders as well. After the two other finals against Saints, people – some of the St Helens players included - claimed we weren't worthy champions because they had finished above us on the table. There is a big debate about whether the title should go to the league leaders, who are the most consistent team over the course of the year, or if a Grand Final is a fair way to decide it. I can see both sides of the argument.

Finishing top isn't the be-all and end-all now. It just gives you a slightly better chance of getting to Old Trafford. With the top-eight play-offs, in theory a team finishing in the bottom half of the table could be crowned champions, which is a bit ridiculous. The system is good in that it keeps the season alive for a lot more teams, but it does take a lot of credit away from the side who come top. Having said that, Old Trafford is a great spectacle and the play-offs do produce some exciting games, as well as a lot of revenue for the RFL. Overall, I like the concept. It is all about timing your run and peaking at the business end of the year, which we became very good at.

Probably my only regret from our four Grand Final wins is that I didn't score in any of them. I helped set up a few tries, but it would have been nice to get over the whitewash myself. As long as we win, though, I am not too bothered; I will leave all the glory to Danny and Lee. I am pretty happy with how I played in all of them so that is good enough for me.

The Grand Final is a different situation to the Challenge Cup decider. In the Cup you get at least two weeks, and sometimes a month or more, to get ready for the final. Under the old top-six play-offs system the preparation time depended on what happened in your qualifying matches. It could be a two-week build-up if you won the qualifying semi, or just seven days for the victors in the final eliminator. Now both finalists play the week before Old Trafford, which is a good thing. One of the problems with the top-six format was that whoever came out on top in the qualifying semi would only play once in a month before the title decider. The top two teams in the table had a weekend off at the end of the league campaign and then the winners of their match – the team finishing first played the runners-up in a Grand Final qualifier – then had another break the week before the decider. Their opponents were thrown into a sudden-death final eliminator and therefore played for three successive weekends, including the final. You can make a case either way for which is best. At the end of a long, tough season any time off is welcome, but on the other hand maybe it is better to keep playing, to build or maintain some momentum. The latter definitely worked for us. Under the old system, the one time we won the qualifying semi, 2005, was the year we went on to lose the final. In 2004, 2007 and 2008 we won at Old Trafford after we'd been beaten in our first play-off.

The week before Old Trafford is pretty similar every year. There's a press conference on the Monday, which is the night of the Man of Steel awards do in Manchester, an event at which Rhinos usually get overlooked. From 2004-2009 the only major honour we picked up in the end-of-season awards was Tony Smith's coach of the year in 2005, when he probably shouldn't have won it. He didn't collect the gong in 2004 or 2007 when he clearly should have done. In 2010 Wigan got the Man of Steel, young player, coach and club of the year awards, but they didn't achieve anything we hadn't in 2004.

After the press conference and awards ceremony you try to keep preparations as normal as possible through the week and then go into camp the night before the game. It is an enjoyable time, especially with the final being played at Old Trafford. You get to have a look around at some stage before the final and it is an impressive stadium even when it's empty. Knowing you are going to be playing there in front of 65-70,000 people a day or two later is an exciting feeling.

Having said that, the first time we had a tour of the ground it was a big thrill, but that quickly wore off. By the second year it had become routine and I just sat in the changing room with a few of the other boys having a laugh and a joke.

The more often you win a Grand Final, in a way the easier it becomes. I know it's harder to defend a title because everyone's out to get you, but when it comes to the championship game itself, previous experience is really important. You do refine and tinker with things as you go on but basically we stuck to a similar formula each year because we knew it worked.

I always try to enjoy the build-up. I feel fortunate to have played in so many finals, but you never know when it's going to be your last. In 2004, for example, we couldn't have known that we'd be involved in four of the next five Grand Finals.

It is the culmination of the season. That's the good thing about the play-offs system, your most important game of the campaign is the last one and you have worked hard for virtually a whole year to get that far. All teams set goals at the beginning of the year. For some sides it might be to improve on the previous season or to qualify for the play-offs. At Leeds, and I am sure Wigan and Saints are the same, the aim is always to win everything possible. Win all your games, win all your home matches, get to Wembley, win the Challenge Cup and take out the Grand Final. That's not being arrogant, it is just a reflection of what sort of club it is. When you've got as far as qualifying for Old Trafford it would be a shame to get too tense or not have a good time in the build-up. It is deadly serious because there's so much at stake but I try to stay relaxed, make sure I take it all in and enjoy what's going on. I feel a bit like a kid in a sweet shop going into Grand Finals. If you have had a bad spell at some time during the year – and we did in each one apart from 2004 – all that is forgotten.

The occasion itself is fantastic. There was a lot of scepticism when the RFL introduced the Grand Final system in 1998. Up until then, the team finishing top of the table were the champions and there was a Premiership competition at the end of the year, based on league positions. Leeds played Wigan in the first Grand Final and the crowd was 43,000, which was pretty good. By 2004 it was up to 65,000 and it was more than 70,000 a couple of years later. It has dropped a bit recently but the game usually attracts around 65,000, which is a good effort considering the finalists only have a week to sell tickets.

The warm-up and walking out for kick-off are the best moments, though if anyone from the RFL is reading this, the fireworks are too loud! The initial time you go out is for the warm-up. That's the first time the crowd get to see you and, even though the stadium is not full at that stage, the noise is tremendous, the crowd erupts and it's an electric feeling. It is great running out at Headingley when it's a packed house but in front of four times as many people the feeling you get is incredible. It's even louder when you walk out of the tunnel, side by side with your opponents, for the actual match. Afterwards it's always moments like that which I remember more than the game itself. Once the match begins you are involved and all the outside factors like the crowd and the atmosphere tend to get pushed to one side because you are focusing on the bigger picture, which is the game and making sure you do your job properly.

I am always really relaxed before a match so I can enjoy it. It's not the same for everybody. You get certain people, Jamie Peacock for example, who like to bang their head against a wall to get motivated. If that works for them, fine, but I like to have a laugh and a joke and just go with the flow. When I go out to warm-up I can take everything in and have a bit of fun. I know some coaches tell you not to, but I do like to look at the crowd to see who I can spot. Some players need to concentrate totally on what they are doing and I think that's a shame in a way because they miss some parts of the experience. But if their approach helps them to aid the team in reaching the ultimate goal, it's worth it because winning the game is most important of all.

If you are in front on the scoreboard when the final hooter goes it is an amazing feeling. You have achieved what you've been working towards and dreaming about for 10 or so months. It's a combination of relief, delight and exhaustion, depending on the circumstances. Believe it or not, in some ways it can also feel like a bit of an anti-climax. You've done it, now what? You have a few beers after the game but you are so drained you tend to save yourself for the next day when the fun really starts. Our routine has been to go back to Headingley for a bit of a party, mainly with friends and family, though supporters get in as well, which is fantastic for them. I can't imagine many sports in which that would happen. To be honest, the fans are usually more euphoric than the players. I have tended to have a drink or two, maybe something to eat, listen to a few speeches and then slope off home.

The couple of hours between the end of the game and the celebration party are a special time. After the final whistle you have the presentation, the pictures and the lap of honour and then it's off to the changing room. What happens then usually depends on circumstances. In 2004, for example, Dave Furner made a speech thanking the boys for sending him out on such a high. He told us he had considered packing in the year before, but he had hung on because he knew the group of players we had at the time could go on to win something and he wanted to be part of it. In 2008 we were all thinking about someone who wasn't there, Brent Webb. Because of his back injury he couldn't even go to the game. More or less as soon as we got into the changing room, after the presentation and the lap of honour, someone rang him and we all sang 'Brent Webb is Superman' down the phone. That was a pretty good moment and I think it showed what a tight-knit bunch we are.

For me, the coach journey back to Headingley after a Grand Final win is probably the best couple of hours of the entire season. The rest of the time you are public property, you are continually signing autographs or posing for pictures and you have to be on your best behaviour. That's fair enough, it's nice and I do appreciate the attention we get. It can be a bit intrusive at times but it's better than being ignored! I always sign my name if I'm asked and I know all that's going to intensify after we've won a big game, but on the coach it's just the players and backroom staff - the people you've worked with, suffered with and achieved with all year.

There are a few beers on the bus, which is a very rare thing, and there is usually a special song on the stereo. In 2004 it was Green Day, Time of Our Life. The entire coach sings and cheers all the way back to Leeds. You'll hear a lot of the players say that their best memory of a Grand Final win is the trip back. When we're back at the party it's about the supporters. On the coach trip it's all about us; we can enjoy each other's company, relax, be ourselves and relish the moment. Once we're off the bus we are public property and role models again. Players always say a big final is for the crowd and that is true to an extent, but the thing that really counts is doing it for your mates, your family and yourself.

CHAPTER 16
EBAY GUM

When I first started flogging off my old rugby gear I had no idea it would turn me into a socks symbol. Being a typical tight Yorkshireman - something I am quite proud of – I'm always on the lookout for a bargain or something for nothing. Selling old shirts, training gear and the like started as a way of making a quick buck but it has developed into a serious hobby and it is something I am now quite notorious for. It has even made headlines in a national newspaper.

As the years have gone on I have developed a network of regular customers and I don't mind admitting some of the requests I get are pretty strange. Believe it or not I have been asked if I'd be willing to sell old jock straps or underpants. So far I have resisted the temptation, though if the money was right.....

The oddest regular is a guy who buys my old playing socks. This is perfectly true. At first we washed them before we sent them off because, to be honest, they stank. Then he e-mailed Vic and said "Next time please don't bother washing them." She mailed back and said: "You don't want Keith's smelly socks," but he replied: "Yes, I really do - the sweatier the better." Every Friday he would send Vic £20 and she'd post off a pair of my socks - that's £1,000 per year! And he pays more for Grand Final or international socks, as long as I've worn them and they haven't been washed. I prefer not to think what he does with them. Tesco, where I get them for about 50p per pair, must think I'm the one with a fetish.

There's a guy in Australia who buys players' boots. I met up with him after the 2008 World Cup and took him Danny McGuire's and Gareth Ellis'. Top players get boot sponsorship so once the tournament was finished the footwear would just have been left lying around in the changing rooms. He wanted everybody's boots apart from, for some reason, Rob Burrow's. Rob was quite upset about that. It is something that has carried on and I've sent the guy boots from most of our overseas players. Greg Eastwood was a big favourite of his. I think the man is just a collector with a pretty odd hobby.

I got into the eBay business more or less by accident. The grand Senior jumble sale began when Vic and I moved into our new country house which sits in ten acres of land. It hadn't been lived in for more than a decade and it was a wreck. We badly under-estimated how much the renovations would cost. The initial estimate was £50,000 and it ended up costing £120,000. Half way through the work, everything was costing too much and we had totally run out of money. Cash was coming in and going straight back out again to the builders.

Fortunately, up until then I had been a hoarder. I had kept every bit of training gear I'd had, plus all my old playing kits, boots, medals, the works. There were tonnes of it filling virtually an entire room. It was all kept in boxes, some of which hadn't been opened for years. It was all sitting there gathering dust, literally with all the building work going on, so the idea occurred to me that somebody might like to have it and make me a few quid towards the building work in the process. The alternative was to re-mortgage and that was the last thing we wanted to do.

The first thing I put up for sale on eBay was a split Leeds Rhinos/Canterbury Bulldogs shirt from the 2005 World Club Challenge. It was literally half of a Rhinos shirt and half of one from the Bulldogs, stitched together. Things like that are quite a popular testimonial fundraiser. That was the guinea pig. We – Vic is actually more into this than I am - put it up for sale with no reserve, starting at 99p, just to see what would happen. We also said that if the buyer lived within a 25 mile radius of Leeds I would go round and deliver the shirt personally for no extra charge, which turned out to be an inspired idea.

To our astonishment that shirt went for £760 and I had 40 more jerseys just lying around the house! Do the maths. From that point on I started clearing out all my old shirts, then moved on to unwanted training gear. Some of the training vests raised £70 each and I had hundreds of those. The money that came in from eBay paid the builders and then some. It funded a full stable block, an equestrian training arena and the purchase of a thoroughbred horse.

To be honest I think we got a bit addicted to it. We started to get a list of regular customers, plus people were coming to us. We'd get people saying, for example: "Can you get a shirt off Brent Webb and get it signed for my son's birthday?" We'd do that and pass the money on. The whole thing snowballed and orders began to come in from all over the place, not just England, but Australia, New Zealand, the United States, you name it. Now I can't leave any rugby gear lying around the house because if I do Vic will have it straight up for sale.

It is all genuine stuff and the feedback we get is generally very good, although we do get the occasional complaint from someone claiming a shirt or whatever is a fake. Vic usually replies to those. It's hard to prove something is genuine but most people take it on trust and I think we've got a fairly good reputation among the collecting community.

Not everyone approves. I get a lot of stick from fans of the Rhinos and other clubs, plus some former players, for my eBay activities. A lot of it is good natured. Sometimes, especially at smaller grounds like Salford, I can hear supporters in the crowd shouting: "Will you sell me your shirt after the game Keith?" and things like that. I quite enjoy that and it's good to have a bit of banter back. I either tell them I'll have to, otherwise I won't be able to afford to eat that night, or I need the cash because it isn't cheap to fuel up a Ferrari.

People seem to think that because I am selling my gear I must be skint. That's not the case at all and it makes me laugh when people say it. At the end of the day, I have made a lot of money out of eBay, so who is having the last laugh? It is all stuff I've been given so it's 100 per cent profit.

I am not the only player doing it. Quite a few of the Leeds boys have sold gear but they tend to do it through me because they don't want people to know what they are doing. We sell to people on our mailing list, our regulars, so it's not generally known. I am past caring what people think and it doesn't bother me.

Obviously I am doing it for the money but I also think it is providing a service and meeting a demand. People like to own something that has genuinely belonged to a player; it's a unique sort of gift and it wouldn't be available otherwise. If I've got something I don't want but someone else is prepared to pay for and will get enjoyment out of, why not? Prices have dropped since I started because to an extent I have saturated the market, so I've been a bit of a victim of my own success. If you can get a few hundred quid for a match shirt nowadays you have done well.

Not all players are willing to do it. Rob Burrow, for example, won't sell anything. People sometimes say I shouldn't be selling stuff. Their attitude is you've worked hard for that, so you should keep it. I know some old-time players who don't approve of replica shirts. They believe that they had to toil away to get a jersey and they don't like seeing some fat bloke in the street wearing one. But I don't part with absolutely everything. I will sell loser's medals, shirts I've worn in games we've lost and that sort of thing, but I have kept my Grand Final winning jerseys and my Super League rings. They are in a shoe box somewhere. Everything has a price and I probably would be willing to part with them it if came to it, but only for 10 grand or more. As far as I am concerned, objects are objects. They don't really have any sentimental value for me. I can't sell my memories and they are what's most precious. I don't need gold rings to tell me I won the title in 2004, 2007/8/9. DVDs of the game and pictures of the celebrations are much more important to me.

We get four sets of training kit from the club every year and if I didn't get rid of it there would be no room in the house. If you were given a set of pens - or a laptop case or whatever - by your employer every year, you didn't want it and someone else did who was willing to pay good money, what would you do?

The club have no objection and they actually sell off shirts on their own eBay shop, so they couldn't complain. They have, though, brought in a rule saying we can't flog the current season's training gear. That was my fault. I don't wear things like waterproofs so I sold some off. ISC, the kit supplier, saw it and complained to the club. They said: "If Keith's selling his gear we must be giving you too much," so the club put a stop to it. That's fair enough, but we get a new set every pre-season and you aren't allowed to wear previous years' kit anyway, so they aren't bothered about what happens to the old stuff.

The biggest controversy my eBay habit has got me involved in came at the start of 2009, a few months after the World Cup. Everybody who took part received a memento - a player participation medal it was called - and I put mine up for sale. A reporter, Julie Stott from *The Sun*, spotted it and did an article, slagging me off for selling my World Cup medal. That attracted a lot of publicity and I couldn't have been happier. I was in Jacksonville, Florida, at the time, on Rhinos' pre-season camp. Before *The Sun* article appeared, the top bid was £30 and that was after about four days. The day of the article it went up to more than £1,000. It created so much interest it eventually went for stupid money - £2,200. And the person with the highest bid paid up, so thanks very much.

The attitude most people had was 'good for you, it's your medal and you can do what you want with it'. One or two, on the other hand, were less than impressed. We replied saying: "I am completely skint, please give generously so I can have beans on my toast tonight." That made a few people laugh.

We had a big debate among the players in Jacksonville about it and opinion was divided. I remember discussing it over a coffee with Jason Davidson, our conditioner who had the same job with England, Jamie

Jones-Buchanan and his half-brother Jodie Broughton. When it started getting to stupid money, people's morals began to change. Jonesy was saying he wouldn't sell his when it was at £100, but when it got to £1,000 he wasn't so sure. At £2,000, players were queuing up to offer me their medals.

Jodie, who hadn't made his Super League debut at that point, was adamant he wouldn't have sold his. That was fair enough, but I turned around and said to him: "Yes, but you haven't done anything in the game – so it would mean a lot more to you." That didn't come out how I meant it to and I got a lot of stick about it at the time. I say the same thing to Jodie every time I see him now: "What have you done in the game?" Jodie's a good kid. He didn't make it at Leeds but went to Salford, scored a load of tries in his first season and got called into the England squad, so he is somebody who could have a big future and maybe one day he'll have the last laugh. Good on him if he does.

In 2010 I got fined by the RFL for telling the media what I thought about referee Richard Silverwood after we lost to Melbourne Storm in the World Club Challenge. I accepted I was out of order, but I wasn't happy about having to stump up so I paid the fine by flogging my loser's medal, plus the player's security pass to get me into the ground and my shirt, on eBay. I got £480 for the lot and the fine was £500. When I put the items up for sale I added a note saying: "Please give generously to pay my fine." One or two people said they had bid a bit extra because it was such a good cause. I think my comments about the referee must have struck a chord because one or two people did offer to pay off the punishment for me, though I declined.

Like I say, I don't mind people accusing me of being tight, though I prefer to think of myself as careful. eBay is a means of making money out of something that would otherwise get thrown away or lie around unused. As well as selling stuff, I also donate old kit to charity and to amateur clubs, who can give it a good home. In terms of eBay, it is an easy way to bring in a few extra quid and I know it is not a source of income that is going to last forever. When I retire, the gravy train will hit the buffers, so it's a case of cashing in while I can. I do have an eye on what's going to happen when I hang up my boots. Whatever I sell goes into stocks and shares. We have invested everything, nothing has been frittered away. The ultimate aim is to be able to live a life of leisure when I pack in playing. I'm probably not there yet, but I'd like not to have to work for long when I do retire.

Full-time Super League players are well-paid, though not to the extent

Premiership footballers are, for example. An established England rugby league international will earn something in the region of £100,000 per year. Players just coming through earn a lot less and some of the high-profile stars - especially the Aussies and Kiwis - can bring in much more.

Rugby league has given me a comfortable lifestyle and I realise how lucky I have been. Most players are the same. We recognise that we are getting paid a good wage for doing something we love - and most of us would play amateur for nowt if we weren't good enough to earn a living from the game. If they are sensible and do things right, the top earners can bring in enough during a career to retire on. Gary Connolly, the former St Helens, Wigan and Great Britain player, who also had a spell at Leeds, proved that and good on him. You have to be smart about it though.

Sometimes there is a bit too much money on offer for the best young kids. If you are 19 years old and earning silly money, say a £100,000 contract, it is going to change you and not always in a positive way. It can give you an attitude and I know quite a few lads who have got hooked on gambling, which has ended up bringing them to their knees.

I have never resented players who get paid more than me. If they are smart enough to negotiate a better contract, well done and credit to them. I know there are players who bring in more than I do but I have always been more concerned about what I earn than how much anybody else does. After we won the Grand Final in 2009, Kevin Sinfield made a speech saying most players at Leeds could earn a lot more somewhere else, but they stayed loyal because of the other benefits, like the mateship we have and the trophies we've won.

After reading this chapter you might not believe me, but I do think there's more to life than money. I want to be comfortably off and not to have to go without things, which might be a reflection of my upbringing, but quality of life, working with people I like and being part of a good set-up and a successful team is equally important.

Super League's salary cap - which restricts the amount clubs can spend on their playing staff - has had a strong effect on limiting players' wages and in general that has been a good thing. It has certainly evened out the competition, which makes our three successive Grand Final wins all the more of an achievement. I do know some clubs find ways to get around it. A few have been fined and deducted points, but others have got away with it. I am not going to name names, but I know it happens because players have told me. I am aware of one very high-profile international player who was on the point of leaving his club to go to rugby union. He had a lucrative offer from one of the top Premiership sides on the table and his Super League outfit couldn't afford to match that and stay within the salary cap. They didn't want to lose him so they paid him one wage on the books and the rest was handed over in the proverbial brown paper bag.

I don't know if this still goes on but at other clubs, wives and girlfriends were sometimes put on the payroll as office workers or whatever. They didn't actually do any work for the club but they got paid a salary as a way of boosting the player's wages, off the books. That's at other clubs; I can honestly say that when it comes to the salary cap, Leeds are whiter than white, which is a bit annoying! It is Gary Hetherington's philosophy: if you want to play for Leeds Rhinos, then you will play for x-amount of pounds and money is not an issue. Gary uses that in contract negotiations all the time and once he has decided what you are worth, he never, ever budges. It is what Kevin was talking about that evening at Old Trafford. We do have a lot of Leeds lads in the team and they are willing to play for their hometown club for a lot less than other sides would offer. We are looked after well at Leeds and you would struggle to do better elsewhere, even if you were financially better off. A fair number of players have moved on over the last few years but I can't think of too many whose career has gone to a higher level.

When I was negotiating with Leeds way back in 1999, Wigan offered me a lot more money to go there. I thought Leeds had extra to give in other ways and I have never regretted that decision. If I had gone to Wigan I would have had to either travel over every day or move there, which - with respect to the place - I didn't want to do. And I wouldn't have got four Grand Final rings.

Staying loyal has also cost me a few quid. The way things work, I could have increased my wages if I had swapped clubs every few years, but on the other hand I had a good testimonial at Leeds, which probably made up the difference, and I have been happy here. The grass isn't always greener. I am a big believer in playing for money; we are professionals and it is how we make a living. But once you reach a certain amount, enough to make you comfortably well off, other things become just as important. For the sake of another 10 or 20 grand, it is not worth the hassle of changing clubs. If you like it where you are, there's no point taking a gamble and moving on.

CHAPTER 17

A WEEK IN THE LIFE

I sometimes get asked what being a 'full-time' player means. Games last 80 minutes and we only play once a week, so what do we do for the rest of the time?

What you see on a Friday night or Sunday afternoon is the most important part of my job, but only a small part of what being a professional rugby league player is all about.

There's training, of course, which is a vital part of any professional player's workload. In the modern game it is no longer just a case of running around a field for a couple of hours, practicing passing and tackling.

Preparation is very scientific and that is something that has really developed since I started playing. Nowadays there's a lot of emphasis placed on diet and on recovering from and trying to prevent injuries. We also spend a lot of time on analysis, reviewing both our performances and those of the opposition. Every game is either televised or recorded by one or both of the teams involved. Coaches swap videos of forthcoming opponents and we'll have seen every rival in action before we come up against them on the field.

Training itself includes weights sessions in the gym and work-outs on the field, as well as things like swimming or – in pre-season – running on the hills. Some days we are finished by lunchtime and on others we train twice, morning and afternoon. Occasionally we may have an evening session.

It's not a nine to five occupation and we are lucky in that we do get a fair amount of free time and afternoons off, but the club expects to get its money's worth from us, and everyone – from JP and Kev to the academy boys just promoted into the squad – has to pitch in with community work.

Players are viewed very much as ambassadors for the club and the sport. We all have a certain number of personal appearances to fulfil each year, which can be anything from attending a press conference to coaching kids, attending a dinner or presenting prizes at a local amateur club.

That might sound like a piece of cake but it's not as easy as it sounds. The coaching is all right but some of the meeting and greeting can be a bit awkward. For example, before the 2010 season we had a training camp in Cumbria, which ended with a dinner to raise money for the Whitehaven club. The whole first team squad were there and before the food we were lined up at the front of the room, our names were pulled out of a hat one by one and we were all allocated a table to sit at.

Making interesting conversation with nine or 10 people you have never met before isn't the easiest thing in the world. It doesn't bother me but I know some of the younger boys find it pretty daunting. We attend quite a lot of events when one of the attractions for the paying customers is to sit with a Rhinos player.

Anyway, to give you an idea of how I earn my living, I thought I would keep a diary of a typical week early in the 2011 season, when I was putting the finishing touches to this book. I chose this particular week, in February, because we had a full seven days between matches, but other than that it was picked completely at random. So here's my as-it-happened account of a week in the life of Keith Senior.

Saturday, February 19, 2011

We played Hull away last night and recorded a 32-18 win. That's two from two at the start of the season, after the Millennium Magic victory over Bradford Bulls. We weren't great in that one, but last night was much better. I was pretty pleased with the way I played and my winger Ryan Hall was among the try scorers, so that was good. I always enjoy playing at Hull; there's usually a decent-sized crowd and a good atmosphere. It can be an intimidating place to go, but I like to think I thrive in an environment like that.

It was an 8pm kick-off and we left the ground just before 11. I get home around 12.30 this morning and I am in bed more or less straight away because we have an early start this morning. I don't get much sleep because I am sore from the game, so I am wide awake at 6am. I have to be back in Leeds for 8.30am for a 30 minute swimming session, to loosen up after last night's match.

I have a coffee and a bacon and egg McMuffin on the way home. I deserve a bit of junk food after my exertions last night. We all have to watch what we eat during the week, but you're allowed a bit of a blow-out at the weekend if you've played on Friday night.

Once home, I spend the rest of the morning moving hay, repairing fences which the horses have broken and chopping wood for the fire, because it's blooming freezing. That's the trouble with having Yorkshire stone flags down in your kitchen.

At 1pm I have pie and peas for lunch, followed by digestive biscuits and two pints of orange squash. I spend a couple of hours watching last night's game, which we will review properly during the week. More nosh at 4pm - four Ryvita, pumpkin seed and nut, with Philadelphia. That is an appetiser for some proper eating this evening. There is a get-together arranged at Rob Burrow's house, but on the way I call in to see a neighbour's friend, who is battling cancer. He is a big Leeds fan so I take him a signed shirt as a surprise. I hope that cheers him up.

We get to Rob's at around 7.30pm. It is a Jamie Oliver-themed party. The girls spend the early part of the evening looking at the cookware, while the lads have a chat and a few drinks. Brent Webb is a good cook and he comes up trumps: curried chicken with a couscous salad. Chile con carne is also available. I need a good feed because I haven't eaten well today. It is a good night and I am back home and in bed around 1am.

Sunday, February 20

No training today so I have a lie in. Am up at around 9am for breakfast: two Weetabix and Crunchy Nut Cornflakes. After that, the morning is spent sorting the horses out and making sure they are fed and watered. It is an easy job because we chucked them out into some woodland yesterday to save having to muck out, as we knew we would be having a late night.

At about noon, Vic and I meet up with some friends at a local pub for a feed. It is a Sunday carvery – all you can eat, which I usually see as a bit of a challenge. I take it easy today: turkey, beef and ham, with veggies, Yorkshire pudding and potatoes. Coffee to follow.

I spend a relaxing afternoon, picking at food: chocolate mousse followed by two pints of water, a protein bar, banana and strawberry smoothie and Multipower flapjack. At 5.30 I feed and water the horses and muck out the stables, then for tea it is pizza, followed by apple pie and custard. Two pints of orange cordial to wash it down.

Household chores in the evening: getting my training kit ready for tomorrow and ironing my shirt because we've got a sponsor's dinner at Headingley. I also clean the bedrooms and do some general tidying up before settling down in front of Dancing on Ice.

One Weetabix for supper.

Monday, February 21

I am up at 6am. First job is to pee into a cup – I have to take a urine sample into training for a hydration test. I help that along with a banana, blueberry and strawberry smoothie, with wheatgrass and barley grass mixed in. It's not too much of a problem. In this job you get used to giving samples for drugs tests and the like.

I get to training – at our Kirkstall base a couple of miles from the Headingley ground - about 7.15am and have a bowl of porridge before a massage at 7.30am, then a bowl of beans and scrambled egg, with coffee.

Between 7-8am we do grip testing, weigh ourselves and complete a wellbeing survey, checking how we feel, where we're sore, how we slept and our nutrition over the weekend. We also do a jump (squat) test to check our power output and see if our legs are tired.

At 9am we have a team meeting and review Friday's game. The good news is we aren't going out on to the field, so we do weights, conditioning cardiovascular work and a boxing session.

I drink about one litre of water during training and have a protein shake afterwards.

At 1pm we have a team lunch in the Carnegie café bar at Headingley. That's something we do once most weeks. The café bar is in the new Carnegie Stand, which opened a few years ago and is also used as a campus for Leeds Met University. It's open to the public, so it's usually busy with students and passers-by. Leeds Carnegie rugby union team and Yorkshire County Cricket Club share the same complex, so it's a good place for star spotting – and the food and service is excellent. I have a ham salad sandwich and a bowl of soup, plus two pints of cordial.

As you can imagine, I am feeling a little peckish by 2pm so I have a banana and apple flapjack bar to keep me going and also to help with the boredom. I spend a while hanging around at Kirkstall waiting for Kev, because we're going to a sauna for hot and colds.

Sauna at 3.30pm, then at 5pm off to Trio – a local restaurant – for a feed, with Kev, Barrie McDermott, Jay Pitts, Ryan Hall and Paul McShane. I have chicken chorizo salad with two pints of water, followed by a mocha.

At 6.30 I get changed into my suit in the hotel at Headingley, ready for the sponsors' evening. Hope the grub's good.

8.30pm, dinner: chicken with veg and trio of desserts, plus two bottles of water. It's the first home game of the season on Friday so this is a chance for all the sponsors to mingle with the players and listen to the club's plans for the year ahead. There's at least one player sitting with the guests at each table. Gary Hetherington outlines Leeds Rugby's business plan for 2011 and afterwards Jamie Jones-Buchanan interviews a few of the players before the Do finishes at around 10pm.

Tuesday, February 22

A day off. I get up at 9am and have my special banana, blueberry and strawberry milk smoothie – with wheatgrass and barley grass mixed in – to start the morning, as I do every day. Breakfast is four Weetabix, with Crunchy Nut Cornflakes, which are very, very tasty.

The horses have been in all night, so the stables look like a bomb site and mucking out takes 90 minutes or so. Vic is off for a hack with her sister so I act as groom and help get the horses ready.

Lunch is one bacon sandwich with two pints of water. Vic gets back from her ride so we worm the horses – it's a glamorous life – and give them a feed.

The weather's okay today, so the afternoon is spent tidying up around the garden, leaf-blowing and so on. I snack on a Tracker bar and a pint of water.

I can't be bothered to cook, so it's off to the local pub for tea: chicken pie with veg, plus two pints of cordial.

Supper is four Weetabix.

Wednesday, February 23

Up at 6am. I have my usual smoothie to drink and then hit the road, arriving at Kirkstall at around 7.15am, in time for a massage 15 minutes later. Breakfast at 8am is coffee with beans and scrambled egg on toast.

9am: Weights, stretching and then a session in the combat room – an old office which has been cleared, with crash mats placed on the floor around the walls – so we can knock seven bells out of each other.

I recuperate with a protein shake and a flapjack bar and I drink around two litres of water throughout training.

10.30am: Team meeting, to go through a video of Friday's opponents – Harlequins – and consider our game plan. After that we are out on to the field for team prep and to go through the game plan.

After training head to Trio for a feed: pizza and chicken chorizo salad, with two pints of orange and water – and a mocha.

Hang about Kirkstall for an hour or so as I am coaching later. Have a chat with Barrie Mac, Rob and Chris Plume, the academy coach.

6pm: Coaching the under-15s at Crawshaw School, Pudsey, for an hour.

After that I head back to Kirkstall to do weights and combat for an hour. I have a sandwich, apple and banana en route to Kirkstall, plus a bottle of water.

I set off home at around 9pm and have four Weetabix for supper before bed.

Thursday, February 24

Wake at 6pm, smoothie and then porridge for breakfast. I head to Leeds and have a massage at 7.45am, followed by treatment on my knee at 8.45am. It has been feeling a bit sore this week but hopefully it's nothing to get too concerned about.

9.30am: The final training session of the week, at Stanningley amateur rugby league club. It is a good set-up and the academy and reserves play their home matches there when Headingley is not available. Stanningley has produced loads of Super League players, including Jonesy and Jamie Peacock.

After training we have a team lunch at Trio. All the players are there. We have a pasta dish and garlic bread, with a jug of orange juice and water. Afterwards a group of us go to Costa for a coffee and a chat.

On my way home I pop into Huddersfield to buy Vic a birthday present. I also call to see my bank manager. I am home about 4pm, shattered. I have a sit down for 10 minutes and then drag myself outside to muck out and feed the horses.

Back out at 5pm to meet Jonesy at Ainley Top. We have been invited to attend a meeting for players who are hoping to go into coaching. This has been organised by the RFL and the idea is they will get us coaching under-15s, 16s and 18s. Traffic there is terrible but eventually we arrive in one piece and tuck into a buffet meal the organisers have laid on.

I arrive home at 8.45 and have Cornflakes for supper, watch TV for an hour and then fall into bed.

Friday, February 25

Game day. I am up at 9am, have four Weetabix for breakfast before mucking out and feeding the horses. I then jump in the shower, as I'm heading off to a meeting with the Laura Crane Youth Cancer Trust, for which I am an ambassador.

On the way I drop Vic off at the hairdresser and then post some items I have sold on eBay. I arrive at the meeting at 11.30am and have chicken pasta for lunch while waiting for Huddersfield Giants' Andy Raleigh, who is also a Laura Crane ambassador.

On the way home I call into a car dealership in Huddersfield. I am getting a new car on March 1st and there's some paperwork to sign. I also collect Vic, then relax for the rest of the afternoon before sorting the horses out and then getting ready to head off to the game, after munching on a tuna sandwich.

It is an 8pm kick-off and I set off nice and early to make sure I don't get caught in traffic. I have a meeting planned at Headingley at around 5pm, to discuss this book. That takes an hour and I head off to the changing room at 6pm, which is when I'd normally arrive at the ground. On the way I get stopped by a few fans wanting autographs – probably future competition on eBay.

When I get to the changing room I'm greeted by the legend Billy Watts, one of rugby league's great characters. Billy's about 105, but he is at training when we arrive every day, helping out with kit and such like. He is the club's official time keeper and has missed one game – when he was ill – in the past 30 years. He has a cup of coffee ready and I am always pleased to see him. It's good to have somebody older than me around the place.

By the time I arrive, Rob Burrow is already changed, kitted up and ready to play. Only two hours to go. The first thing I do is get my ankles strapped. I read the programme, sip coffee and chat while that is being done. Sometimes there's an under-20s curtain-raiser, which we watch a bit of. Their game is being played at Stanningley tonight, to protect the Headingley pitch, so the boys have a natter instead.

We all have to weigh ourselves before the game and again afterwards, to see how dehydrated we are and how much water we need to drink to get our weight back up.

The Doc, Jon Greenwell, gives me my pain-killers. I take Tramadol, two Paracetamol and a stomach tab, as I get bad guts. I'm not the only one, as we find out later.

I slowly get my shorts, socks and warm-up top on and do the spot the difference and word search puzzles in the programme, with Ryan Hall. He's a smart kid so we nail them pretty easily.

About 7pm Brian Mac has a chat about tactics and so on and then, with 20 minutes to go, talk about the game picks up. The headphones all come off and preparations become more intense. Kev and Rob are the main talkers – we backs are a bit more relaxed about things and we generally chill in the corner, out of the way of the head-bangers. Those are the lads who like to get themselves fired up. JP – who is still recovering from his knee reconstruction and so isn't playing tonight - is a big one for that, pacing up and down. Weller Hauraki seems to be similar. We respect their wishes and keep clear so they can go through their usual routine.

I have a massage on my calves and hamstrings and then get my shoulder strapped. I have grade four osteoarthritis, so I'm in a fair bit of pain. I'm waiting until I retire and then I'm going to treat myself to a new shoulder; I fancy a Titanium one. It's not too bad - after so long you get used to the pain.

With kick-off approaching, we all gather to do our pre-match stretching in the social room at the end of the changing room corridor. The idea is to get muscles warmed-up before the game. Then it's back into the changing room for a quick pee – if you need it – and we all wait until everyone's ready before heading out on to the field together for the pre-match warm-up. I like to be at the back.

We regroup on the field and then do half a lap together in front of the South Stand, which is where our most vocal supporters gather. After that we go through our warm-up before returning to the changing room for final preparations.

The warm-up is position-specific. We do a bit of ball work, passing along the line just to get the ball in our hands. Backs do catching, kickers do kicking and forwards concentrate on ruck work, as well as some contact on the tackle pads. We regroup and do 'some shots on shields' – basically tackle practice – in our defensive units, left, middle and right. We also stretch and do high knees to get the legs going.

Back in the changing room the talk is intense now and everyone is ready to go. The coach and captain – and whoever else wants to chip in – have a few last words. At this time I sit in my place, fold my shirt with my name facing me – I haven't put it on yet because I never warm-up in my playing jersey - and have a few moments to myself.

Most of the boys have their own routine. Kylie, Ali and JJB are all Christians and they have a quiet moment to pray.

Our conditioner Jason Davidson gives us the call and we are on to our feet and into a circle for a rapid chat about what we need to do over the next couple of hours. Jason counts us down and we do 10 fast feet – basically running on the spot – before hand slaps, hugs all round and good luck wishes to each other. Then it's into the tunnel, out on to the field and let battle commence.

Tonight, things don't go well. We get an early try when Chris Clarkson goes over and we are playing at 100 miles an hour, but we can't add to our total. A couple of mistakes let Harlequins into the game, totally against the run of play, and before we know it we are 18-6 down. Kev scores just before the break, so the gap is cut to six at half-time. There has been one bizarre incident in the first half, which fortunately goes unnoticed by most people in the ground. There's been a bout of illness going around the camp in recent weeks and one of my team-mates gets caught short a few minutes into the match. He has to nip – or rather dash at full speed – behind the scoreboard on the Western Terrace. Fortunately, that section of the ground is closed tonight due to building work. I have no idea what would have happened if it had been open!

In the changing room at half-time we have five minutes to sort ourselves out, get injuries strapped and generally calm down. Then Brian Mac has his say. The talk is quite positive and the only criticism is constructive. We are only a converted try behind and we know when we stick to the game plan and carry out what we set out to do, we can break them down. It is just a case of getting back to how we started the game. There's also talk about our attitude. When we play against teams like Wigan and Saints we are always fired up. Against the supposed lesser teams we sometimes tend to do just enough. The word goes round that we can't expect things just to happen for us, we have to work hard, raise the intensity and be more aggressive. Harlequins have won their opening two games and they are definitely no mugs. Jason counts down again, 10 fast feet and back out for the second half.

We get an early try so Quins' lead is just two points and I suppose at that point most people in the ground expect us to run away with it, but again we can't kick on. Our defence doesn't work the way it should and they run in three soft tries to make it 36-16. Hally and JJB go in for consolation scores but it finishes 36-26 to Quins; a very bad day at the office.

At the end of the game Jason and the other on-field assistants bring protein shakes to us on the pitch. Everyone's feeling down, so we trudge into the changing room and sulk for a while in our seats. Brian says a few words and one or two of the players chip in. Despite what you might expect, there's no shouting or carrying on, no kicking doors or anything like that. We are at a stage where we don't need that. We know what we need to put right. With the ball, we are still at an early stage and we're confident things will come good as we go on. The main talk is about our defence, which hasn't been good enough. We are conceding too many points and letting sides score soft tries against us.

It always seems to take ages to get changed when you've lost. Slowly we take our kit off, get strapping removed and bags of ice applied where needed. We shower and then have ice baths. Food is available in the changing room: Müller Rice, burgers and pizza. I tend not to eat after a game, preferring to wait until later, so I give that a miss.

I am one of the last out of the changing room today and the media are hanging around outside. Nobody really likes to talk after a loss but it is part of the job and it's very rare that any player refuses an interview. I speak to Dave Craven from the Yorkshire Post and Peter Smith of the Yorkshire Evening Post and then do a filmed interview for Phil Daly, the Rhinos media manager. That will go on the club website. I tell the press we are confident things will come good, we are on the right track and there's no need to change the new, expansive style of rugby we are playing under Brian.

Once that's done I head up to the Long Bar in the cricket stand. There's food available there and I sign a few autographs and mingle with fans, though I am not really in the mood. There are interviews and speeches over the microphone but the atmosphere is pretty glum.

That's not quite the end of the working week. When Long Bar duties are over we head as a team for the Virgin fitness centre in Kirkstall, a mile or so from the ground, for a swim. I can't swim because of my shoulder, but do stretching exercises in the pool.

There's a McDonald's at the other end of the car park, so a few of us head there for a burger and a chat and, on this occasion, more sulking. Then it's home, wind down and off to bed.

CHAPTER 18

LIFE WITH BRIAN

At the time Brian McDermott was announced as our new assistant-coach, towards the end of the 2010 season, it was obvious he was being groomed for the top job when Bluey eventually left the club, which was expected to be at the end of the following year.

I was unsure how the two of them would have worked together, but that wasn't an issue after Bluey decided to return home in the autumn of 2010 and Mac came straight into the hot seat – four years after leaving Leeds to be head coach at Harlequins. I was happy to see him back and felt he was the right appointment for Leeds. Having worked with Brian before, I knew his qualities and I was sure he would bring something new and exciting to the club. I was also pretty certain he could get the best out of the players we had in the squad and the young ones beginning to come through.

The new era didn't start too well. In April, 2011 we lost at home to Huddersfield Giants – the first time my hometown club had won at Headingley for 51 years – and that was our fifth defeat in 10 league games. Brian was already under pressure and some of the fans were starting to get on his back. After that, we won six on the spin, we got a few key players – like JP and Danny Mags – back from injury, our defence tightened up and we cut down on the silly errors. That shows how quickly things can turn around, but then we went into another nose dive. Five of the next seven games were lost as we dipped to eighth in the table and the pressure was back on. I was out of the door by then and I wasn't happy about Brian's role in my departure, but even so I hope he can turn things around and ride out the storm, because I think he has got a lot to offer as a coach.

To be fair to Brian, right from the start he said it would be mid-way through his first season before we really began to show what he was all about as a coach. It takes time to get new ideas across and he was aware of that. When he came in, all the players were right behind him and we were happy with his appointment as team boss. The poor form we were in at the start of 2011 was down to us, not the backroom staff. No matter how well he prepares a side, there's not much a coach can do when the players cross the whitewash. It wasn't Brian who was dropping passes and missing tackles. In training we were looking good but it all seemed to go wrong on game day. That wasn't Brian's fault, it was ours.

Before the season started, Gary Hetherington came out with a statement about wanting the team to play expansive rugby. That is something Brian bought into and he got a lot of stick from the supporters because it wasn't working. When you throw the ball around you are bound to make mistakes and your defence has to be good enough to handle that. Ours wasn't, but I would not have been in favour of changing our style of play to something more conservative. When it stuck, it was effective, but the mistakes we were making were basic errors, not down to the changes Brian implemented.

Brian's a bit different to any other coach I have had, though I think you have to be quite a strange character to take that sort of job on. He is an ex-Marine and a former professional heavyweight boxer and he operated in the front-row in his playing days, so you wouldn't expect him to be an intellectual. Everyone knows the backs are the intelligent ones in a rugby team, but he is as smart as they come; he is a deep thinker and he has an opinion on everything, not just rugby. You could ask him about grass being green and he would have a theory on it. Whether that would be right or wrong is another thing, but he would definitely have an opinion. The Apollo moon landings are one of his favourite topics - he is certain they never happened and he can come up with quite a convincing argument to back that up. Brian is a tough guy but he is not a bawler and shouter. He would rather think things through.

After retiring as a player with Bradford he had a spell on Tony Smith's coaching staff at Huddersfield and then came to Leeds as Tony's assistant. He left midway through 2006 and I think going to London to be in charge of his own team definitely helped him grow and develop as acoach. Rather than being involved with Tony Smith, he went away, learned and came back with his own ideas and systems. I reckon a lot of the people who were criticising him in early 2011 were the same ones who said we went downhill after he left five years earlier. He came back and gave us a lot of structure, which we didn't have the previous year under Bluey.

I was quite surprised about how technically astute he was when he came back. He definitely brought in some good things, but we didn't click, at least at the start of the year. People were saying it was the worst rugby we had played in a long time, but I wouldn't necessarily agree with that. I think we actually played some quite good stuff but it all got ruined by silly, fundamental errors and holes in our defence. An example was our home game against the champions Wigan on April Fool's Day. With 15 minutes to go we were 22-4 up and had totally dominated the game, but we completely ran out of gas and they scored three late tries to snatch a draw.

It could have been worse; we were two points up inside the last minute and they made a break right to our line. Danny Buderus pulled Liam Farrell down and they would probably have scored a try on the next play – which would have been the last of the match – because we were out on our feet. Bedsy decided not to take the chance, so he held on to Farrell. The ref told him to get off a couple of times, and then awarded a penalty and Sam Tomkins kicked the equalising goal after the hooter had sounded. That was smart play by Bedsy, as you'd expect. He did the right thing, because there was always a chance Tomkins would have missed with his kick. It was actually a good point and I am sure fans would have settled for that beforehand, but it felt like a loss. It is always tough when you have given absolutely everything and still not come away with a win. What that game did show, though, was that we could play good rugby when we got our game together.

On the other hand, sometimes we were so bad, you just had to laugh about it. I have taken some criticism for smiling and laughing during our game against Huddersfield. Fans might think that shows I don't care, but they could not be more wrong. It was a case of if you don't laugh, you would cry. Everybody in the team cares deeply about what we do and we take it hard when things go wrong. We were a very frustrated team because we were given a game plan – and one we all thought was right – but we weren't able to stick to it. That was nobody's fault but our own. Confidence was low and it was hard to see a way out of the slump, but that was a good test for Brian, to see if he could get us back on track. When your back is against the wall, that's when you get to show what you are made of.

Sometimes you have to look at negatives in a positive way and on occasions a bit of adversity can be good for everybody. It toughens you up and builds character. Everybody expected Brian to come in and make everything rosy overnight and it didn't happen. That was similar to when I first signed at Leeds and I was supposed to be the final piece in a trophy-winning jigsaw. As you've already read, I had a torrid time for the first few months. If you don't start superbly, you get a lot of critics and the pressure builds. That can make your job a lot tougher but it also makes you more thick-skinned. In sport you are always happy to take the plaudits but you also have to listen to criticism. The key thing is not to listen to it too much or really take it to heart. Anyone who took what's written on fans' message boards seriously would never play another game. If I had listened to the supporters, I would have retired when I was 21! At the end of the day, the externals – the fans – don't know our game structure or how we are supposed to be playing.

We are in a great job but we are scrutinised all the time. At a club like Leeds you are in a goldfish bowl – and sometimes no matter what you do and how hard you try it is not good enough. Daryl Powell used to say it is the hardest job in the world because everybody's a coach and everybody knows better. You have to accept that and it is one of the pitfalls of playing for such a big club. You're not under the same pressure at a club like Salford or Harlequins; their supporters care just as much, but there are not as many of them and expectations aren't as high. Having said that, the rewards aren't as great either. I have learned that you have to be a bit tongue in cheek with spectators. I honestly do value opinions and constructive criticism, but as long as I believe what I am doing is right, that is the most important thing for me. I am sure Brian feels the same way. For as long as he believes in his methods and he is strong enough to stick to them, he will be okay.

One of the successes Brian did have at the start of his time at Leeds was in promoting some exciting young players from the academy. He did the same in London, but that was probably through necessity rather than choice. While he was there, loads of young Londoners got an opportunity in the first team because he had such a small squad. I once told him I had never heard of some of the lads he had brought through – and he said he hadn't either! If he needed a winger, for example, he'd ask the youth manager if there was anyone suitable and that player would get chucked straight in, even if he had never trained with the Super League team. At Leeds there's more choice and players don't get into the elite side until they are ready.

Ben Jones-Bishop, who played with Brian during a loan spell in 2010, had a fantastic start to the season until he dislocated his shoulder in a home game against Salford. He had just been called into the England elite training squad and it was a massive shame for him because he is a talented kid who has a big future in the game. He is a natural try scorer, with a deceptive running style; he doesn't seem to be moving that fast, he glides, but once he gets into space he doesn't get caught. I just hope he is getting his bad luck with injuries out of the way early. He had a long spell on the sidelines at Harlequins after he fractured his skull. He made a full recovery but he has still got quite a spectacular scar and that's why he wears a scrum cap when he plays.

Another one to burst on to the scene was Kallum Watkins. I have taken a close interest in his progress because he is being touted as my long-term successor at Leeds. I have spoken to Kallum about that: everyone is saying he is a left-centre, Kallum sees himself more as a utility-centre and I think, with how he plays the game, the right-centre suits him best. What nobody is arguing about is the fact he is a real talent. He has a right-handed carry, a right-handed flick and a left-handed fend, whereas I am a left-handed carry and right-handed fend. He broke into the team in 2009, but suffered an anterior cruciate ligament injury early the following year, which kept him out of action for 11 months. That set him back a bit but he doesn't turn 20 until December, 2011, so he has got time on his side. He has played a bit at full-back and also had a run on the wing, because of injuries to Lee Smith, Bish and Zak Hardaker, who is another young kid who could have a big future, but I hope he can go on and establish himself in the centre.

Kallum has great feet, he is strong, quick and has terrific skills with ball in hand. He needs a bit of schooling and he has to work on his game-awareness, especially on the defensive side of things. That's something which comes with messing up: you have to make mistakes to be able to correct them. In a couple of games early in the 2011 season, Kallum sent his winger over for a try from a flick pass. And on a couple of other occasions he tried the same thing and the ball went into touch. When it comes off, you're a great player. If it doesn't, you are an idiot. That is something I have learned to live with.

Eighty per cent of the time it does come off. The other 20 per cent can bite you on the backside but you have to look at the bigger picture. Players with special talent can sometimes get you out of the mire in close games. I would rather see Kallum – or any talented young kid - try things than adopt a cautious approach. You can't stop players expressing themselves and the game would be very boring if you did. I hope he doesn't get some of his natural flair coached out of him and with Brian in charge I don't think that will happen. Brian's more likely to encourage him to play than to try and rein him in. A lot of the coaches I have had have told players to chance their arm: never stop playing and don't die wondering.

Kallum has already played for England at youth level and he was named in the Knights squad in 2010. I have no doubt he will go on and play Test match rugby - and before very long. Sadly, he is from Manchester, but I won't hold that against him. He has all the attributes, but the thing I really like about him is his attitude, which is first class. For me, that is the most important thing. Over the years I have seen countless players who had great talent but didn't make it in the game because their attitude wasn't right. The amateur code is full of them. Go to any parks pitch on a winter Saturday afternoon and you will see players who look like they could have made it in the professional ranks. The reason they didn't was because they liked a beer too much or they weren't prepared to put the effort in. I have seen just as many who weren't the best in terms of ability, but made it to the top because they were willing to work hard and learn.

At Leeds, because of the work ethic we have and the support the club gives in terms of lifestyle, most of the kids coming through have the right attitude. Ones that don't tend to get moved on. The academy lads don't quite have the free role they might at other clubs. At Leeds they are looked after a bit more. Players here have to play by the rules and fit into the club structure.

Attitude is hard to coach into players. You can drip feed it and show them how it benefits them, but it is one of the hardest things to see in a young player coming through. Coaching the under-15s I can see some players with great skill, but until you have worked with them for a while you don't know if they have the right character to make it in the game. You either want it or you don't and there are not that many players who have the right mix of ability and attitude.

I think developing a good work ethic is actually tougher for the best players than the less talented ones, because things are easier for them. When they are playing junior or youth rugby, those kids are big stars and everything is set around them. When you put them into a team environment, sharing the workload, sometimes it doesn't suit them because the whole game doesn't revolve around what they do.

It's a shame that a lot of players go straight from school into full-time rugby. They miss out by not being in the job market and living in the real world. There's now virtually a whole generation of players who've never done a proper day's work in their life. They don't realise what a great lifestyle they have. There are highs and lows in the game but at the end of the day we are getting well paid to do our hobby. Most of us would still play the game even if we weren't good enough to earn a living from it. I only worked for three years or so but that was invaluable. It keeps your feet on the ground. A lot of these players are going to have to go into the workplace once their playing days are over because – unless you are an exceptional talent – there's not enough money in the game to live on once you have hung up your boots. It would be good to give kids a taste of real life before they get into the full-time rugby environment.

A young kid called Stevie Ward has been training with the Leeds first team during the school holidays and he is a good example of someone with talent, plus a good attitude. He is studying for 'A' Levels and playing in the under-20s, even though he is only 17. He is a loose-forward who can also play stand-off and he is as good a prospect as I have seen for a while. He's one of those youngsters who has been a star at every age group, but I think he will make it in the game because he has been able to handle that and the transition into a professional environment, when the game is not just about him. He is a nice kid, he has loads of ability and, crucially, his attitude is spot on. He is willing to work hard and he wants to learn. His nickname around the academy is Kev, which says a lot about him.

Anyone who gets compared with Kevin Sinfield must have a lot going for him, as well as big shoes to fill. Kev is probably the perfect mix of attitude and talent. He is an ideal captain: he does everything right, he says everything right and he is 100 committed to rugby league; he lives and breathes the game. As a skipper he is someone who leads from the front, which is what you need from a captain. He rarely has a bad game and he comes up trumps when it really matters.

Now into his 30s, he is beginning to get a bit more relaxed in his old age. He has a wife and family and is starting to realise there is more to life than rugby league, but he is the sort of player who is a genuine role model for young kids to aspire to – which I am definitely not!

As a player, I think Kev is under-rated. Everyone knows he is the most successful captain Leeds has ever had, but his ability sometimes goes unnoticed. He is very talented and as a goal kicker he is up there among the best I have seen. That's down to a combination of natural ability and hard work. He is always practicing and he does all the little extras after every training session. I think Brian McDermott has brought a new dimension to Kev's passing play and that shows, even at this stage of his career, he is still learning and trying to improve, which is credit to him.

I've been lucky to play with and against some great players and Paul Sculthorpe would be high up the list. I played with him at international level and against him in some tremendous Leeds-St Helens battles and he was a fantastic competitor, with good skill and the right attitude.

He was a very tough, no-nonsense type of player. He had a great engine and an impressive work-rate and good ball skills as well. He could play at stand-off or loose-forward and he was in a similar mould to Kev, but in a bit bigger frame. He loved working out and he was a bit of a gym monster. I was disappointed for him when his career got cut short by injury, because he still had a lot to offer and I think he could have gone on to even bigger and better things. It was a massive loss to Saints, Great Britain, England and Super League.

Jason Robinson was also a big loss to our game when he went to rugby union, but I am sure I wasn't the only player secretly a bit relieved to see the back of him – after having that experience on the field, literally, a few times.

He was up there among the best I have played with. I had a brief spell playing alongside him at international level and he made a lasting impression. He was a complete freak - his footwork was electric and he was one of the hardest men to play against. You don't mind big guys running straight at you, because you know more or less what they are going to do. It's when you come up against these little wick so-and-so's, who you can't get hold of, that problems arise. He definitely embarrassed me a few times early in my career. You would think you had him nailed and whoosh, he was gone. A perfect example was the try he scored against Leeds in the 1998 Grand Final, the season before I joined the club. He got the ball from acting-half, cut infield and stepped past Darren Fleary, Jamie Mathiou and Daryl Powell before accelerating between the posts. Nobody else in the world could have done that.

It's a funny thing, but I find the smaller men much more difficult as opponents. I've never had to play against Rob Burrow and I am glad about that because he must be a nightmare to try and grab hold of. With the big guys, there's not much deviation in what they do, though a few of them have started stepping a bit now. Usually though, the massive props are quite predictable and you'd rather have someone who weighs 20 stone coming at you than somebody who is 70 kilos and runs like a little jack rabbit.

Rob is only 5ft 5in and 11 stone, but pound for pound, he must be one of the toughest players in the game. One of the funniest things I have seen in a long time was Rob squaring up to Hull's Epalahame Lauaki – who is about a foot taller and twice as heavy – in a Challenge Cup tie at the KC in 2010. Lauaki was basically holding Rob at arm's length, while our man swung punches at him, without getting anywhere near landing. To make it even funnier, Rob got sin-binned for his trouble.

Rob has copped more than his fair share of head knocks but he will take on the big guys when he has got the ball and defensively he never gives an inch. Because he's so small you'd expect him to get a battering every week, but it's a case of getting hold of him first. Rob is also one of the characters in rugby league; he is a real joker and he has SMS – Small Man Syndrome. I think because he is so small he must have been picked on as a kid and he has become very thick skinned over the years. Now whenever there's any banter going off, he is always at the forefront of it.

I never enjoy coming up against the little guys, like Luke Robinson at Huddersfield or Saints' Jonny Lomax, who I think could go a long way in the game. They are small in stature but they duck and dive, they've got fast footwork and it's tough getting to grips with them. Everyone talks about how tough they are, which they have to be, but they'd need to be a lot harder if we big guys could actually get our hands on them!

In terms of centres, some of the ones I have most enjoyed playing against are Matt Gidley, Toa Kohe-Love, Martin Gleeson and Nigel Vagana; all top class players. These players bring the best out in me because I know if I am not on my game against them I could get embarrassed. Gidley had a fantastic spell at St Helens and he was definitely a winger's type of centre: you only have to look at how many tries his winger Ade Gardner scored to realise the quality he had. I reckon 70 per cent of those would be down to his centre. He was similar to me in that he would enjoy creating tries as much as scoring them. Gidley was blessed with excellent ball skills and we had some great battles over the years, for club and country. When he was at Saints it made playing against them a bit more enjoyable because we had a mutual respect.

Kohe-Love didn't get the credit he deserved. In my eyes he was a superb player and he was hard to go up against. He was tough, was prepared to give you a whack round the head and when he had the ball in hand he had great footwork and raw strength.

More than once Martin Gleeson has made me look silly in a game, but that gives you a kick up the backside and makes you try all the harder, so it's not necessarily a bad thing. I remember one game against Warrington when he stepped round me and scored a try; that woke me up a bit and I went on and scored a hat-trick. I knew I had to pull my finger out. You need challenges like that.

I always loved playing against Vagana. We started at international level at around the same time and had some terrific contests at Test and club level when he had a spell at Warrington. He was a good player and a tough cookie. I think we were similar in a lot of ways: always got picked, always played and had a lot of respect for each other.

Another one was Inga Tuigamala during his spell at Wigan. He had it all: size, speed and muscle and some footwork as well. He was also one of the nicest guys you could come across. I remember playing against him one time and putting a good shot on. I was standing in front of him at marker and as he got up to play the ball, he patted me on the shoulder and said: "Good tackle mate, well done." I was a bit dumbfounded; you don't expect that from an opponent in the heat of battle. He was a class act.

I remember playing in the centre against Ruben Wiki, maybe New Zealand's greatest-ever rugby league player. He was the first player to earn 50 international caps, which is a staggering achievement. He began as a centre and about a year after I came up against him for the first time, he was playing at prop! How on earth does that happen? He was a remarkable player and he had a presence about him. I am not often star struck, but he was one of those players you looked up to and, I don't mind admitting, I was a bit in awe of him. He was like royalty, you felt rude if you said anything bad about him. It was something of an honour to play against him but I was delighted when he moved to prop so he became somebody else's problem.

These are all players I enjoyed playing with and/or against, but to be honest I didn't have any rugby league heroes or role models when I was growing up. I didn't really follow the sport and I got into rugby through union, so I wasn't steeped in the game before I started playing. As a union kid, Jonathan Davies was someone I admired.

When it comes to coaches, technically Tony Smith was the best I have worked with and David Waite was also very good, though he was a bit over-complicated at times. For motivational skills, I think John Kear is the best and I would put him ahead of Bluey, who was also excellent in that department.

I have known John a long, long time and I think we'll always have a bit of a bond after Wembley in 1998. John has had his ups and downs, but two Challenge Cup final wins as head coach tells its own story. He has done an amazing job at Wakefield Trinity Wildcats on a very limited budget. When he took over in 2006 they seemed doomed to relegation, but they won four of their last six matches – including victory over Castleford in a final round shoot-out which sent Tigers down instead. I think that was one of the great coaching feats of the Super League era. John's ability to get teams up for one-off games is well known, but he also does a good job with youngsters and with players who have been cast off by other clubs and have a point to prove. He has a lot of passion about the game, he is a blokes' coach and he is very easy to get on with. I wouldn't like to go out for a beer with all the coaches I have played under, but I definitely would with John, especially if he was paying. A lot of coaches can't get away with doing that, but it has worked for John.

CHAPTER 19

AC-HELL

The day before I was due to send this book to the publisher we played Harlequins at Headingley in the Challenge Cup fifth round. It was May 20, 2011, the 560th game of my career and my 365th for Leeds.

With about five minutes left I went into a tackle, heard my right knee pop and my leg went numb. I collapsed in a heap and the medical staff came on. It was obvious I would not be able to continue, so they asked if I wanted a stretcher. My reply was something along the lines of "no thank you!"

A couple of the support staff grabbed an arm each and I hobbled off the pitch and straight into the medical room for an assessment with the team doctor Jon Greenwell. He wasn't certain what the problem was so my knee was strapped, I was given some crutches and I went home.

I was back in on the Saturday for some physio and more tests but the knee was too swollen for the medical staff to diagnose the extent of the damage, so I had a light massage to loosen the muscles in my calf and quad, the leg was strapped up again and I was sent back home. I spent the rest of Saturday and all Sunday with my leg up, icing it.

On the Sunday night I had to cut the strapping off as my calf and ankle had swollen up due to internal bleeding. They were really painful but my knee felt okay, other than the fact it was so stiff I had no movement.

On the Monday morning Kev Sinfield picked me up at home and drove me to Leeds for treatment, more tests and another massage of my calf and quad, but still no answers. By this stage I was beginning to fear the worst.

On Monday lunchtime I went for an MRI scan at a local clinic. Basically, that involves lying very still in a big tube for 25 minutes listening to music. I hadn't had much sleep the two previous nights because of the pain in my calf and ankle so I actually nodded off.

Once that was over and done with and they had woken me up I was sent to see a specialist in Bradford. He tested my knee, went for a look at the scan results and then came back with the bad news, which I was dreading but also expecting: "I am sorry but you have torn your acl, damaged some cartilage and chipped a bone. You won't be able to play again this season." He even produced a plastic knee to show me the areas which had snapped or broken, then he booked me in for an operation date in a couple of weeks' time, at the start of June, when the swelling had time to go down.

The operation seemed to be a success, at first. Initially, the specialist felt it had gone better than expected and the good news was I didn't need micro-fractures. In layman's terms, that means they take a hammer and chisel and crack all your bones to cause bleeding, which aids the recovery process. If they'd had to do that I would have been on crutches for at least six weeks.

I felt pretty good immediately after surgery, but about a week later it was obvious there was something wrong. I had been off my food, which is unusual and though I had a bit of range in my leg I wasn't feeling good. Vic went away on holiday for a few days and when she came back I started getting feverish. At night I was lying in bed in a cold sweat, I had a high temperature and I wasn't eating at all. The leg was aching and I felt absolutely terrible.

I came into Leeds on the Monday and told Meirion Jones, the head physio, how I was feeling. Without being too graphic, the wound was seeping a bit as well so Mei sent me straight to see a specialist, he admitted me to hospital immediately and they operated again that night. I was in hospital for four nights.

It turned out I'd picked up an infection. Not just an ordinary one, it was a superbug – Staphylococcus. I had to go on to antibiotics and after a few weeks they needed to up the dose because the infection had risen. It was a strong little bugger. I was taking two tablets every six hours, every day.

I felt a bit better for a while, but then went downhill again and on July 10, which was almost two months after I suffered the injury, I was back in hospital for my third operation. The final operation – so far at least – was at the end of July, to remove one of the pins that was placed in my knee when I had the initial surgery. There were two pins, top and bottom and the lower one was removed, because that was the source of the infection. That seemed to do the trick, though it didn't completely cure the problem. Fortunately, there has been no issue with the acl repair, that all went according to plan. As it turned out, the infection was worse than the injury itself – and that was the worst I have had in my professional career.

Acl are probably the three letters most dreaded by sportsmen or women. They stand for anterior cruciate ligament – which is basically the front of the knee. Tear your acl and it means major surgery and anything up to a year on the sidelines.

Sadly, it is a fairly common injury in rugby league and a few years ago it would have been career-ending. Nowadays, because surgery is so advanced, most players make a full recovery. Jamie Peacock and Danny McGuire both suffered acl injuries in 2010 and they returned a week apart the following Easter with no ill-effects. Kallum Watkins and Carl Ablett are two other players in the Leeds team who have been through it, but none of them was 35 when it happened.

That went through my mind as soon as I felt my knee go and it is one of the reasons why I refused the stretcher. If that was going to be my last time on a rugby pitch I wanted to leave it under my own steam.

I think I always knew my luck would run out at some point, but the timing could not have been much worse. Ironically, just a few days earlier I had been chatting with our coach Brian McDermott and he told me "you are bound to get broken at some time".

Up until my knee went I had managed to go through my whole career without a single serious injury. In fact, one of the questions I got asked most often, along with "Why did you punch BJ Mather?" and "Can I buy your shirt?" was: "Why don't you ever get injured?"

The truth was that I did. I have had my fair share of breaks, dislocations, tears and the like, but I had been fortunate never to be sidelined long-term. It was probably down to sheer luck, but the injuries I'd had previously were the sort that tend to clear up in a month or so. This one was very different, though fortunately not as bad as the damage JP and Danny Mags had suffered. They were out for nine and eight months, respectively. Kallum injured his knee in March and got back on the field – though not for the first team – in August. My injury was more similar to his.

However bad it is, anyone who suffers an acl tear has a long road ahead. First it's a case of waiting for the swelling to go down before the surgeon can operate. After that you need at least five months' recovery and re-hab before you can even think of playing again.

I will be 36 in April, 2012, so time is not on my side. It is without a doubt the biggest challenge I have faced in my career, but as soon as the specialist told me the bad news my first thought was that I am not going to let my career end this way. Realistically I don't know how the wound is going to heal but I am still in decent shape and my body usually recovers pretty well, so I am confident I am not going to have to hang my boots up just yet. I want to go out on my own terms and that is going to be a big part of my motivation as I go through the recovery period. Physically I am confident I will cope, though the mental side of it is in some ways a bigger challenge. Having never been through a long-term injury before, I am not sure of how to handle it. Being injured is the worst part of professional sport and I know I am incredibly lucky to have missed so few games, though I have had my fair share of setbacks.

My first serious injury was in my second season at Sheffield, 1995, when I hurt my back. It was a strange one, a muscle-spasm type problem, which just happened. I was having shooting pains when I ran, I didn't do anything particular to cause it and eventually it just cleared up by itself. I missed quite a few matches that season because of it but one day the pain simply disappeared. Now when we do long-distance running in pre-season, after I have not done anything physical for a while, I get backache but nothing as bad as it was that year.

My first Leeds injury was a broken left thumb. I did that on my old team-mate Waisale Sovatabua's head in a game at home to Wakefield in 2001. I went in to tackle him, got it wrong and cracked my thumb on his rock-hard noggin. I carried on playing but the fracture was diagnosed afterwards and I had to have surgery. The thumb was pinned and I had a cast on for a while, but I played the week after that came off. I missed three Super League matches – all of which we lost - and the Challenge Cup semi-final defeat against St Helens. Dean Lance got sacked during my spell on the sidelines, so I was injured for his last game and Daryl Powell's first as coach.

I dislocated a finger against Bradford, but I didn't miss any matches due to that one because it got put back in place during the game. I went into a tackle, got up at marker and couldn't feel my finger. I looked down and the finger on my right hand was pointing to the left. I got back into position and played on until the physio, Patrick Moran, could get on to deal with it. That sort of thing looks bad on TV but to be honest it's not actually that painful, because of the adrenaline. It hurts when you first do it but after that it goes numb. It feels strange but there's not really any pain.

I have done both thumbs. I dislocated and broke the right one playing for Great Britain in the second Test against Australia at Hull in 2001, when I tried to fend-off Luke Ricketson. The best thing about that one was I got to have gas and air for the pain. It's what they give women in labour. It's the only time that has happened and it gets rid of everything, it was fantastic. The team doctor, Chris Brookes, had a canister of gas and air in the changing room, so I was on that afterwards and then straight to hospital. Super League clubs have private health cover so there's no waiting around in casualty if you have to make a hospital visit. The Hull physio Keith Warner was there that day, so he made sure I was well looked after and I got bumped straight to the front of the queue. I carried on for a while in that game as well before I got taken off. I missed the third Test, which was a dead rubber, but it was post-season so I didn't have to sit out any club matches.

Cut heads have been a regular occurrence and, because I don't have hair, that can be quite spectacular. One time was against Wigan when I banged my head on Terry Newton's hip. It was only a little nick which needed three stitches but there was blood everywhere. It looked like a scene out of a Quentin Tarantino movie. Another time I banged my head on Scott Naylor's knee during a game against Bradford at Headingley. That was another gory one and I had ten stitches that time.

Up until the acl, the worst injury I'd had was the damaged ankle – ruptured ligaments to my tibia and fibula - against Bradford when big Joe Vagana fell on me in 2005, the week before the Challenge Cup final. I missed more games because of that one than any other, apart from the knee reconstruction, but that was partly my fault. If I hadn't played in the Cup final, which made it a lot worse, I would have been back sooner. You've read the full story about that one in an earlier chapter. That injury happened in August and, apart from 40 minutes in the Cup final, I didn't play again until the Tri-Nations two months later.

Another big one playing for Leeds was a torn calf. It was a 10 centimetre tear, though some of the papers said 10 inches, which would have been quite spectacular. I "defied medical science" by getting back from that one, according to the physios. I trained all week and it felt like I had a bit of cramp. I went to see Patrick, he sent me for a scan and that showed I had torn my calf. I only missed two games because of it, a Super League match at Huddersfield which we lost and a big home win over Halifax. Missing the Huddersfield game wasn't too much of a hardship as it turned out because the team got absolutely flogged in training as a punishment and I was glad to sit that out.

I have also had a long-term shoulder problem which needed surgery at the end of 2009 and still bothered me for most of the following year, resulting in another operation 12 months later. I had restricted movement in my arm and shoulder because of that, but fortunately it wasn't severe enough to keep me off the field and I'm pleased that people outside the camp didn't seem to realise I had a problem. It is always good if you are going to have surgery to get it done at the end of the season. Then, of course, you don't miss any matches, you get to duck out of a bit of pre-season and you don't have to play in the annual Boxing Day friendly.

Apart from that lot, until that May Cup tie I had got through my career pretty much unscathed, which I was quite proud of. I don't think there was a secret to that, it was largely down to good luck and my knee injury proved that doesn't last forever. I do look after myself, I am strong physically and I'm a good healer but it's hard to explain why I have been so fortunate for the majority of my career.

Various physios have told me they can't understand why I have never torn my hamstrings, which is a fairly common problem in professional sport and something that can keep players out of action for weeks or months. I have very short hamstrings – I can't touch my toes – and I have no flexibility at all. I am not the most agile of players and sometimes I struggle to put my socks on.

I very rarely miss training and that is something else I am proud of. Some players will sit a session out if they have a slight knock, but unless it's really serious I will try to get out there and get stuck in. Determination plays a big part. Because I have played so many games I hate missing out. That was the worst thing when the specialist told me I wouldn't play again for the rest of the 2011 season. We were half way through the year and the thought of missing so many matches was almost unbearable. The previous year I had been rested for a game away to Salford and I was devastated because that broke my ever-present record for the year. Having a week off did me the world of good but I was pretty upset about it at the time because until then I was the only player in the squad with a 100 per cent record.

Before the acl, most of the games I missed in Super League were due to being rested, suspended or on international duty, rather than having an injury. My longest lay-off during my time at Leeds was after the ankle injury in 2005 when I missed seven. I was ever-present in 2000 and 2006 and I played in all 16 before the knee injury in 2011. That's a total of 365 appearances out of the 393 Rhinos played between me joining them and my knee giving way, which I reckon is a record to be proud of.

One of the reasons rugby league is such a non-stop sport is the fact players are treated on the field while the game carries on, unless it's a bad injury and play has to be stopped. That usually only happens for a head wound or if someone needs stretchering off.

When the physio comes on the first thing he or she says is "are you all right?" It's as simple as that. Sometimes you'll call for the medic to come on but most of the time they'll spot there's a problem and run out to see what's what. You'll either wave away him or her – there's quite a lot of female medics in the sport - or ask for some treatment there and then. It's down to the player; if you feel you can play on you'll tell the physio to get lost. If it is serious they'll take over but most players don't like having to go off – and especially not on a stretcher.

In the 2011 season our young back-rower Chris Clarkson got hurt in a televised Challenge Cup game against Crusaders at Headingley. He and the medics thought he had broken an ankle and he was stretchered off with everyone in the stands clapping. It turned out to be just bad bruising and all the boys let him know what a wuss he was, being carried off with a stubbed toe.

Head injuries are something chances are never taken with. I've never been knocked out, but I've had the Bambi legs a few times. You get hit and start seeing stars, but that usually clears in a minute or two. Concussion is taken very seriously. If you get a serious bang to the noggin you get stood down for a couple of weeks and you have to pass a cog test before you're allowed back. That's a fairly simple sort of exercise, now done on computer, to check you've got all your marbles back. I know a few players who can't pass those tests even if they haven't had a bang to the head. Everyone does the test pre-season and then if you get a bang you do it again and they compare the results. In theory you shouldn't be allowed to play again until the marks match.

One of the worst injuries I have seen on a pitch was Chev Walker's when he was playing for Hull KR against us in the play-offs in 2009. That was doubly upsetting because he is a mate of mine and I was involved, though it was a total accident. It was another case of a player being a bit too brave for his own good and battling on when he really should have been sitting on the sidelines. Chev told me he'd had a small fracture for a few months; he was having injections to play, but he was in pain with it. It was bound to go at some time, but looking back on the tackle, if Chev hadn't been as strong as he is, it wouldn't have happened. He was carrying the ball and I was trying to put him to ground. He had my weight on his back, but being the beast he is he carried me for a few steps before his leg went. At first I didn't realise anything had happened but when we were on the ground I saw his foot flapping about and I could see the bone sticking out. I immediately waved to the physio and I tried to comfort Chev as best I could. Basically, all I told him was "Don't look at your leg!"

That was a nasty one because it was a compound fracture, with the skin being broken by the bone coming through. That's not uncommon and I've seen players – bystanders, not the one who's hurt - being sick on the pitch because of an injury like that. Chev is a fit, strong, tough guy, but he was out of action for 11 months and didn't play a first team game for Hull KR again, which tells you how bad that injury was. He came back at the start of the 2011 season after signing for Bradford. Ironically, his debut was against us, in Cardiff. I was chuffed to bits for him when he got back on the field, though he has had more bad luck with injuries since.

In hindsight, Chev shouldn't have been playing in the first place, but lots of guys carry on when they have quite bad injuries. Matt Adamson played in the 2005 Challenge Cup final exactly two weeks after he had suffered a fractured cheekbone in the semi-final. Kev Sinfield did a similar injury at the end of the 2009 campaign, but the club played down the extent of the damage. Officially they told everyone it was just badly bruised so he wouldn't get targeted. His face still hadn't healed fully when we won the Grand Final.

In rugby league there is a 'get up and get on with it' attitude to injury. It's probably a macho thing; nobody wants to show they are hurt. There's not much fabrication in our game, like players rolling around trying to waste time or win penalties, though the latter does happen sometimes. In our sport we just can't do that. If we get an injury, unless it's a broken leg, we are expected to get back into the defensive line and if we don't, we get absolutely slaughtered for it. It is just the way we are brought up; we enjoy the rough, tough aspect of it, the bangs on the head and the bumps and bruises. You do get a buzz from getting a wallop, then fighting the pain to get back into the defensive line and make the next tackle. It is a team sport and you never, ever want to let your mates down. If you are not back in the defensive line, someone else has to cover for you.

Footballers get a lot of criticism for their so-called play-acting and that's because the laws of the game allow them to take advantage of that sort of situation. For me it has spoiled the game because they've got to a situation where there's virtually no contact allowed in certain areas of the field.

Another bad injury was the one Paul Deacon suffered playing for Great Britain in the 2005 Tri-Nations against New Zealand at Huddersfield, which was a real shocker. He got hit high by my old adversary Nigel Vagana and suffered a badly broken nose and a fracture to the roof of his mouth. Chris Brookes, the GB team doctor, and the physios did a fantastic job and we were told later that if he hadn't had such prompt treatment he might have died.

Nobody likes to see a player hurt. It affects you more if it's a team-mate, but bad injuries to opponents can shake you up as well. There's always a feeling of 'that could have been me'. The Chev one certainly set me back a bit and I didn't have the greatest of games after it happened. He claims I was in a worse state than he was. I have heard him telling interviewers he was calming me down while he was getting treated on the field, which isn't true, but it was a bad situation.

Injuries like that don't happen very often, thank goodness. Acl ruptures are more common and they can be just as bad. Franny Cummins decided to retire after he did his acl - and he is younger than I am. Probably the saddest one of those we've had at Leeds was Jamie Peacock's. He got hurt two weeks before the 2010 Challenge Cup final, which was a devastating blow for him and for the team. Having been through it now, I can say it is one of those injuries which isn't that painful but the consequences are extremely serious. Stepping is a major part of the game, so when you suffer an injury like that it has a bit of a psychological effect as well, because you feel like you can't step or you are nervous about it going again.

Rugby league is a contact sport and everyone accepts injuries as part of the game. We all like to put big shots on, but nobody enjoys seeing a team mate or an opponent get hurt. In 2010 I got into bother for kicking Wigan's Joel Tomkins in the head during a Cup tie at Headingley. He was trying to prevent me from playing the ball and I lashed out. I got called up before the disciplinary but I didn't get a ban for it. As the game was going on I did apologise to him and I said sorry again the next time we played Wigan. I got in touch with Chev after his broken leg and he told me there were no hard feelings, which I really appreciated. I knew he wouldn't hold me responsible but it was nice to hear that from him anyway. It's not often injuries are intentional and hurting someone deliberately is actually quite hard to do.

I have heard people say the game is getting too fast and too physical now and that there are more injuries than there used to be. The game is played at a quicker pace than it was 15 years ago and full-time training has made players stronger, so the collisions are tougher. But I don't think any more players are getting hurt now than when I first started playing the game and from what players from the 1960s and 70s have told me, it is nothing like as brutal as it was then.

There is a lot of controversy over tackle techniques, people diving in at the knees and that sort of thing. We have picked up a lot of dead legs and knee and ankle injuries during the past couple of seasons, but I wouldn't say the injury toll is getting heavier. At Leeds we have been quite fortunate with injuries, certainly since Tony Smith's time as coach. We had a couple of years when we didn't seem to get any, but then in 2010 they all came at once and it was similar early in 2011. At one stage we didn't have any senior props available, with JP, Kylie Leuluai, Luke Burgess and Ryan Bailey all injured and Ben Cross suspended. Then they started returning and the outside-backs copped it. Ben Jones-Bishop suffered a dislocated shoulder, Lee Smith (hamstring) and Brett Delaney (foot) were also out, so Zak

Hardaker was recalled from a loan spell at Featherstone and he suffered a broken thumb in an accident at home. Then Kallum Watkins damaged some ligaments in a wrist and he was sidelined as well. It goes around in circles and a lot of it is down to luck, though what you do in training and in the gym can also have a bearing. At one stage we had more of an emphasis on weights than we do now and that seemed to lead to a lot of injury problems. In recent years the injuries we have had have tended to be non-preventable ones, like knee ligaments and breaks.

I definitely don't agree that the game is too fast and physical, in fact I actually believe the authorities are trying to protect players a bit too much at times. An example of that in a high-profile game was the 2010 Challenge Cup semi-final against St Helens. We were lucky to get a couple of penalties for alleged late tackles, one on Kevin Sinfield and the other on Rob Burrow. Both of those were harsh calls, though we didn't argue at the time. With the way the game is, you have to act on suspicion and as a player you accept that and you're ready for it. By that I mean if someone is running on to the ball you don't know whether he is going to receive a pass or not, so you've got to perhaps anticipate what you think is going to happen. If you don't you are maybe going to allow a try to be scored. Sometimes that might lead to a late challenge but I think that's part of the game.

I don't mind taking or giving the odd head-butt or jab in the ribs. I wouldn't want to see that eradicated from the game. If a tackle is a second or more late, fair enough, but if the ball has just been passed I reckon you have to accept that. I am prepared to cop a few cheap shots. As a player that's why you are in the game; if somebody sticks the nut on me in a tackle I don't mind it. Anyone who doesn't enjoy the contact aspect is in the wrong sport. I expect it and I will give it back. In my opinion it is an integral part of the code. It is what makes rugby league special to play, the enjoyable physicality of it. We aren't playing tennis. I love it when somebody tries to have a go at me, when you go into a scrum and the opposition second-row tries to butt you or whatever. That sort of thing still does go on, though probably not as much as it used to.

You create enemies on the field and it gives the game a bit of extra spice. If somebody does me, my attitude is 'fair play to you, you got me there, now I will try and get you back'. Having said that, there are taboos, things that I would not do: gouging for example. That is decidedly dodgy and I would never attack another player's eyes. Biting is the same, though that can happen by accident. In a tackle sometimes a hand or arm gets put across your mouth and it is a natural instinct to have a chomp. I am more one for using my head. I always get my head in close and often when I am tackled I will put a bit of a head butt on. That is something I have mastered over the years. In 2009 and 2010, when I was struggling with movement in my shoulder, I couldn't fend with my arm so I perfected the technique of doing it with my bonce. When we played Huddersfield a couple of years ago their centre Jamahl Lolesi tackled me and I head butted him as I was standing up. I played the ball and out of the corner of my eye I saw him fall and I managed to catch him before he hit the deck. That was one of those unacceptable things that I got away with. I butted him and then I made sure he was all right, which probably showed both sides of my character – the dirty aspect and my caring self.

As tough as Super League is, more injuries seem to occur in training than matches. In a game everything is 100 per cent, but in training you tend to hold back a bit and that's when injuries can happen. You can't be full-on all the time, but some players give more in training than others and when they are coming up against someone who is taking it easy, the consequences can be quite drastic. You do get spats between players and training ground bust-ups, but those are usually forgotten about quite quickly

In training we sometimes have opposed sessions, under-20s against the first team squad. That's always a bit hairy because the young kids are trying to impress and they'll come at you 100 miles an hour. They are trying to make an impact, while we are focusing more on the technical aspects than having to deal with an 18-year-old prop running full pelt at you. Sometimes you have to have a little word and tell them to calm down.

We used to have a wrestling coach and those sessions were always intense because of the macho caveman instinct. Everybody wanted to show how tough they were, so there was never any holding back. We are all competitive people and we'd all want to win a wrestle. Probably the most competitive bloke in the Leeds squad is Jamie Jones-Buchanan. He can't stand it if anyone beats him at anything and he'll do everything possible to win. He is not that big so he will find a different way to beat you. If you're having a wrestle and you are starting to get the upper hand, he'll stick his finger on your temple, try to bite you, grab you in the balls, whatever he can to steal the advantage.

Nick Scruton found that out in a wrestling session when he was coming back from a bad ankle injury. Nick spoke to Jonesy before they started and asked him not to go anywhere near the ankle. Jonesy agreed, but Scroots is a big, strong kid and he started getting the upper hand. Straight away Jonesy grabbed hold of Scroots' foot and started twisting it. I think Jonesy must have got picked on as a kid because he knows all the dirty tricks.

I approve of that. I have a saying 'if you're not cheating, you're not trying'. Of course I would never deliberately break the laws of the game (!) but you have to try and find a way to win, whether that's in training or a match. That might involve sticking a knee or your head in, putting the ball up your jumper or kicking a spare ball back into play, like Tommy Martyn did against us in the play-offs tie I mentioned earlier.

Rugby league isn't a dangerous profession in the way motor sport or horse riding, for example, are, but over the last couple of years we have had a couple of deaths, which have rocked everybody involved in the game. One was Adam Watene, the Wakefield Trinity Wildcats front-rower, who passed away after collapsing during a pre-season gym session in 2008. The following year a young kid called Leon Walker, who had been with Leeds' academy, died during a second team game for Wakefield at Celtic Crusaders.

Both incidents were absolutely tragic and for it to happen to the same club twice was especially shocking. I knew Adam to say hello to and, like everybody else in the sport, I was deeply moved by what happened. The way everyone in rugby league rallied around to support Adam's and Leon's families and the Wakefield club was very touching.

Adam was the same age as me when he died, so naturally it does make you think and it puts things into perspective. You never know how long you have got or what is around the corner. He was a tough, fit bloke and nobody would have forseen that. Because we look after ourselves, keep ourselves fit and get very good medical care, you would never expect something like that to happen.

In terms of playing the game I can honestly say what happened to Adam and Leon didn't change my attitude or approach at all. It's like crossing the road; that's dangerous but you just get on with it. I ride motorbikes and horses, which carries a lot more risk than playing or training for rugby league. Horse riding has the highest injury rate of any sport. You can't wrap yourself in cotton wool. My attitude is you have to live life to the full and do what you enjoy. I just hope that after my knee heals I will get that opportunity again.

CHAPTER 20

LEAVING LEEDS

Despite what people might think, I didn't leave Leeds Rhinos for more money. I left because they no longer wanted me - and after 13 seasons that hurt, a lot.

What came out at the time was not the full story. It wasn't a case of me not being offered a new deal, or turning one down; in fact my contract was terminated. Rhinos' management were happy for everyone to think I was out of contract at the end of 2011, but that wasn't true. At the time I left the club I actually had almost a year and a half remaining, until the autumn of 2012.

We had been in negotiations, but that was over an extension rather than a new deal. My position was that I was keen for two more years, in other words I wanted to play on at Leeds until the conclusion of the 2013 campaign.

I was always under the impression the club would be happy for me to do that, at least until Brian McDermott called me into a meeting in the spring of 2011. This was before I suffered the knee injury which ended my season and, as it turned out, my Rhinos career.

I played every game in the first part of the season, when everyone else was dropping like flies. At one stage we had no senior props available because of injuries or suspensions and then we copped a crisis in the outside-backs, with Ben Jones-Bishop dislocating his shoulder and Brent Webb, Ryan Hall, Kallum Watkins, Zak Hardaker and Brett Delaney all getting sidelined for one reason or another.

It wasn't easy playing with a different winger every week – which is what it seemed like – but I got my head down and I thought I was going along pretty well. Maybe not at the absolute top of my game, but still I was coming off the field most weeks thinking I had done a decent job.

Anyway, Brian Mac said he wanted a chat and what he came out with left me shocked. It amounted to this: "I am not sure about you for next year. At the moment, you are Leeds' No 1 centre, but we need to start thinking about bringing younger players on and finding the next Keith Senior."

He said he saw me being the third-choice centre in 2012 and a squad player. I couldn't believe what I was hearing, with half of the season still to go. How can you decide so far in advance what your team is going to be for the following year? I don't think it is right to fix positions before the season has begun, and therefore regardless of performances.

If Mac had said to me: "We are starting with a clean slate, we have got three or four centres and you are all fighting for positions on an even footing," fair enough, I would have been happy with that. He didn't tell me who I was third choice behind, but I guess it would have been Kallum Watkins and either Brett Delaney or Carl Ablett, two players who want to play in the back-row; Lee Smith, who wants to be a winger or full-back, or a new signing, who the club hadn't even brought in yet.

Had Brian told me they'd signed a centre to take my position because they were thinking about the future, I could have accepted that. But to hear I was falling behind players who weren't specialists in my position, didn't want to play there or hadn't been identified yet was hard to take. I can only assume they had been in negotiations with a centre for a while.

A few days after that conversation, Brian came back to me and apologised, as he felt what he had said might have seemed a bit insulting. It did feel that and I don't know how he could have got what he needed to say so wrong, though I appreciated the apology. Anyway, the gist was I was no longer top dog.

I could have stayed with the club, taken the money and played a bit part as and when they needed me, but that's not my style. I am not going to stay where I am not wanted, never have done and never will. I was 35 at the time they dropped that bombshell, but I still felt I had a lot to offer and if it wasn't going to be at Leeds then I would carry on with someone else.

That was not my first choice. After so long as a Rhino I had always assumed I would finish my career at Leeds, but I wasn't going to retire just because Brian Mac felt I was no longer up to the job; when I hang up my boots I want it to be on my terms.

Rhinos' management said I was free to look for somewhere else and I was grateful to them for that. Gary Hetherington has always said he would look after my best interests and he agreed to terminate my contract so I could get on with my career and my life. But I want to make it clear it wasn't a matter of my deal coming to an end. I was released.

It certainly is not how I wanted my Rhinos career to finish. We parted on reasonable terms, but I would be lying if I said there were no hard feelings at all. I was massively disappointed with the way I was treated after being there so long and I was pleased I wasn't the only one who felt that way.

A lot of well-wishers got in touch to say they were sorry I was leaving.

One or two even said they were in tears at the news, which was quite touching. Kevin Sinfield told Brian he was making a big mistake, so it was good to have the full support of the captain, as well as some of the other players. But the coach is in charge, it's what he thinks that matters and there was nothing I could do about that.

I wasn't being precious about it and I can understand them wanting to look to the future and bring young players through. I have no problem with that, but I reckon it has to be done on form. One thing Brian said to me, which turned out to be quite prophetic, was that one day my body was going to break.

He got that right because my acl went a few weeks later, but Jamie Peacock is only a year and a half younger than me and he came back from a similar injury with no ill-effects or loss of form. Ironically, the day after the club announced I was leaving they confirmed that JP had signed a new one-year contract, which was a good thing and I was pleased about that. But Brian was quoted as saying age was just a number and it had no bearing on JP's ability to do his job. The reason they let me go was because I was too old, so there was some double standards there.

Do I resent what happened? Actually, yes I do. I want to make it clear I like Brian as a person, I liked him when I played against him and I like him as a coach, but I think he needs to get better at his man-management. Sometimes there's a thin line between being brutally honest and downright insulting. I think Brian pushed those boundaries a bit too far at times and that did cause some disruption in the camp. I know there were Rhinos players who were upset by what he had said to them.

I wasn't the only player to leave mid-way through the season. A couple of weeks before they got shut of me Ben Cross and Luke Burgess were both released. Ben was an Aussie prop, brought in from Newcastle Knights after JP got his knee injury. It was pretty obvious from the start that Brian didn't rate him. He struggled to hold down a place, lost it altogether and was then told he wasn't in Mac's plans, even though he had a year and a half left on his contract. He was paid-off and then signed for two different clubs on the same day, which must be unique. He joined Wigan until the end of the season and agreed a deal with Widnes Vikings for 2012, so he fell on his feet. Cross might even have played in the Challenge Cup final against Leeds, which would have been ironic, but he broke an arm playing for Wigan a couple of weeks before Wembley and missed out.

What happened to Biff Burgess was disappointing. He was offered a contract by Leeds and wanted to stay, but felt he was worth a bit more than was on the table. The club weren't willing to budge on that and it all went sour. Biff got dropped and he believed that was because he wouldn't sign his new deal. He asked for a release so he could go and join his brothers Sam and George in Australia.

At first Gary said he could go on loan to another Super League club until his contract expired at the end of the season. There were plenty of clubs interested, but Biff didn't want to do that and after he made it clear he would stay at Leeds and kick his heels on the sidelines until the end of the year if necessary, they did the right thing and released him. He signed for South Sydney straight away and made his NRL debut a week after he arrived Down Under, so it worked out well for him, but I think with a bit more effort on the club's part he might have stayed. The club made out he wanted to go to Australia come what may, but that wasn't true. He would have remained at Leeds if they had been willing to improve their offer.

With that in mind, I wanted to make it fully clear when my departure was announced that I wasn't looking to leave, but what had happened made it impossible, in my eyes, for me to stay. Once it was obvious I had no future at Leeds I asked my agent to spread the word and I was flattered by the amount of interest shown. Hull KR were keen to talk to me and I also spoke to John Kear, at Wakefield. It would have been good to work with John again, but at that stage he had his hands tied. The problem was he didn't know whether Wildcats would be in Super League the following year, or even if he would still be working there, as he was out of contract at the end of the season. Wakefield were everybody's favourites to lose their Super League licence, so it wouldn't have made a lot of sense to sign there on a top-flight contract and then have to start looking all over again a few weeks later, if they had their elite status taken away. Little did I know...

I didn't get as far as actually negotiating with anyone in Super League, or with a couple of French rugby union clubs who put some feelers out to see if I would be willing to go over there. I would have followed up the foreign interest, but I got word that Crusaders were keen on me and right from the start that seemed like the right option. For one thing they were coached by Iestyn Harris, someone I knew well from our days playing together for Leeds and Great Britain. I also felt I could do some good there and, being totally honest, I liked the idea of being a big fish in a small pond.

Iestyn got in touch with my agent who asked me if it was okay to pass my phone number on. He gave me a ring and we met at Hartshead Moor services on the M62, near Huddersfield. That wasn't the most discreet of locations, but we had a chat for a couple of hours and he sold me on the idea of going to Wrexham and being part of what he was trying to achieve there.

I wanted to go somewhere I could make a difference and Crusaders were ideal in that regard. At the time I signed they were bottom of the table and had won only four of their 20 league games that season. I saw it as a massive challenge to go to a club like that, but I have played the game long enough to know I could make an impact there.

Iestyn didn't try and feed me any bullshit. He wasn't promising Grand Final victories or anything like that; he admitted it was going to be a tough couple of seasons and there was a lot of work to do in terms of changing the mentality and the culture of the place. On the day my signing was announced, July 7, the club suspended seven players – including my old mucker Jordan Tansey – for a breach of discipline.

Iestyn wasn't talking about even getting into the top-eight in my first season there, though he wanted us to be challenging around the fringes. The plan was to set some foundations and then go for it in 2013, which I thought was realistic.

I was aware a lot of people felt Crusaders' licence should not be renewed in 2011: they were struggling on the pitch, crowds were low and they had been in administration the previous winter. The RFL had invested a lot in the Welsh franchise and obviously they did not want to see that go to waste, so I was pretty confident they would get another three years.

As far as I could tell from the little time I spent there and from what people connected with the club told me, there was a lot of potential in Wrexham. They had a good ground and excellent facilities. A new gym was being built; I spoke to the physio and conditioner before I signed – which is very important when you get to my age - and was highly impressed with them. Also, the club got on well with the council, which seemed like a handy safety net.

It seemed to me the club had a lot of ambition and it was the job of the players and coaching staff to make that a reality. The way I went into it, I reckoned if I could help do that, it would be just as satisfying as my Grand Final wins with Leeds.

I think it's fair to say my decision to join Crusaders wasn't universally welcomed by the Welsh fans. I soon had people Tweeting me about something I was quoted as saying in the national press at the start of the 2010 season.

We played Crusaders in our first match that year, which was their debut in Wrexham after moving from Bridgend and dropping the Celtic prefix from their name. As defending champions we were big news and the fact it was the first Super League game played at the Racecourse Ground created a lot of interest in the media.

I was asked what I thought about the move to Wrexham and told pressmen I believed it was a backwards step and that they should not have been allowed in the competition, playing at their new base. You always need to be careful what you reveal to the press, because what you say can get twisted or blown out of all proportion. That was one example, but I admit I did object to the idea of the club relocating from south Wales to the north, around half an hour's drive from established clubs like Warrington and Widnes. Wrexham is exactly the same distance from my house, near Huddersfield, as Hull KR's ground. That is not expanding rugby league, which is what Crusaders should have been all about. I wasn't saying Crusaders should be chucked out of Super League, but I did feel the RFL ought to have done more to keep the club in Bridgend. A lot of time, money and effort was put into building a club in south Wales and at the first sign of trouble they were allowed to up sticks and move to within 30 miles of a traditional club, Widnes Vikings, who weren't at that time deemed good enough to be in the competition. I didn't think that was right, I still don't and in fact, after what happened in July, 2011, I was proved right. After the comments of a year before, I had a lot of Crusaders fans telling me I needed to play out of my skin for them to make amends. I wish I had got chance to do that.

Signing for Crusaders was not just a challenge on the field. Vic and I planned to move to north Wales and that was a big deal for someone who has lived in Yorkshire his entire life. We were going to get tenants into our place and were set to rent somewhere over there. That proves I wasn't going into the Welsh venture half-heartedly. It was definitely not a long-term thing - as a die-hard Yorkshireman the White Rose county is in my blood and I couldn't see myself staying in Wales permanently – but I was going to give it everything I had.

All this is in the past tense, because my big move never happened. Even now the dust has settled, I can't quite believe what went on and I am still very, very angry about it. On July 26, 2011, the RFL announced which clubs were to receive a Super League licence for the next three years.

The announcement was made at Old Trafford and broadcast live on Sky

Sports News. I watched it at home on TV and I honestly had no warning of the bombshell that Richard Lewis, the sport's chairman, was going to drop.

In alphabetical order, he announced which clubs had received A grade licences, then the B grade ones. When he came to the C grade, he announced Castleford Tigers, then Harlequins. I may not be the most academic of blokes, but I know my alphabet and Cr comes after Ca. Salford, Wakefield and Widnes were all in, but no mention of Crusaders.

Lewis went on to announce that Crusaders had decided to withdraw their application. Apparently they felt their short and medium term future wasn't strong. Well, they didn't seem to feel that when they signed me on a two-year deal three weeks earlier, or when other players, Gareth Thomas for instance, were given contract extensions.

Anyone who follows me on Twitter will know exactly what I thought about that. I was furious and I made that quite clear, in some fairly strong language. What I said was (with the expletives included): "Crusaders have just f***** me over what a b****** joke, excuse my language I'm absolutely furious".

That was in the heat of the moment and I regret the words I used, though not the sentiments I was expressing. I did later apologise for what the national media described as a "rant". I got a lot of coverage after the announcement and Sky Sports News had a camera crew on my doorstep very quickly.

I wasn't so much angry about the club's decision, though they must have known all was not well when they signed me. What really upset me was the fact there was no advanced notice, no warning, no phone call. Surely the club owed it to me – and especially to the guys who were actually playing for them at the time - to give us a heads-up?

To add insult to injury, weeks after the licence announcement I still hadn't had any contact from Crusaders advising me that my contract was actually terminated. I have taken legal advice and proceedings may well follow.

Frustrating and upsetting as it was, I was actually better off than the guys who were already on the books and who had families to support, cars to fund and mortgages to pay. They were dropped right in it and I really felt for them. The RFL stepped in to grant the overseas players among them special dispensation so they didn't count on the quota and most of them found new clubs pretty quickly. That was great for them, but what about the rest of us, the English guys who were looking for a gig somewhere? It meant the market was suddenly flooded with cheap Aussie/Kiwi labour and that messed it up for home-grown players. Typical RFL, well-meaning, but ill-thought out.

Anyway, as far as I am concerned what is done is done. I'd had a second contract terminated inside a month and I was back on the jobs market. I spoke to John Kear fairly soon after the announcement and a move to Wakefield was back on the agenda, but four days later Wildcats announced his contract wouldn't be renewed at the end of the season. They were still keen on me, as were a few other clubs, but at the time of writing nothing has been decided and my future is still up in the air.

There was even a bit of contact with the Rhinos and whatever happens between now and the end of my playing career, I would like to return to Leeds at some stage. Gary said publicly when I left I would be a "friend of the club for life" and that maybe there would be a position for me on the Rhinos' backroom staff in the future. He has told me that privately as well, which was good to hear. He has always insisted he will look after my best interests, at least he did before he read this book!

Gary is a businessman and if he sees a way of using me to help Leeds Rhinos and promote the club, he will do that. Without being big-headed, I am one of the most recognisable players in Super League – and that hit home to me in the week the club announced I was leaving.

I thought it might make a line or two in the papers, but it was the main sports story in the Yorkshire Evening Post, all the daily papers covered the news and when I turned up for lunch with the players that afternoon Sky and ITV were both waiting to interview me. It was an item on Sky Sports News all day, which was flattering and a bit overwhelming.

Leeds can use that fame, or notoriety, in some capacity in a couple of years' time when I hang up my boots and – while I don't know what else might crop up in the meantime – I would be happy to go back.

As I have said, I was disappointed and a bit bitter about the way I left the club. At the time of writing that is still fresh and the hurt is quite strong. I am still getting used to being a "former Leeds Rhinos player" and it was quite a shock when I read that in the press for the first time.

But I was at Leeds for 13 seasons and the club was a massive part of me. I have made lasting friends and memories which will stay with me forever. I will give 100 per cent to which ever club I finish my playing career with and in whatever I do in the future, but part of me will always be a Rhino.

CHAPTER 21
SENIOR CITIZEN

For as long as I have been involved in the game, people have been saying rugby league is dying – and that's not just the sport's enemies. If you read the letters pages in the trade press they are dominated by supposed fans moaning about everything that's allegedly wrong with the code. Well I disagree. I think rugby league has a healthy future and I expect the game to get bigger and better over the next few years.

The switch to summer, back in 1996, was the best thing rugby league has ever done. It is better for the fans and players and it has allowed more people to play the game. If you are keen enough you can play union in the winter and league when summer comes round. That's not really possible at the very top level but plenty of players do it lower down the pecking order.

Where we lead, the other code tends to follow and I expect one day union will see the light and switch seasons. But league is much more suited to summer than union: the 13-a-side version is a faster, top of the ground game, whereas union is more tactical and muddy conditions sometimes suit their forward-dominated battles.

Super League is a big improvement on the old first division; it is a strong competition and it is getting closer every year. A few years ago there were only four teams, Leeds, Saints, Wigan and Bradford, in with a realistic chance of winning silverware. Now Huddersfield and Warrington have joined that list and Hull KR and Hull aren't far off. Castleford have made big strides as well and Catalan finished third a few seasons ago.

There are now more people playing the game, it is strong in the universities and at amateur level and the Rugby League Conference has more than 100 teams, based all over the country. Good young players are coming through all the time and there is still a real passion for the sport in areas like Yorkshire, Lancashire and Cumbria. Rugby league has had a lot thrown at it over the last 100 years or more, yet it has always come back punching and I don't see that changing.

Where we do struggle is at international level. England play, at most, four or five games per year – a mid-season Test and the Four Nations in the autumn. That is just not enough. Union is thriving because of its international set-up. It is a global game and league is only really strong in three countries, Australia, New Zealand and England – or four if you count

Papua New Guinea where it is the national sport.

I have been to America four times with the Rhinos and England and there are league teams up and running in the States, but the sport is virtually unknown and the standard isn't high. Their national team would struggle to compete in Co-op Championship One. It's a similar situation in Ireland and Scotland and maybe even France. Rugby league is beginning to take off in places like Jamaica, Eastern Europe and the Middle East, but there is still a long, long way to go before we have a world-wide sport.

We have to find a way of making those nations stronger because at the moment if you are an up and coming rugby player in one of those countries there's not much incentive to play league. At international level you could play union a dozen or so times each year in front of 70,000 people, or league on a couple of occasions with 4-500 watching. It's a no-brainer.

That is something which needs to change, though obviously that's easier said than done. Winning the 2003 World Cup probably set the England union boys up for life financially and they became household names. If we had won our version in 2008 we would have got about £12,000, we wouldn't have been on the Honours List and the national media would have done their best to ignore the achievement.

That's the difference. With Leeds Carnegie being based at Kirkstall, players from both codes mix and we chat about each other's sport; you always want to know how much the other lot are earning. The salary cap in the Aviva Premiership is £4m and ours is £1.6m. No wonder Bath can come along and poach Kyle Eastmond from St Helens. The RFU give their clubs a massive hand-out because they've got more cash than they know what to do with. In those terms the codes are worlds apart.

I started in union but I have no regrets at all about choosing league as my game. When you are a kid, rugby is rugby; you just like running with the ball and tackling and things like game plans and structures don't matter. I wasn't really aware of the difference between the two codes, I just enjoyed being involved, and I would probably have stayed in union if my team had continued. That said, I didn't have much of an impact. I never got any sort of representative recognition and I don't think I would have made a good living from the sport, which I have in league.

I don't like to compare which is the toughest or the better of the two codes. I can honestly see merits in both games and the Carnegie boys are a good set of lads but, size-wise as much as anything else, I could probably only play in the centre in union and I honestly think I would get a little bit bored. As a back, I don't think the work-rate and the involvement would keep me as interested as it does in league and I'm definitely not big enough to play in the pack.

In union I would probably be an inside centre, going on to the crash ball, but I'd be looking at five hit-ups per game and if I did five tackles I would be having a busy day. In league you make 15-20 hit-ups and 20 to 30 tackles every game. You are constantly involved and that's what I enjoy, rather than waiting for the game to unfold and come to me.

Some critics say league is more predictable than union because of the five drives and a kick element. I don't agree with that. The ball is in play more in league and there's more emphasis on handling and less on kicking. That's because possession isn't so crucial. In league you hand the ball over after every six tackles, whereas in union the priority is keeping hold of it at all costs. There's more of an opportunity to take risks in league and to attack.

We spend a lot of time looking at ways of creating one-on-ones, whereas in union that is frowned upon because there's a chance of losing the ball. I believe there is more flair and excitement in league: the sort of tries Chris Ashton has captured the headlines for scoring in union are seen every game in Super League – sometimes by prop-forwards.

League keeps evolving and the game is a lot different now to when I started. In those days, for instance, we didn't have video referees or 40-20 kicks, there were only two substitutes, we didn't have Grand Finals to decide the title and the game was winter-based.

Most of the changes have worked and the game is better for them. The 40-20 rule – which means if you kick from your 40 into touch in the opposition's 20-metre area you get the put-in at the subsequent scrum – is superb because it promotes attacking skills.

The biggest issue in the game at the moment is the ruck, or play-the-ball. The rules seem to keep changing and the authorities can't decide whether they want to speed things up or slow them down. That is frustrating for coaches, players and fans and confusing for referees. There's a lot of inconsistency in refs' interpretation of what is a fast play-the-ball and I think that's something which needs to be resolved.

There are at least two rule changes I would like to bring in. Firstly, I think ball steals should be allowed. At the moment you can't rip the ball away from an attacker if you have more than one defender in the tackle, but that leads to a lot of confusion. It is tough for referees to tell whether the ball has been stolen or just dropped. You see a lot of penalties awarded against the defending side when it has been a loose carry by the attacker. The emphasis should be put back on the ball-carrier and on respecting possession. If you lose the ball that should be your problem.

I also think the rule-makers could look at just allowing two defenders in a tackle. That would be a massive change and it would alter the way the game is played, but I believe it would lead to more open rugby. Again, it would be a hard concept to referee and maybe we should be taking decisions away from match officials, rather than giving them more to think about, but it would speed the game up. I think at the moment there is too much stress placed on the wrestle and on getting players into the tackle. It all stems from how well Melbourne Storm played against us in the 2010 World Club Challenge. Full credit to them, they pushed the rules to the limit and they did a job on us, but they didn't win too many admirers for the way they played.

Wigan won that year's Super League by playing a similar way, which isn't surprising considering their coach Michael Maguire joined them from Melbourne. Their success has turned Super League into a defence-oriented game, which I don't think is particularly exciting to watch. That's probably why we are moving back towards faster play-the-balls. It is interesting how the way the game is played has changed every few years. When Super League started, teams weren't that fit because only Wigan were used to being full-time.

Bradford were a powerful team and they had size everywhere. Their wingers were as big as props and they dominated the competition for a while. Then things began evolving and the hardest-working team became the most successful, which was us. When Tony Smith came to Leeds he instilled a very strong work-ethic and that worked. We became dominant for a period. Now everybody is a hard-working team and that alone won't win you a game.

Therefore you have to look at other ways of creating openings, by being ball-players and forging opportunities through vision and skill, rather than using size or hard work. Creative teams are coming back into fashion.

Flair has always been there, in the shape of players like Danny McGuire or Kyle Eastmond, but their game is based more on individual skills, rather than making chances for the team. Danny and Kyle are both great players and they will score tries out of nothing, but their style isn't based on putting team-mates through a gap or creating an opening for someone else.

People like Andrew Johns or Brett Kimmorley, two great Aussie pivots, will create space in the defence by the way they take the ball to the line.

That is one reason we are still lagging behind the Aussies at Test level. We don't have the half-backs to organise a team and implement a game plan.

Switching Sam Tomkins from stand-off to full-back has been a great move because it gives him a free role. The Wigan youngster is a magnificent individual talent and at full-back he can do what he wants. At stand-off he has to play within a structure and he finds that harder.

Another big change in recent years has been the expansion of the sport into Wales and France. Catalan Dragons have made a much better stab at Super League than Paris did at the dawn of the competition all those years ago. That's because the south of France is a rugby league heartland; they still rely heavily on overseas players, but they also have some of their own talent coming through and the foundations were in place before they started.

Perpignan is a nice city, it's close to the coast and the weather's usually good. When you go there for a match you can tell there is a game on as you wander around the place. For instance, the waiters in the bars and restaurants dress up in replica shirts of whoever the visitors are, which adds to the atmosphere. It is a good place to go for a weekend and I think their presence has enhanced the competition.

Despite what happened with my ill-fated move to Crusaders, I hope rugby league does take off in Wales. The sport can only benefit if that is the case. It goes back to the international game, if more French and Welsh rugby league players are coming through, the code is going to be stronger for that. There is a long way to go, but Welsh players like Elliot Kear and Rhys Evans are beginning to break through into Super League and make an impact. Crusaders are hoping to carry on in the Championship and I hope the young, local player route is the one they go down in the future. When you have got 15, 16 or 17 Aussies or Kiwis in the squad it defeats the object of having a club in a so-called development area. It may be a quick-fix, but it isn't a long-term one.

Harlequins haven't really taken off as a Super League club but there's a lot of good work being done in London development-wise and again local youngsters are starting to come through, people like Tony Clubb and Louie McCarthy-Scarsbrook. The professional game hasn't exactly been a success in the capital but it definitely isn't a failure. Fulham/Crusaders/Broncos/ Harlequins have survived for a long time against all the odds and the people involved down there are as committed to the game as anyone you'll meet inside the M62 corridor.

We definitely need a club in the capital and as far as I am concerned, the more Londoners who play the game the better. If we're going to compete with the Aussies we need to widen our player-base. Rhinos have a link with the south west, which is a big union area, and if we can unearth some promising playing talent down there it will be good for the game as a whole.

Cumbria should be the next venue for a Super League club. Rhinos have been there on pre-season camps a couple of times and it really is a rugby league heartland with a passionate fan base and loads of amateur clubs. There are three semi-professional clubs there, Barrow, Whitehaven and Workington, but the problem is they all hate each other – particularly the latter two, who are based just a few miles apart. Back at the start of the summer era there was a plan to merge the Cumbrian clubs into one Super League franchise, but that got shouted down. I think a new Super League outfit there would be a huge success, with Barrow, Whitehaven and Workington all continuing as feeder clubs in the lower divisions. The problem would be finding somewhere to base the top-flight set-up and I don't think there's the will to make that happen.

Rugby league has a lot of work to do, but – whatever the critics might claim – it definitely isn't dying. As for my own future, I am still keen to play on for two more years, despite the Crusaders fiasco. I will have to see how my knee recovers and what offers come along, but I am confident I've got a couple more good seasons in the tank, which will take me up to the age of 37. What happens after that remains to be seen, but if I am still feeling good I may well play on. Steve Menzies was outstanding for Catalan in 2011 at the age of 37 and has decided to go round for at least one more year, so there's no reason why I can't do the same.

You are a long time retired and former players tell me there's nothing like the buzz you get from playing the game, even if you stay involved as a coach or administrator. As long as I can still make a positive contribution I will carry on, though I am not sure I would do that if I couldn't get a gig at a Super League club.

I am passionate about rugby and I will always give 100 per cent, but after such a successful career, I just can't see myself playing in a lower division team in front of crowds of a few hundred. I don't know if that sounds arrogant; it isn't meant to be, it's just the way I am. I wouldn't drop a division just to carry on playing.

I am not a one-club man like Kev Sinfield is. I have seen a lot of players being cast to the wayside after showing a lot of loyalty themselves, but Gary Hetherington has always looked after me, we have a good relationship and – as I mentioned in the previous chapter – I would like to work with him again when I do hang up my boots.

Long-term, coaching may well be my next career move, though not at first team level. I have had a bit of experience at that in the amateur game and, even that low down the chain, it's a thankless task. It is a ruthless industry and I can do without the hassle. Coaches can't win; at some stage, no matter how good they are, things are going to go wrong and they'll get the bullet. I have seen the effect the pressure has had on some of my coaches – in fact I have probably caused some of it – and it is not something I would do for a gold pig.

You get a lot of aggro from fans and the media, who will be your friend if things are going well but turn on you when they aren't. I don't need to get involved with that and I think I would get a lot more satisfaction helping to bring through the next generation of players.

If I do go into coaching it will probably be at junior or youth level. Barrie McDermott's job as Rhinos' head of youth would be ideal! He has got too many fingers in too many pies at the moment – media work, his job at Leeds, after dinner speaking and so on – so I think he needs to focus on one job, not 17. I would be happy to take the Leeds role off his hands.

I had a bit of a mentoring role at Leeds and that's something I enjoy. I have made a lot of mistakes in my time – on and off the field – so I feel qualified to speak about what to do and what not to. I think taking someone as a 15 or 16-year-old, helping him through the early stages of his career and seeing him make his debut in the first team would give me a lot of satisfaction.

During my final few years at Leeds I was involved with the under-15s on a voluntary basis and that is another aspect I really enjoy. Keeping training interesting for kids is a big challenge, because there are a lot of distractions at that age; most of them can also play football or cricket and they also have an interest in members of the opposite sex.

Rugby-wise, the key is to get them young, get them interested and keep them interested. That's especially the case with the under-15s, who are on the scholarship scheme but haven't yet been signed by the club. They will be free to move on when they turn 16, so it is important to make training fun for them and to show them that Leeds is the right place for their future development. That is a really challenging role and one I enjoyed.

There are a lot of talented young players out there but I am surprised at how naïve some of them are in terms of their rugby league education. When they come into the scholarship system at Leeds, the coaches are having to teach them the basics of the game, which should be second nature by the time they get to age 15 or 16. Coaching needs to be better at amateur and junior level, so when the kids get to a professional club the coaches there just need to apply a bit of polish.

The amateur game doesn't really act as a feeder for the professional ranks. There's too much emphasis on the social side of things which, to be fair, is why I coached at that level. I did it to have a bit of a laugh and to enjoy a few beers and a night out with the lads. And that was in a good standard of rugby league at St Joseph's.

I know some amateur clubs resent it when their best young players get signed up by Super League or Championship teams, which is a ridiculous attitude. Their job should be to help kids go as far as they can in the game. It ought to be a matter of pride for any amateur club if one of their youngsters goes on to Super League or international level and, as often as not, the ones who don't make it go back to their old side either to play or coach.

Fortunately not all clubs have that attitude. East Leeds, for example, are as proud as punch at the success Danny McGuire and Richard Mathers have enjoyed and it's the same at Stanningley, where Jamie Jones-Buchanan and Jamie Peacock came from.

As I say, there's no shortage of ability knocking around and I think some of the youngsters I have seen coming into the system at Leeds could go on to make a big future for themselves. Here's a couple of names of kids you won't have heard of, but who I think could do well in the next few years: George Milton and Elliott Minchella.

George is a quiet kid, one of those who puts his head down and gets on with it. He plays prop in Leeds' under-15s, but I see him more as a back-rower, though that depends on how he fills out and grows. He has great skill. Defensively he is solid and workmanlike and on attack he has a good offload and a fine passing game. I like him as an all-round player.

Elliott is a kid from Bradford with great potential. He has all the attributes to be a great loose-forward. He just has to make sure his attitude is right. As I have already mentioned, for me that is the biggest factor. I have seen so many players with terrific skill fall by the wayside because they didn't have the heart or the brains to go all the way.

Apart from coaching, something else I have thought about doing is player-management. Rugby league doesn't have a big attraction for sponsors and while most of the top stars have an agent, there's not really any player-management out there.

You might find someone who can get you a boot deal but there's nobody to get the players the recognition they deserve and to help them take advantage of the position they are in. I think our top stars deserve far more credit than they get. If Danny McGuire played rugby union he would be a household name. As a rugby player he has got far more ability than just about anybody I can think of in the 15-a-side code.

He would be on adverts, in lifestyle magazines and a regular on Question of Sport. But in rugby league there's nothing. Danny is well-known in Leeds but if he walked down the street in London, Birmingham or Newcastle, nobody would recognise him. That's a shame.

Chris Ashton would probably have been a big success if he had stayed in league, but he wouldn't have got the attention or the money he now receives in union. There's a lot of concern in league about players defecting to the other code, but I can understand why they do it. Because union is so strong internationally – the Six Nations and the World Cup are a licence to print money – the pay is a lot better. There's also an opportunity to play in front of bigger crowds if you get to Test level and to become much better known. Lee Smith and Kris Smith – no relation – are exceptions, but I can't think of many league players who have dated famous actresses or pop stars and, as far as I know, nobody in our game is married to royalty.

Union players have a far higher profile, even if their skills aren't as good. It should not be like that: Rhinos average well into five figures for home games, the crowds in the sport generally match what you get in union's Premiership and the lower divisions in the Football League, and Super League is one of the most-watched sports on Sky.

Players deserve more recognition and I would like to help them get that. It needs somebody to help with the players' image and to take advantage of what they have got. It is a short career, it could end at any minute if you get a bad injury and you need to make the most of it while you can.

Since I got into horse riding, Vic has been my negotiator. She could sell sand in a desert. She has helped me get free gear and she's blagged us top corporate tickets for the Horse of the Year Show. I have learned off a master and that has shown me that there are avenues out there for players to take, if they get the right advice.

Another part of player-management is negotiating contracts and I reckon I would be pretty good at that. I have certainly had enough practice over the years and if you can get money out of Gary Hetherington you can bargain with anyone.

I remember when I was young, negotiating with Gary. What an

experience that was: you would go into the meeting believing 'I am quite a good player' and you'd come out thinking 'I must be the worst player in the world, why is he even offering me a contract? I should be paying him.'

So I can understand why players need agents at a young age. I have got wiser over the years and as you get older it is something you pick up. You learn what pay structures are, what other people are earning and you get an idea of what you are really worth. Obviously you ask for more than that but you realise what a realistic offer is.

To be an agent all you need is a bit of front and contacts at all the clubs. The player sells himself really, with the work he does on the field. If you have a superb player, negotiations are easy. The challenging aspect is representing the young kids coming through the ranks.

A lot of former players dabble in media work but I am not sure that would suit me. The media, not just in rugby league but generally, are very negative in this country. I suppose it is a case of bad news sells, so the papers and TV aren't really interested in happy stories; they want to know about the rubbish that happens in people's lives. I don't think it is particularly the fault of the reporters, most of them anyway; it is just human nature and a reflection of society. People want to read and hear about others' misery, especially if it involves a so-called celebrity or someone who is well-known.

In football, players are often kept at arm's length from the media, but that isn't the case in rugby league, which needs all the publicity it can get. Dealing with the press boys, radio or TV is part of the job. I haven't had any training in how to handle being interviewed and I think that's something the RFL should make sure young players are aware of. I seem to get interviewed more than most, which I suppose is a compliment in a lot of ways, and overall the rugby league journalists have been pretty fair to me; it is the news reporters who cause the problems.

Because rugby league is a small world we are quite lucky in that there's a fairly limited corps of press men, who we see on a regular basis. I probably know all of the national rugby league press boys – and a few girls – and they are aware that if they print something I don't like, I'll take it up with them the next time we meet. Generally – and I'm not just saying this because one of them helped me write this book – you get treated pretty well by the local media. They aren't looking for scandal as much as the nationals and they tend to work with us on an even closer basis, so it's not in their interests to start making stuff up. If they did we would stop talking to them.

Dealing with the media does get a bit tedious at times, because you tend to get asked the same questions over and over again. On the other hand you have to be careful about what you say because words can get twisted sometimes, so the answers you give aren't always very interesting. When someone like me comes out of the changing rooms and starts having a pop at the referee, or the pitch or the state of the game in Wales, you can see the press rubbing their hands together because I have just made their evening. It is no good saying something and regretting it later, because by then it will be too late. In the internet age you can make a comment one minute and literally the next it is being read on a website somewhere.

I have enjoyed putting this book together and a lot of the broadcast work I have done has been good fun, so if an opportunity to get involved in the the media came along I would consider it. One thing I definitely plan to do after I retire from playing is continue with my charity work. I am the Laura Crane Youth Cancer Trust's corporate ambassador and it is an involvement I get a lot of satisfaction from.

Laura Crane was from Huddersfield, where the charity is based. She was diagnosed with cancer in 1995, when she was 15. Tests revealed she had four forms of the disease and she passed away in 1996, just after her 17th birthday. It is a tragic story but one that is happening to families all over the country all the time.

The Laura Crane Trust is the only UK charity dedicated to raising funds for research into cancers affecting 13 to 24 year olds. Apparently, in this country six teenagers every day are diagnosed with some form of cancer and when you hear a statistic like that, how could you not give the Trust your support?

My involvement came about after I attended a touch and pass tournament for kids at Moldgreen, which is a Huddersfield amateur rugby league club. Representatives of the Laura Crane Trust were there and I got talking to them. They were looking for somebody in Leeds to represent the charity in the city and asked if I would be interested. I said I'd be happy to help. At the Rhinos we visit local hospitals every Christmas and I have been in and chatted to kids on the cancer ward and it really puts everything into perspective. I am known as a grumpy old man but what these youngsters have to cope with is way beyond anything I have ever experienced. The brave way they and their families deal with a horribly traumatic situation is truly inspiring. You might have a bad day at training or be on a bit of a losing run, but what these kids are going through is heart-wrenching. It makes you sit back and think about things.

I am lucky in that I have got spare time away from my job; it is a local charity so I can be hands-on and get involved and because I am quite well-known in the area, they can use my name to raise their profile.

Andy Raleigh, who plays for Huddersfield Giants, is involved as their youth ambassador. They have four full-time staff who organise fundraising events and I help out when I can. To be honest, it doesn't entail doing much, just turning up and showing my face, talking to people about what the charity does or even just attending dinners. If, for example, a business in Leeds is willing to organise an event for the charity I will go along and show my support. It sometimes helps sell tickets if they can say a local sportsman will be attending. One thing we are looking at trying to do is organise a charity polo match. They did one a while ago which Katie Price went to, so it is quite a big event.

Like so many families, mine has been affected by cancer. Both my grandmas died of the disease; my gran on my dad's side passed away from bowel cancer in September, 1988 and my mum's mum of lung cancer on September 19, 2010. She had asked for a visit from Saskia a few weeks before she died and that was the last time I saw my daughter. I remember the date of her death, because I was in Newcastle supporting Vic as she competed in the Great North run, for the Meningitis Trust. After I hang up my rugby boots I will do the same event in Gran's memory. They don't know it yet, but my family on my mum's side will be joining me, to raise money for a cause which is close to my heart. The Laura Crane Trust does fantastic work and I would urge anyone to have a look at their website: www.lauracranetrust.org.

I have been through a lot in my rugby career and my private life. There have been a lot of downs and occasions when I have questioned myself and what I am doing. At times – for example during the 2008 World Cup and its aftermath - I have felt at the end of my tether, but compared with what the kids the Laura Crane Trust are trying to help have to deal with, it has all been a piece of cake.

I have made mistakes and had bad times on and off the field, but overall, I've had a good life so far and a fantastic career. There are things I regret and with hindsight I would change, but not many. And that is the bald truth.

Afterword

By Kevin Sinfield

Keith Senior played for Sheffield Eagles in the game when I made my Leeds Rhinos debut, way back in 1997, but my first real memory of him is from a couple of years later.

I played 21 times in 1999, which was my breakthrough season. One of those matches was against Sheffield at Don Valley Stadium and we lost 22-16. Keith earned me a massive rollicking from our coach Graham Murray and that is something I have never forgotten, mainly because he has reminded me about it on a regular basis ever since.

I had come off the bench, someone made a break and I was in support. I took the pass and I should have scored, but Keith ripped the ball off me. There was another defender in the tackle, so it ought to have been our penalty, but the ref gave a knock-on and the chance went begging. With the game being so close, that was a crucial moment.

Graham Murray was furious and at half-time he made it clear what he thought about me messing up. I was only an 18-year-old kid at the time.

Keith signed for us later the same season and he brought that incident up straight away, but we hit it off from the start and I feel privileged to have played alongside him – and to have been his mate – for so long.

There's a four-year age gap, but we have always got on really well and the time that brought us closest together was the 2000 World Cup. We had spent many hours in each other's company that year on club duty, but in the international set-up we found ourselves sharing a room and we basically lived out of one another's pockets for the entire tournament.

That's when I first got to see another side to Keith, apart from the Mr Grumpy image he tries to portray. Keith has the reputation of being a typical Yorkshireman, liking a pint, not saying a lot and being as tight as a duck's proverbial. With the stubble on his face and the shaved head, he looks like a bit of a hard case, but in 2000 I got to discover what he is really like.

And yes, he is as tight as they come and all those years ago he enjoyed more than the odd beer, but if you peel away some of the layers, he is a really caring bloke. Underneath the gruff exterior he is good fun, with a lot of good qualities and he can be genuinely funny.

In my early years in the international set-up we spent a lot of time together as room-mates and we got on very well. We had some adventures on and off the field. We roomed together during the build-up to the ill-fated one-off mid-season Test in Australia in 2003 and having Keith there made it a lot more enjoyable for me.

On tour it always takes a while for club affinities to break down, but that trip we were only away for a week or so and therefore there wasn't really time to build up new friendships. Having Keith alongside helped me get through a difficult experience.

Since he has met Vic he has become a country gent and that really makes me laugh, because he is a million miles away from the fella I first knew in 1999. Over the years you expect blokes to mellow, but with Keith the opposite is true – he has got easier and easier to wind up as time has gone by. Now he's well into his 30s, you can get a rise out of him within seconds. I dread to think what he'll be like when he's 80.

A classic example was the time – which he talks about in this book – when he went to a party at Terry George's house, the gate was left open when he went home and Terry's dogs got out. They were spotted worrying a farmer's sheep and they ended up being shot.

It wasn't a funny incident and I know Keith – being an animal lover – took it hard, but it got some press attention and of course being blokes and rugby players, we took the mickey out of him relentlessly at the next training session.

He turned up to "baa" noises from me and Jamie Jones-Buchanan, followed by chants of "who let the dogs out". Keith flipped, which was really good fun. You can tell when Keith's about to go: he turns red, his eyes start bulging and his bottom lip begins to quiver. That's when you know you've got him.

He told me he was going to see me after training in the wrestle room, for a fight. I burst out laughing, Jonesy said something else to him and he told Jamie "And I'll have you too." We were both in hysterics and all the other boys were falling about as well. Things like that happen roughly once every week.

Rugby players get a bad press sometimes for their lifestyle, which can be detrimental to their performance. If you drink too much, it is going to affect the way you play. When I first knew Keith he probably drank at least once a week, now it'll be a handful of times per year.

He is really conscious of what he eats and he looks after himself. He is smart about how he lives his life now. It is evident throughout this book that he has made mistakes; he would be the first to hold his hand up and acknowledge that. The mark of a man is if you can learn from your mistakes and he has certainly done that. What you see now is a more rounded person.

Keith is a bit accident-prone and he never seems to be far away from the headlines, but as a player, I think he is up there with the very best of the modern era. His longevity alone marks him out as someone special.

To have played around 550 career games and to still be going strong is remarkable in the modern era, when the game has got faster and the collisions bigger. He is still in good shape, he has got all his marbles – more or less – and that is credit to him.

In my opinion, the best British centres of the Super League era have been Paul Newlove, Gary Connolly and Keith Senior. I didn't have the privilege of playing with Paul Newlove, but I lined up alongside Gary Connolly for Leeds and at international level and I know they are both fantastic players who achieved a lot in the game, but I would have Keith in my team ahead of either of them.

I love playing alongside Keith and I think he is the best centre Super League has seen. That's not just my view, there are plenty of others in the game who would say the same. He has got size, pace, power and skill and I think Keith in full flight is one of the best sights in the sport. I would not like to try and stop him, so I am thankful I haven't been on the opposing team for more than a handful of occasions.

He holds the record for most Super League appearances and tries and it will be a while before anyone gets near either of those. To have played in every Super League season, from 1996-2011, is an unbelievable achievement and in that regard I think Keith is a bit of a freak. He will look back on his career with a lot of fond memories.

In terms of his influence on the team, Keith doesn't say a lot, but when he does open his mouth you tend to sit up and take notice. He is not one to call a spade a gardening implement, he says it how it is and he doesn't hold back. He can be brutally honest with people, he doesn't try and dress things up and he isn't one for looking after people's feelings. There have been times when he has spoken up and been very negative, but that's not always a bad thing. If people are getting carried away, a few words from Keith usually brings them back down to earth – and having Keith around regularly reminds the rest of us how lucky we are.

I remember the last time we were in Australia together, for the 2008 World Cup. We met up with our old team-mate Marcus Bai, who is someone I know Keith has a lot of time for. When we were on the Gold Coast, Marcus got in touch and invited us to go for lunch. It is fair to say Marcus has put a bit of weight on since his playing days, though he is still in decent shape. I saw him first, so it was handshakes and man hugs all round and I told him how good it was to see him and how well he was looking. Then along came Keith. He took one look at Marcus and said to him: "For f***'s sake – look at the size of you. What have you been eating?" I think he hurt Marcus' feelings a bit, but that's Keith all over. He didn't mean to upset him; that was just what came out of his mouth.

Over the years I have travelled a bit with Keith, to and from training. That dates back to the days when Barrie McDermott still played and we shared a car over from Oldham, stopping off in Huddersfield en route to collect the big fella.

He would get in the car and scoff a giant bag of peanut M&Ms for breakfast. He has really bad morning breath, so we liked to keep the windows open. Every morning we'd ask him if he had brushed his teeth. He always said he had, but I think he was too tight to pay for toothpaste.

eBay has certainly helped with his finances in recent years and earned him plenty of publicity. I don't really understand why flogging off his old gear has gained Keith so much bad press, not that he is bothered. It has become a nice sideline for him and I don't see anything wrong with it, most of the time.

Back in 2007 we played New Zealand in a home Test series. We trained at the Rhinos' Kirkstall base and after one session, I left my England hoodie behind. We were in the next day, but I couldn't find it anywhere. The kitman didn't have any spares, so I was without a hoodie for the entire series – which wasn't much fun because it was October/November and absolutely freezing.

I'm sure you know where this story's leading. The next time I saw my hoodie, it was on eBay. Keith had picked it up and put it straight on the website – he got £50 quid for it. I didn't know anything about it.

On a related topic – and this may be a case of too much information – I am probably the only player in the game who still wears a jockstrap. I have found that recently after a game, when I have thrown my jockstrap on the floor in the changing room, I come back from the shower and it has gone missing. I am wearing trunks now, like everyone else, but I am sure Keith is selling them, to some seriously weird punters.

*

Kevin Sinfield made his Rhinos debut as a 16-year-old in 1996 and has gone on to become the most successful captain in the club's history, having skippered them to four Grand Final triumphs.

Keith's record

KEITH SENIOR

Born: 24.4.76

Signed by Sheffield Eagles from Huddersfield YMCA Rugby Union
Sheffield Eagles debut: v Widnes (H) Lost 0-22   Left wing ... 2.10.94
Leeds Rhinos debut: v London Broncos (H) Won 14-8 Left centre ... 10.9.99

	App + Sub		T	G	Pts	
Sheffield Eagles						
1994-95	20	3	3	0	12	
1995-96	8	3	3	0	12	
1996	21	1	17	0	68	
1997	27	2	7	0	28	
1998	25	0	19	0	76	+ 1t GB
1999	30	0	7	0	28	
Leeds Rhinos						
1999	3	0	0	0	0	
2000	35	0	17	0	68	
2001	28	0	16	0	64	+ 1t Yorks.
2002	32	1	24	0	96	+ 1t GB, 1t Yorks.
2003	32	0	12	0	48	+ 2t GB (Inc. 1 non-Test) 2t Yorks.
2004	30	0	13	0	52	+ 2t GB
2005	29	0	25	0	100	+ 2t GB
2006	33	0	16	0	64	+ 2t GB
2007	30	0	7	0	28	+ 2t GB
2008	34	0	15	0	60	+ 1t England
2009	28	0	12	0	48	
2010	33	1	10	0	40	
2011	16	0	4	0	16	
Totals						
Sheffield Eagles	131	9	56	0	224	
Leeds Rhinos	363	2	171	0	684	
Great Britain	31	2	12	0	48	
GB v NZ Maoris 1999*	1	0	0	0	0	
GB v New Z'land A 2003*	1	0	1	0	4	
GB v Newcastle Div 2006*	1	0	0	0	0	
1996 Tour	4	0	2	0	8	Not inc. 0+2 app., 1t Tests
England	10	0	2	0	8	
Emerging England	1	0	0	0	0	
Yorkshire	4	0	4	0	16	
GRAND TOTALS	**547**	**13**	**248**	**0**	**992**	
* Non-Test						

Also available from Great Northern Books:

Dominic Matteo
In My Defence
The Autobiography

Bremner
The Complete Biography by Richard Sutcliffe

Revie
Revered and Reviled
The Authorised Biography by Richard Sutcliffe

Lucas
From the Streets of Soweto to Soccer Superstar
The Authorised Biography of Lucas Radebe by Richard Coomber

Magnificent Seven
Yorkshire's Championship years
The men, the magic, the memories
by Andrew Collomosse

Frith On Cricket
Half a Century of Cricket Writing
by David Frith

Sweet Summers
The Classic Cricket Writing of JM Kilburn
Winner of Wisden Book of the Year

From Bust To Boom
*Hull City AFC: from the brink of extinction
to the Barclays Premier League*
by John Fieldhouse

Deano
From Gipsyville to the Premiership
By Dean Windass

www.greatnorthernbooks.co.uk